# The
# Baby Signing
## Book

# The Baby Signing Book

## SECOND EDITION

## Includes **450** ASL Signs for Babies & Toddlers

# Sara Bingham

B.A. (Linguistics), B.A. (Psychology), Honors Diploma
(Communicative Disorders Assistant)
Founder of WeeHands

## Illustrated by Jamie Villanueva

Robert
ROSE

*To my husband, Angelo, our two children,*
*and all the families WeeHands has taught.*
*Thank you all.*

For complete cataloguing information, see page 285.

*Disclaimer*
This book is a general guide only and should never be a substitute for the skill, knowledge, and experience of a qualified medical professional dealing with the facts, circumstances, and symptoms of a particular case.

The nutritional, medical, and health information presented in this book is based on the research, training, and professional experience of the author, and is true and complete to the best of her knowledge. However, this book is intended only as an informative guide for those wishing to know more about health, nutrition, and medicine; it is not intended to replace or countermand the advice given by the reader's personal physician. Because each person and situation is unique, the author and the publisher urge the reader to check with a qualified health-care professional before using any procedure where there is a question as to its appropriateness. A physician should be consulted before beginning any exercise program. The author and the publisher are not responsible for any adverse effects or consequences resulting from the use of the information in this book. It is the responsibility of the reader to consult a physician or other qualified health-care professional regarding his or her personal care.

Design and page composition: Joseph Gisini/PageWave Graphics Inc.
Illustrator: Jamie Villanueva
Cover photograph: © Larry Williams/zefa/Corbis
Editor: Bob Hilderley, Senior Editor, Health
Copyeditor: Sue Sumeraj
Proofreader: Sheila Wawanash
Indexer: Gillian Watts

The publisher acknowledges the financial support of the Government of Canada through the Book Publishing Industry Development Program.

Published by Robert Rose Inc.,
120 Eglinton Ave. E., Suite 800, Toronto, Ontario Canada M4P 1E2
Tel: (416) 322-6552   Fax: (416) 322-6936
www.robertrose.ca

Printed and bound in Canada.

1  2  3  4  5  6  7  8  9  MI  21  20  19  18  17  16  15  14  13

MIX
Paper from
responsible sources
FSC® C103567

# Contents

# Preface

IKE MANY PARENTS WHO SIGN WITH THEIR baby, my initial motivation for teaching my son American Sign Language (ASL) vocabulary was to give him a way to express his wants and needs before he was able to speak. Joshua started signing at 9 months of age, and by the time he was 18 months old, he could use at least 80 words, a combination of spoken words and signs. He was able to communicate his needs and wants. He could request a cookie by signing COOKIE. He could ask for more fruit cocktail by signing FRUIT. He could even ask to have the family minivan cooled down in the middle of a heat wave by pointing to the dashboard and signing COLD WIND — a better phrase, really, than air conditioner! Joshua's ability to make clear requests using signs delighted my husband and me.

What truly impressed us, though, was Joshua's ability to comment on his world and share his experiences with us. I have a clear memory of one cloudy, chilly, windy, miserable spring day when I took Joshua for a walk and he was able to sign about the weather. We were walking along the streets in a new housing development — no houses up, but the streets were paved — with nothing to block the wind. It was cold! I just wanted to get our walk over with and go home. What brought me back to the moment was when Joshua pulled on my jacket and signed WIND. A few seconds later, he signed CLOUD. He was marveling at the weather — not simply making a request, but sharing a moment with me. I could tell from his face that it was a remarkable experience for him as well.

I am often asked why I started signing with my children. Before having children, I worked with the Toronto Preschool Speech and Language Services. Alongside speech-language pathologists and other professionals, I worked with children with Down syndrome, autism, and other developmental delays. These children had difficulty communicating, and we used sign language and pictures to help facilitate their language development. Our therapy included helping parents learn to use sign language and pictures with their children.

Because of my work, I knew the benefits of using ASL with children who are non-verbal or beginning communicators. Together, we learned to sign songs and nursery rhymes. After years of working with this population, I could not sing "Itsy Bitsy Spider" or "Row, Row Your Boat" without signing them.

Because of my work experience, I knew I wanted to sign with my own children. I recognized that if they had an alternative way to communicate before speech developed, I would know what they were thinking, they would present fewer challenging behaviors, and we would just plain have fun. When my son signed FISH at 9 months, I was thrilled. My husband laughed at me and said, "Sara, why are you so excited? You've been teaching others to do this for years!" Quite simply, it is thrilling to see your own children communicate clearly at such an early age.

I am still amazed at what my children have been able to share with us and continue to share with us. At home, we still sign (including fingerspelling) and continue to learn more signs and more ways to use them. Because of this, on a cold January afternoon, I was able to knock on my patio window and sign, NO, STOP! SHOVEL DOWN to my children as they were trying to bury our dog in the snow.

# Baby Signing History

We are not the only family to enjoy the pleasures of signing, and Joshua and Sabrina are not the only hearing children to profit from learning how to sign. In the 2004 movie *Meet the Fokkers,* Ben Stiller's character comments, "Oh yeah, I've heard about this baby signing stuff. This is like cutting edge." Yes, this movie played a part in bringing baby sign language to the public's attention, but the idea of using sign language with hearing children has been around for quite some time. As early as 1867, the American linguist William Dwight Whitney looked at the positive communication abilities of hearing children born to Deaf adults. Interest was revived a century later by a number of researchers, principally Joseph Garcia, an ASL interpreter in Alaska.

Garcia noted that babies born to Deaf members of his community were able to use signs to communicate earlier than babies born to hearing families started to speak, and he began researching what happened when sign language was taught to hearing babies. Garcia's research showed that babies who were exposed to sign language could make signs 5 to 6 months earlier than they could produce spoken words. These results led Garcia to write what would become a landmark resource on the topic of baby sign language, *Toddler Talk,* which was reprinted in 1999 as *Sign with Your Baby.* Shortly thereafter, the idea of signing to babies captured the public's imagination.

# WeeHands

I first started researching sign language and communication development while studying linguistics at the University of Ottawa and psychology at Carleton University. Later, when I was working with young children with special needs and teaching sign language to their parents, I came across Joseph Garcia's work on baby signing and language development. When my son was born, it made sense for me to sign with him. But Garcia's research also inspired me to teach other families.

WeeHands, a workshop in baby signing, was born in 2001 in my empty dining room. WeeHands has grown to become a complete baby signing program that teaches parents how to use ASL vocabulary with their babies. WeeHands classes focus on language development, providing parents with practical, well-researched strategies to help them teach their babies ASL vocabulary. This work is the foundation of *The Baby Signing Book.*

# How to Use This Book

Your baby is growing and learning about the world from the day he is born. Over the next months and years, you can use this book to guide your family through the world of signing with your baby. You will be shown what, how, where, and when to sign throughout your baby's day — during mealtime, playtime, diaper changing time, and a host of other times. Throughout the book, words that are signed are placed in small capital letters.

Part 1 provides an introduction to signing with babies and young children. The first chapter contains a quick guide to signing — the basic knowledge, skills, and strategies you need to get started. Chapter 2 reviews the research that has been conducted on signing, focusing on its immediate and long-term benefits for your child's language and learning development. The remaining chapters in Part 1 are age-specific guides to signing with your baby and toddler, from birth to age 3 and beyond.

Part 2 is a dictionary of more than 350 ASL signs. One of the basics of teaching language skills is to discover what motivates a child and then let him lead the way. Keep this in mind while reading Part 1, and refer to the dictionary in Part 2 to find signs for things and activities your child likes.

Part 3 provides some favorite songs and rhymes you can sign with your child. Don't worry about whether you sound good when you sing. Don't worry if you make mistakes while signing. Have fun signing and singing, and your child will too.

At the back of the book you will find a resource list of other books, videos, and websites that can help you learn additional ASL signs. Keep in mind that the main goal of teaching ASL vocabulary to young children is not to help them become fluent in ASL, although that may be something your family will aim for in the future. The goals are to be able to communicate with your children before they can speak, to reduce their frustration, and to have fun.

## Getting Started

Start with a few basic signs, such as EAT, MILK, and MORE, then add new signs when you and your baby are ready. You can sign any number of signs to your baby or toddler, just as we speak an enormous number of words to them. Incorporate signs into your daily routines while playing, singing, and reading. Provide a language-rich environment for your child through signs and speech. Your child will be able to both hear and see what you are communicating.

Your child has been communicating with you from the day he was born, through his smiles, coos, and cries. By signing, you are connecting with him in a special way. Yes, there are benefits to using ASL with babies and toddlers in terms of improved language development, increased vocabularies, and higher intelligence quotients (IQs). But most important, as can be seen in the stories parents have shared with us (see the boxes called "Notes from a Signing Parent" throughout this book), signing with your child lets you into his world from infancy onward.

You'll be amazed at how quickly the years fly by. Put as much emphasis as you can in these early years on playing, signing, and reading; you will create wonderful memories that will last your family a lifetime.

**eat**

**milk**

**more**

# TOP 5 SIGNING TIPS

## 1. Play face to face

Encourage all family members to get down on the same level as your baby. That way, you can see and learn more about what your baby experiences. At the same time, your baby will be able to watch and learn more about communicating with you. He will also love the attention.

## 2. Imitate

Imitate both the movements and the sounds your baby makes. Do what your baby does. Say what your baby says. Soon he will be imitating you.

## 3. Label your baby's experiences

Give your child names for the things you see and do. Label these items using both signs and speech. For example, if your baby points to a bird, sign BIRD and say "bird." If your child is jumping, say "jump" and sign JUMP.

## 4. Be consistent with your signing

You want your child to think, "When Mommy and Daddy say 'more' or 'ball,' they always sign it too, so that must be how it's done."

## 5. Repeat, repeat, repeat

Find as many different ways as possible to use the same words and signs in a day. For example, to teach the concept of "on," sign and say, "SOCKS ON. SHOES ON. PANTS ON. SHIRT ON." Sign before, during, and after the activity.

# PART 1

# Baby Signing Basics

# CHAPTER 1

# A Quick Course in Baby Signing

W HETHER IT IS A NEWBORN'S CRY TO BE FED or a toddler's tantrum on a grocery store floor, these behaviors are motivated by a desire to connect with another human being. Our ability to communicate puts us in touch with others and allows us to have an effect on our environment. Communication in any form, whether through words, cries, or body language, allows us to bond with those around us. As we grow, it is through communicating that we make mistakes and then acquire new skills and knowledge. The ability to communicate enables us to connect, learn, and grow.

From the day they are born, newborns are able to communicate by crying to let their parents know they are needed. Babies also communicate through coos and gurgles. It is up to their parents and caregivers to interpret these vocalizations — which is not always an easy job. However, learning to sign with your baby will open up new avenues of communication, both useful and pleasurable.

## Toward Better Communication

Our ability to communicate through language, taking in what we have learned and applying this information to new situations, is a uniquely human trait. If we can nurture clear communication at an early age, all the better.

### Hardwired for Language

In her book *What's Going On in There?* Lise Eliot cites evidence that humans are "hardwired" to learn language. All babies and toddlers, regardless of race, religion, geography, or parental language, learn language on the same schedule and in the same way, moving from single sounds to single words to single phrases and sentences, all before the age of 4 years. Eliot suggests that specific areas of the human brain are set up for language because humans are *meant* to communicate through language.

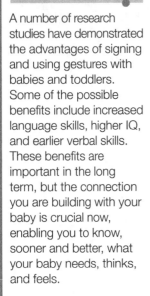

**Did You Know** ?

A number of research studies have demonstrated the advantages of signing and using gestures with babies and toddlers. Some of the possible benefits include increased language skills, higher IQ, and earlier verbal skills. These benefits are important in the long term, but the connection you are building with your baby is crucial now, enabling you to know, sooner and better, what your baby needs, thinks, and feels.

Celebrated linguist Noam Chomsky has proposed that our children's talent for creating new words and phrases is proof that humans have an innate ability to use language. What parent has not smiled at their 3-year-old's use of language and wondered, "Where did she come up with that?"

 **Q** **Is baby signing only for children with hearing loss or special needs?**

**A** No. The sign language vocabulary presented in this book is intended for babies who are hearing well and developing normally. However, because this book teaches ASL vocabulary, the language development strategies described are also useful for children who have special needs, including children who are hearing impaired. These children and their families will need additional professional and community support.

## Parent Participation

Parents definitely have an effect on their child's ability to communicate. A child is not born with the ability to wave bye-bye or to raise her hands to mean "Pick me up." Parents teach their children these communications skills. Each time Daddy leaves for work, he says "bye-bye" and waves goodbye. Mommy repeats what Daddy says and may move the baby's hand up and down to imitate a wave. This is repeated each day, at every departure.

Mom and Dad are modeling both the spoken language and the gestures customary for these departures. Most likely, higher-pitched vocal tones are used, making the words of more interest to the baby. The gesture — a wave — and its verbal equivalent, "bye-bye," are repeated again and again until one morning, their baby moves her hand. Both parents get excited and repeat the movement, exclaiming, "Yes, bye-bye! Wave bye-bye!" Their baby squeals in delight and waves bye-bye more distinctly. Their baby has learned, with the help of her caregivers' reinforcement, to communicate . . . to wave bye-bye.

### Did You Know

Babies often point or gesture toward an item they want, but parents are left guessing exactly what they are asking for. This can turn into a frustrating game of 20 Questions. Learning to sign reduces the frustration many parents and babies experience.

## First Gestures and Signs

Just as they learn to crawl before they can walk, babies can gesture before they are able to talk. Around the age of 7 to 9 months, babies learn to wave bye-bye and to raise their hands and arms toward their parents as if to say "Pick me up." Baby sign language expands on the ability to gesture before and while speech develops. Babies can learn to use signs to request more milk, to comment on the wind and clouds, and to direct attention to the dog next door. They can make the signs for MILK, WIND, CLOUD, and DOG long before they are able to clearly communicate these concepts using speech.

# American Sign Language

American Sign Language (ASL), first designed for the hearing impaired, is the most common sign language taught to babies and toddlers. The baby sign language presented in this book focuses on basic ASL vocabulary.

## ASL Facts

- In 1894, the football team at Gallaudet University (North America's only university for the Deaf) invented the football huddle to keep their opponents from seeing them discuss strategies in ASL.

- William Hoy (1862–1961), the first Deaf major league baseball player, was the reason umpires adopted the hand signals Out, Safe, and Strike.

- In 1970, the Deaf actor Linda Bove was a guest on the popular American children's TV show *Sesame Street*. In 1976, she became a regular on the show.

- In 1983, Diana, Princess of Wales, accepted an invitation to be the Royal Patron of the British Deaf Association. She later studied British Sign Language (BSL).

- In 1983, *The Smurfs* became the first television cartoon in America to use sign language. The "Smurfing in Sign Language" episode had the highest ratings *The Smurfs* had ever had.

- In 1987, Marlee Matlin became the first hard-of-hearing signer to win the Best Actress Oscar, for the role of Sarah in the film *Children of a Lesser God*. In 2000, she was a guest on the children's program *Blue's Clues*. After her appearance, 5 to 10 ASL signs were incorporated into each new show.

(Adapted from Jolanta A. Lapiak, www.handspeak.com)

### ASL Origins

Based on early French Sign Language, American Sign Language is the language of the Deaf in English-speaking North America. ASL is the fourth most used language in North America, after English, Spanish, and French. Other signed languages, such as British Sign Language, French Sign Language, AUSLAN (Australian Sign Language), and Mandarin Sign Language, are used in other countries. Interestingly enough, the signed language used in French-speaking Quebec is based on British Sign Language.

In 1815, Thomas Hopkins Gallaudet, an American minister, traveled to France to learn more about schools for the Deaf there. Gallaudet persuaded a teacher who was Deaf, Laurent Clerc, to return with him to America, and in 1817 they opened the first school for the Deaf in North America, in Hartford, Connecticut. North America's Deaf community used the sign language taught at this school, mixed with the sign language already being used in the United States; this hybrid developed into ASL as it is known today.

ASL is considered a real, or live, language because it has native users and because it changes and evolves. Scholars consider Latin a dead language because there are no native speakers. I am a native speaker of English, a live language, and my generation (when we were teenagers) brought such wonderful words as "awesome," "gross," and "like" to a different light in the English language: "Like, for sure, that was totally awesome!" "He is so gross!" (I am so embarrassed for my generation!)

> *"Through infant signing, babies reveal their minds to us; if we are watchful, we can see their worlds from their perspectives."*
>
> — Claire Vallotton, Michigan State University

---

**Q I learned that sign a different way. Which is correct?**

**A** Just as in English or any language, there are regional differences in ASL signs. The word "boot" in North American English represents a type of footwear; in Britain, it refers to what North Americans call the trunk of a car. In some regions of North America, the word "pop" is used for a soft drink; in other regions, the word "soda" is used.

---

## ASL Dialects

Within each country's sign language, there are dialectal or regional differences, just as there are dialectal or regional differences in spoken English. Think of the words "submarine," "hoagie," and "grinder." These are all North American English words for a sandwich made on a long loaf of bread.

Words vary from region to region and even across generations. Depending on the age of the speaker, the words "smart," "nice," and "sweet" could each refer to an attractive shirt. My mother uses the word "smart" when referring to a new blouse, while I might use the word "nice," and my 6-year-old son would say "sweet." The same differences can be found in American Sign Language.

## ASL Grammar

ASL is not based on any spoken language and therefore does not follow the grammatical rules of English or any other spoken language. However, it does have its own syntax and grammar. Rachel Coleman from Signing Time, an organization that

**red**

**bird**

**look**

provides sign language teaching resources, explains why ASL has a different grammar structure than English.

Rachel's daughter, Leah, is profoundly deaf. Originally, Rachel would sign to Leah using ASL vocabulary in English word order. When Rachel wanted Leah to look at the beautiful cardinal outside the window, Rachel signed, LOOK RED BIRD. As soon as Rachel signed the word LOOK, Leah would look and miss the rest of the sentence. Because Leah was looking where her mother had directed the sign for LOOK, she missed the signs for RED BIRD. When Rachel recognized this problem, a light came on in her mind. Rachel and her family then started using ASL word order (syntax) and grammar. Now, when Rachel signs RED BIRD LOOK, Leah knows what Rachel is referring to (the noun) and what to do (the verb).

**Q**  **Why should I use American Sign Language with my baby?**

**A** Here are three good reasons to use ASL. ASL is a true living language that continues to grow. Research supports its use. ASL resources are widely and readily available. Besides, ASL is the language of the Deaf in our community. Why not celebrate that language? You never know when a basic knowledge of ASL will be useful. You might meet someone at work or on a city bus who is hearing impaired. Your child might make a Deaf friend in a dance class, at church, or at school. *Sesame Street, Blue's Clues,* and *Signing Time* all use ASL. Why would you not want to use it?

## ASL or Made-Up Signs?

Some people advocate using made-up signs rather than ASL signs, fearing that ASL may be too difficult for the baby or toddler. However, research has shown that babies and toddlers can learn ASL signs, and there is no need to modify or simplify the signs. If a signed word is too hard for a child to produce, or if a spoken word is too hard for her to say, she will make an approximation based on her individual motor skills. The key is to learn to recognize the approximations your child makes, respond to them, and model the appropriate signs back on a consistent basis, just as you would repeat the correct pronunciation of a word your toddler is struggling to say.

These approximations, whether signed or spoken, are often very logical and very cute. For example, one day at dinner we were having melon for dessert, and my 4-year-old daughter, Sabrina, said, "I really like candle-lope!" My husband and I have never tried to modify the word "cantaloupe" when we said it to her. Over the holidays, she also talked about staying at a "home-tel" while we visited relatives. There is no need for us to make these spoken words easier for her — and there is no way we could have anticipated her adorable approximations. Similarly, there is no need to simplify ASL signs for our babies and toddlers.

## ASL Resources

A number of wonderful American Sign Language resources are available for your family from libraries and retail outlets. These include some great DVDs, flashcards, books, and games. (See the Resources section at the end of this book for more information.) These resources help bring sign language into mainstream learning and will benefit children with a wide range of language abilities. A little girl in my daughter's class has special needs and cannot speak. Samantha uses ASL signs, pictures, and a little computer to communicate. My daughter thinks nothing of this and signs along with Samantha while they are playing.

✓ **SIGNING TIPS**

To teach ASL vocabulary to your child, try these strategies:

- Use delayed modeling: show the desired item, wait, and then model the sign.
- Teach vocabulary incidentally or informally throughout the day.
- Teach vocabulary in engaging and interactive activities.

**Q  What is the best time to start signing with my baby?**

**A**  It is never too early or too late to start signing with your baby or toddler. I began signing to both my children when they were 6 months old. If I'd known then what I know now, I would have begun even earlier. Start signing as soon as you are ready and comfortable. The earlier you sign to your baby, the earlier she will begin to understand what you sign.

Understanding precedes the ability to use any language expressively, but most babies develop the memory and motor skills to start signing back when they are between 8 and 10 months old. There are exceptions: some will sign earlier and some will sign later. My firstborn, Joshua, made the sign for FISH at 9 months. I thought my daughter, Sabrina, would sign back even earlier, but she waited until she was 11 months old. In one week, though, she made up for lost time, signing back three different signs — for NO, EAT, and MORE — at different times.

### Learning ASL

This book will not teach you to be fluent in American Sign Language. There is much more to learning ASL as a language than memorizing signs. If you choose to further your ASL education by studying additional vocabulary, grammar, and culture, we recommend finding a course taught in your community by someone whose first language is ASL and who is trained to teach ASL to adults. Most community colleges and school-board continuing education departments offer ASL classes for adults. Try to find a course offered live in your community, but if such a course is not currently available, check the online ASL courses in the Resources section of this book.

# Start Signing

As parents and caregivers who are not fluent in American Sign Language, we do not sign every word to our children in ASL. In fact, it may be impossible to speak English and sign ASL fluently at the same time, because each has its own grammar and syntax. Our aim when signing with our hearing babies is not for them to be signers exclusively, but for them to both speak and sign.

### Emphasize Key Words

When signing to your baby or toddler, sign only the key words of your spoken sentences and phrases, mainly nouns and verbs. Key words will be those you have recognized as important for your children to know.

You might say, "Do you want MILK?" while making the ASL sign for MILK. Speaking English (or whatever spoken language you use at home) and pairing it with key ASL signs forces you to slow down your speech and emphasize the key words.

### Repeat Key Words and Signs

More often than not, when you want to emphasize a word, you end up saying and signing that word over and over again, allowing your child to see it frequently. That's good. Repetition helps the brain reinforce existing neural connections and make new ones. Make an effort to repeat signs often throughout the day and in different contexts.

### Slow Down Your Speech

Most parents and caregivers cannot sign as quickly as they speak. This is actually a good thing. Because we are not fluent signers, signing with our children forces us to slow down our speech so they can better understand us.

## Exaggerate Your Speech and Gestures

Exaggerating your spoken words and signs will emphasize the sounds and movements you are making. More distinct sounds and larger gestures will draw your child's attention and allow her to hear and see nuances in the words and signs.

## Sign Back

Once your baby or toddler is signing back to you, she can get your attention and set topics of conversation. If a toddler points to a tree, start talking about trees. If a toddler points to a tree and signs BUTTERFLY because there is a small butterfly on one of the branches, talk about butterflies. Your child's signs allow you to know her interests and carry on a conversation.

## Learn from Mistakes

When babies or toddlers start to play with language, they make a lot of mistakes, as everyone does when learning something new. Toddlers often overgeneralize concepts they are learning. For example, they might call all four-legged animals "dogs." Horses are dogs, cows are dogs, even cats are dogs. When we hear our children do this in spoken language, we correct them and teach them the right word. When we see our children do this in sign language, we model the correct sign. Children learn from their mistakes, whether with spoken language or signed language. When children communicate earlier through signs, they are able to make mistakes and learn about language earlier.

# How to Make Hand Shapes

Typically, you sign with your dominant hand. If you are right-handed, most signs are made with your right hand. If you are left-handed, most signs are made with your left hand. It is very hard to read a person's signs when she keeps switching hands. In one of my ASL classes, I met a mom who was ambidextrous. She made one sign with her right hand, the next sign with her left, the next with her right, and so on. She was very talented, but watching her sign made me dizzy.

## Three Hand Positions

Many signs can be made using your dominant hand alone, but others require the use of both hands. There are three ways that you will use your hands to make signs:

### 1. One-Handed Signs

This type of sign uses only your dominant hand. One-handed signs include those for BOY and DOG.

**SIGNING TIP**

In her book *It Takes Two to Talk*, speech-language pathologist Ayala Manolson suggests using "short, simple phrases and fun exaggerated words and sounds" to help children learn key words readily.

**boy**

**wonderful**

**dance**

## 2. Two-Handed Signs

With this type of sign, both hands make the same movement, so you do not have to worry about what hand does what. Examples include MORE, FINISHED, and WONDERFUL.

## 3. Other-Hand-Supported Signs

In the third type of sign, your dominant hand makes the motion while your other hand stays still or acts as support for the moving hand. Examples are the signs for MUSIC and DANCE. I am right-handed, so when I'm making the sign for MUSIC, my left hand stays still and my right hand moves over my left arm as if strumming an instrument. When I sign DANCE, my left hand acts as a base (the dance floor) and my right hand (V shape) moves, or dances, across my left palm.

Do not be concerned about which hand your baby uses to sign. Babies will watch your models and use what is best for them. When he was a baby, my son switched hands when he signed and when he fed himself. It turns out that he is left-handed. My daughter was very clearly right-handed from the time she was 11 months old.

## How to Make Signs

ASL signs have five distinct characteristics:

### 1. Hand shape
The shape formed by your hand(s) to make the sign.

### 2. Body space (placement)
Where the sign is placed in relation to your body (e.g., at chest level, at shoulder level, above your head).

### 3. Movement
Most signs are not stationary but fluid, involving some hand movement.

### 4. Palm orientation
The direction your palm(s) face while you make the sign.

### 5. Facial expression
These can be used to augment the meaning of your signs. For example, a questioning expression conveys that you are asking a question rather than making a statement, while a vehement expression can be used to convey urgency.

Of these five components, hand shape, body space, and movement will be emphasized here. These components help distinguish the meaning of signs, often in subtle ways. Take, for example, the signs for BATH, PLEASE, and HAPPY. Your baby might use these signs to politely ask for a bath and express how happy she is to have one.

### Hand Shape

The sign for BATH is made with both hands making "A" shapes, while the signs for PLEASE and HAPPY are made with an open "B" hand shape.

**bath**

### Body Space

The ASL signs for PLEASE, BATH, and HAPPY are all made at the same place on your body: the chest area.

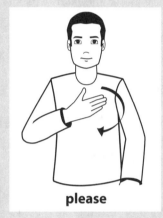

**please**

### Movement

The movement for PLEASE is a circular motion on your chest. In the sign for BATH, both hands move up and down on your chest. The sign for HAPPY involves one hand moving up and away from your body.

**happy**

> **Baby Sign Dictionary**
> In Part 2 of this book, you'll find a dictionary of 450 ASL signs, with directions for making them. You might want to bookmark this Baby Sign Dictionary for quick reference while you're reading this book and signing with your child. Go ahead and compile your own dictionary of the signs you use most often.

## Recognize Approximations

Knowing the components and characteristics of various signs will help you decipher your baby's possible sign approximations. I have found that babies generally get body placement and movement more or less correct, but may have difficulty with hand shape because of the finer motor skills needed for some hand shapes. For example, your little

**apple**

**water**

one may begin by signing APPLE using the correct body space (at the cheek) and movement (a twist), but the hand shape may not be a perfect ASL letter "X."

Before one of my baby signing workshops, a very eager mom told me that, although she was very excited about the idea of signing with her baby, her 8-month-old was not signing yet. During my presentation, I explained that babies often have difficulty with hand shapes. The example I used was the sign for WATER. Babies usually get the movement and body placement correct for this sign, tapping at the chin. However, instead of using the "W" hand shape for the sign, babies often approximate the sign with something easier, such as the "1" hand shape. Her eyes met mine across the room, and her eyes welled up with tears. I knew that her baby was signing! She told me afterwards that, indeed, her daughter had been making an approximation, just as I had described, for WATER.

# How to Sign ASL Numbers and Letters

### ASL Numbers

Each number in the English language has a specific sign in ASL, and many of the hand shapes needed for signs are based on number shapes. Learning the ASL numbers from 1 to 10 will help you with a number of the repetitive songs we typically sing to our children, such as "Five Little Ducks" and "Five Little Monkeys."

ASL numbers are signed with one hand, your dominant hand. When you sign numbers 1 to 5, your palm is facing you. When you sign numbers 6 to 10, your palm is facing away from you, or toward the person you are signing to.

**1**

**6**

## ASL Letters (Fingerspelling)

Each letter of the English alphabet has a specific sign in ASL. When you spell a word out in ASL, it is called fingerspelling. Not all words in the English language are represented by an ASL sign; some words, such as "kiwi," have to be fingerspelled because they have no equivalent in ASL. We might not necessarily fingerspell to our babies and toddlers frequently, because it can be complicated (although I have seen toddlers try to fingerspell), but it is still a useful skill to know.

Learning the alphabet is an important part of a preschooler's educational life. One of the first things we do in kindergarten is sing "The ABC Song," which helps us recognize the letters of the alphabet. Imagine how many times you have sung this song since you were a toddler. Learning to not only sing but also sign "The ABC Song" helps a young child *see* each of the letters in the alphabet. Because the sequence L-M-N-O-P is often sung or said quickly, children often think that it is one letter. Signing the alphabet helps a young child see the letters as separate units. And because we cannot sign the alphabet as quickly as we typically say it, we have to slow down our speech, which helps someone acquiring the language to learn the letters more easily.

ASL letters are signed with your dominant hand, with your palm facing out. When you are fingerspelling a word, your hand remains in the same place, at about shoulder height, unless there is a double letter in the word, and then your hand bounces slightly while showing this letter's shape to indicate a double letter.

Do not expect your baby to sign the whole alphabet back to you, but do use the ASL alphabet to help you with the hand shapes needed for key words, and use "The ABC Song" to entertain your baby.

> *"Movement is an essential part of learning and thinking. Teachers using ASL with their students have expressed that the children's hands are engaged and they seem calmer and more focused. During sign instruction, the children were more attentive and focused because they had to look at the teacher to get the information."*
>
> — A. Brereton (2009)

**A**

**B**

**C**

## Sign and Sing

"The ABC Song" is fun to sign and sing to your little one. Your child will love the one-on-one attention she is given when you sign and sing to her, and you will be amazed at how captivated she is by your hands. Parents have often told me that signing and singing "The ABC Song" has gotten them through many a grocery trip with a young baby or toddler.

**sign**

### The ABC Song
A B C D E F G H I J K L M N O P Q R S T U and V W X Y and Z.
NOW I KNOW my ABCs.
Next time, won't you SIGN with ME?

## Compile Your First Sign Dictionary

Now you can put together a list of about 5 to 6 signs that represent items or activities that interest your child. Whether you are signing with a baby or a 2-year old, you need to consider what would motivate your child to begin signing. At around 9 months of age, my son was very interested in fish, dogs, and different forms of transportation. Signs we used with him included FISH, DOG, CAR, and TRAIN. At the same age, my daughter was focused on all things food. With her, we initially concentrated on the signs for MORE, EAT, and MILK.

To this list, add 5 to 6 signs for activities you and your baby do a few times every day, such as EAT, SLEEP, and CHANGE DIAPER. Your child may not be as motivated by these signs, but they will be useful to her, and seeing them frequently throughout the day will help her learn them.

> ### ✓ SIGNING TIPS
>
> - Sign words for activities that are important to your baby.
> - Sign words for people and objects that interest your baby.
> - Sign words for activities that occur a few times each day.

## Repeat the Signs on Your List

Now that you have your list, try signing the words on it before, during, and after the relevant activities. That way, you are showing your child these signs a number of times throughout the day. For example, in teaching the sign for MILK:

**milk**

- **Before:** Sign MILK before you give her milk (as you are asking, "Do you want some MILK?" or giving her information: "Here comes the MILK").
- **During:** Sign MILK while she is drinking (as you are commenting, "You're drinking your MILK" or "It's good MILK").
- **After:** Sign MILK when it is gone (as you are saying, "Your MILK is finished" or asking, "Do you want more MILK?")

## Find Your Comfort Level

Don't worry about how many signs you use at the beginning. If you are comfortable signing 3 to 4 signs to your baby to start with, then sign 3 to 4 signs. If you are comfortable signing 10 to 15 signs, sign that number. If you are comfortable signing 50+ signs, sign 50+ signs. As long as you are consistent with the signs, you will not confuse or overwhelm your child. The number of spoken words we naturally use with our children doesn't confuse them; signing a larger number of signs will not be overwhelming either.

## Use Parentese and Gesturese

Something happens to most adults when they start talking with a baby. Their voices get higher, and they start speaking in a singsong way. This baby talk is often called parentese or motherese. To keep your child's attention while signing, continue to use parentese, combined with a more sophisticated gesturese: baby sign language.

## Reward Signing

Reward your child's signing behaviors, even if they are not intentional signs. Let's say that, while in her high chair during a mid-morning snack, your 11-month-old baby claps her hands. The clapping movement is similar to the sign for MORE (same movement and body space). You reinforce this approximation by giving your baby a blueberry. Your baby looks at you curiously. You sign and say, "Do you want MORE?" As you say the words, you exaggerate the movement for MORE. You sign and say this a few more times. Your baby imitates you, and you give her another blueberry. She gobbles up the blueberry and smiles. You repeat this process for 15 more blueberries. At the end of this short snack time, both of you are smiling and your baby has learned another sign. You have shaped an unintentional approximation gesture into an intentional sign.

## Get Excited

React to your baby's first attempts at signing with as much excitement as you would give to first words. When your child does sign, whether it is a perfectly formed sign or an approximation, repeat the sign back to her with a lot of energy while saying the word. The fun is just beginning.

more

# CHAPTER 2

# Sign Language Development

T HE IDEA OF USING SIGN LANGUAGE WITH hearing children has been around for quite some time. In 1867, William Dwight Whitney published *Language and the Study of Language: Twelve Lectures on the Principles of Linguistics*, in which he observed the hearing children of teachers at schools for the Deaf. He found that if their parents used both speech and sign language to communicate at home, these children usually had the ability to sign before they could speak.

A century later, in the 1970s, several published reports demonstrated that babies could learn to express their needs and wants through sign language earlier than they could through speech. These studies also showed that children who can sign have larger vocabularies than other children. Many other benefits to signing have been discovered in subsequent research studies.

## Basic Terms

When discussing the language development of pre-verbal babies and verbal toddlers and preschoolers, it is valuable to differentiate among the terms "speech," "language," and "communication."

### Definitions

*The American Heritage Dictionary* defines "speech" as
- something spoken; an utterance.
- vocal communication; conversation.

  *Random House Unabridged Dictionary* defines "language" as
- the system of linguistic signs or symbols considered in the abstract (opposed to SPEECH).
- any set or system of such symbols as used in a more or less uniform fashion by a number of people, who are thus enabled to communicate intelligibly with one another.

---

### Did You Know ?

In 1994, Joseph Garcia's landmark book, *Toddler Talk: The First Signs of Intelligent Life* (later reissued as *Sign with Your Baby*), brought the idea of signing with hearing babies to the public's attention. Garcia, an ASL interpreter, realized that children born to parents who were Deaf were able to communicate earlier, through signs, than babies born to hearing parents.

The same dictionary defines "communication" as
- the imparting or interchange of thoughts, opinions, or information by speech, writing, or signs.
- something imparted, interchanged, or transmitted.

Signing is a form of communication, not oral but visual. To put it simply, speech happens at your mouth, while signing happens at your hands. Language, whether oral or visual, happens in your head. This includes your ability to learn and remember words, and to put them together.

## Receptive and Expressive Language

The idea of language can also be broken down into the concepts of receptive language and expressive language. Receptive language refers to what an individual understands regarding the information received from others. This information is typically received by listening to others speak, but it can also be received by watching others sign. Expressive language refers to what an individual is able to express, either verbally or through sign.

# The Benefits of Signing

Babies who are signed to can often produce their first sign when they are around 8 to 10 months old, much earlier than they develop the ability to produce spoken words. Linguists, speech pathologists, and other researchers have confirmed that when signing babies start to speak, they typically have a better understanding of language and larger vocabularies.

## Intelligence

In addition to acquiring language more readily, these children experience other long-term benefits, including higher IQs and better reading skills. Linda Acredolo and Susan Goodwyn's book *Baby Signs*, published in 1997, demonstrated that children whose parents used gestures when they were babies had an average IQ of 114, 12 points higher than their peers who were not signed to. Although the children's expressive language skills were not measured in these studies, Acredolo and Goodwyn showed that 3-year-old children who had been gestured to as babies had a receptive vocabulary as large as that of the average 4-year-old.

## Reading Skills

Dr. Marilyn Daniels has studied the effect of sign language on reading and other language abilities. One study of signing with older children found that children exposed to sign language throughout their kindergarten year had larger vocabularies than

**Did You Know**

A word is a word, whether signed or spoken. It doesn't matter whether you represent the concept of a four-legged animal that barks and wags its tail by the spoken sounds "dog," "*chien*," or "*perro*," or by the movement of slapping your leg and then snapping. The English word "dog," the French word "*chien*," the Spanish word "*perro*," and the ASL sign for DOG all represent the same object or concept.

**Did You Know**

Children born to Deaf parents may have better reading abilities than their peers who have no exposure to sign language.

their peers who were not taught signing in their kindergarten year. Both groups of children, signing and not signing, were tested again at the end of their next school year. Although sign language instruction was not included in this following year for either group, the children who were taught sign language in their kindergarten year maintained a lead in vocabulary development at the end of grade one.

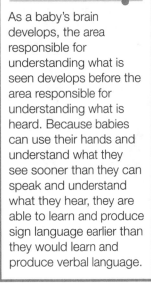

### Note from a Signing Parent

The biggest gift you can give a baby, toddler, or child is the tools to communicate. I always say, "What a beautiful world it would be if all children could communicate to each other, in the same language, 'Do you want to PLAY?'" American Sign Language is such a beautiful language of expression. Our son enjoys using his signs with his Deaf aunt, as well as with other people in the Deaf community. When he is playing shy in public, he sometimes resorts to his second language, ASL. Of course, he still enjoys signing while reading, and he absolutely loves singing and signing. We also enjoy signing through windows when we are leaving for school or work. We always include the sign for I LOVE YOU.

— Joanne Davis, Brooklin, Ontario

### Neurological Growth

There may be a neurological explanation for this phenomenon. In *What's Going On in There?* Lise Eliot discusses language development and the plasticity of a young child's brain: "Early life, when the number of synapses in a child's brain is at its peak, presents the greatest opportunity for selecting the optimal neural pathways for mediating language."

A young child's brain, and in particular his cerebral cortex (the outer layers of the brain), triples in thickness during the first year of life. Neurons and synapses continue to be produced and grow after birth. Babies are born ready to learn language and have specific areas of the brain dedicated to this task. With each new experience, these parts of a baby's brain further connect and develop. Children who are signed to as well as spoken to are able to use vision, hearing, and touch to learn language. Each time a word is heard, an auditory neural connection is made. Visual neural connections are made each time a sign is seen. Neural motor connections are made each time a word is said and signed. These areas of the brain become well developed because, first, the child has been signed to and, then, is able to use sign language to express himself.

**Q** **When is it too late to begin signing with my child?**

**A** It's never too late! Dr. Marilyn Daniels showed that children who started to learn sign language in kindergarten had larger vocabularies. Using sign language with young children adds an additional sensory component to learning language, a kinesthetic one. "Using sign language literally allows a child to feel language," Dr. Daniels noted.

## Motor and Speech Skills

In 1983, the research team of John Bonvillian, Michael Orlansky, and Lesley Novack found that, although children first develop the motor skills for speech and then develop the cognitive ability for language, these two skills, though related, are not reliant on each other. They suggested that speech areas of the brain develop later and more slowly than related motor areas of the brain, while motor control of the hands develops earlier than the motor control needed for speech.

Their research also looked at the sign acquisition and language development of children born to Deaf parents. They found that these babies and toddlers exhibited motor development similar to that of other children. However, standard language development milestones, particularly vocabulary development, were met much earlier. Babies and toddlers who were signed to had larger vocabularies. Most babies produced their first sign between $5\frac{1}{2}$ and 10 months of age and had an average vocabulary of 10 signs at their first birthday. By the time their subjects were 18 months of age, they produced between 15 and 136 signs.

## Overcoming Language Problems

Signing has also proven to be helpful in helping children overcome language problems. I once worked with a family whose 3-year-old son had great difficulty speaking. We offered speech therapy and taught him to sign. He picked up signs quite easily, particularly the sign for COOKIE. When he did begin speaking, his mother was amazed at his hand motions: "It was as if he had to look at his hands sign COOKIE and feel his hands sign COOKIE, and then he could get the word out."

However, Tricia Davis, an audiologist, noted that, "Statistically, there will be children who will have oral speech and language delays regardless of whether they are signed to, or not, as babies or toddlers. The percentage as reported in a number of studies is 10% minimum."

**Did You Know**

One out of 10 children will have a speech or language delay. Sign language gives them an alternative way to communicate, to learn how to use language, and to build their vocabularies until they are able to speak.

# Long-Term Applications

You will find opportunities to use the ASL signs you learn with your babies as they get older. You may sign to other caregivers when your child is asleep and you do not want to wake him. You might sign to your children or other caregivers when you are separated by distance or a window. I remember signing to my husband that my son (at 3 years of age) needed to go to the bathroom. I was in one car and my husband was in another (we had both just pulled in to our driveway). My husband quickly came and got Joshua into the bathroom while I brought my infant daughter, her car seat, and the groceries into the house.

Now that my children are older (4 and 6 years old) and very verbal, I continue to see the benefits of signing with them. Signing adds a visual and motor component to learning to read, for example, engaging more areas of the brain and thus improving retention of new words. My son now both sounds out words and uses the ASL alphabet to fingerspell them when he is reading.

> *"Providing infants and toddlers with symbolic tools earlier may help them engage parents and build knowledge of social-emotional concepts."*
>
> — Vallotton & Ayoub (2010)

# Sign Language Development Stages

Joseph Garcia, author of *Sign with Your Baby*, has shown that a baby who is signed to regularly and consistently at 6 to 7 months of age may begin signing by his eighth or ninth month. However, as with any of the skills your baby or toddler is developing, such as first smiles, sitting up, and first steps, the production of a baby's first sign depends on the baby. All babies are different.

As with the acquisition of any language, you will find that your baby will show that he understands this new language receptively before he is able to use it expressively. Other factors that will influence the production of your baby's first sign include how often you sign and what you sign. Choosing sign vocabulary that is motivating and useful to your baby will encourage him to sign.

### Imitation Stage

Before your baby produces his first sign, you will notice that he watches you intently when you are signing to him. He may even laugh and smile at your movements, as if he is wondering what you are doing. After some time, he will seem to be imitating your movements, as if he is thinking, "Mommy waves her hands around, so I guess I should too!" This process is similar to how a baby babbles and plays with sounds when learning to speak. Your baby is both imitating your movements and practicing his developing motor skills.

**Q** **Will signing with my baby delay his speech development later on?**

**A** Quite the contrary. A number of studies have shown that children who were signed to as babies have larger vocabularies and stronger verbal language abilities later in life. Teaching your baby to sign allows him to receive information about his world both visually (through signs) and through hearing (speech). Since your baby's ability to understand what he sees develops earlier than his ability to understand what he hears, he will understand what you sign to him before he understands what you say to him.

## Signing Progression

1. Your baby watches you when you sign. The movement seems to fascinate him.

2. Your baby imitates you when you sign. You may find him babbling with his hands as well as with his voice.

3. Your baby seems to recognize or understand your signs. He calms down when you sign MILK or gets excited when you sign BATH.

4. Your baby seems to produce meaningful patterns of movement at different times of the day or in specific situations. You find yourself asking, "Could that be a sign?"

5. Your baby makes his first sign! It may not be the exact hand shape, but you know it is consistent.

(Adapted by permission from Brandy Brass-Rafeek, Sweet Signs)

### Patterning Stage

After your baby has been imitating you for a few days or weeks, you will notice that some of his movements have a pattern to them. You may find yourself thinking, "He's been making the same movement for a few days, but it's not a sign and I can't figure it out." These more organized, patterned movements are your baby's way of practicing until he is ready for his first signed word. They may also be your baby's first attempts at approximating your signs.

**Q** **Our baby has begun to cry when my partner waves and signs GOODBYE as he leaves for work. What's going on?**

**A** Around the time your baby is 8 or 9 months old, he will start to wave goodbye when you wave goodbye, much to your delight. He has now developed the motor skills to raise his hand up and down, and the memory skills to realize that waving is a fun way to communicate with you.

However, as he develops further and understands that "goodbye" means that someone he loves is leaving, your baby may start to whimper or cry when you say "bye-bye" or wave goodbye. This separation anxiety can lead to "making strange" behavior. Your baby, who would once go to anyone, may now start crying when placed in the hands of another person. Babies at this age may also start crying when their parent leaves the room. The term "Velcro baby" is sometimes used to describe this behavior.

Be comforted. In the development of memory and understanding skills, separation anxiety is actually a positive milestone (although it doesn't seem like it): it means your baby's memory is developing. The ability to remember that "bye-bye" means that someone is leaving is a sign of your baby's developing comprehension skills.

## Approximation Stage

In this stage, your baby may approximate your sign, but the body placement, the movement, or, most likely, the hand shape may be wrong. When his approximations do not use the correct body placement, the reasons why often make a lot of sense. When my son first signed the word BIRD, for example, he made the correct hand shape and movement (one hand making an L shape that opens and closes like a bird's beak) but the incorrect body placement. The correct placement for BIRD is in front of your mouth; he would make the sign in the air over his head. This is logical when you consider where birds are typically seen — up in the sky. Whenever he made this sign, I would acknowledge it, then model the correct sign.

**bird**

## Acquisition Stage

Once your child makes his first sign, duly rewarded by your enthusiastic response, he will begin to acquire new signs, slowly at first, and then in sudden bursts after 12 or so signs are in his repertoire. When a child's efforts are rewarded positively, he is more motivated to expand his vocabulary of signs.

**Q** **How quickly will my baby acquire signs?**

**A** Your baby's second sign may come 2 weeks after his first sign, and his third sign may come 2 weeks later. His fourth sign may come $1\frac{1}{2}$ weeks after that, and so on. By the time, your baby has learned his 10th sign, each new sign may come every 4 to 5 days or less. After a baby has 10 to 12 signs in his repertoire, at around 14 to 16 months of age, he may experience a signing explosion or a vocabulary burst. He then starts to pick up words quite rapidly. Still, children learn at their own individual pace.

My son learned a new sign every 2 to 3 weeks when he was younger than 14 months old. This gap lessened between 14 and 16 months. One day, when he was 16 months old, I saw something click in his eyes, and he spent the day pointing to things and looking at me, as if to say, "What's the sign for this?" From that point on, he learned about two to three new signs or spoken words a day.

# Sign Language Development Strategies

How and when babies and toddlers develop the ability to sign has been a subject of considerable research, though larger and longer research studies of signing children and their parents are still needed.

In the foreword to Joseph Garcia's book *Sign with Your Baby*, Dr. Burton White notes that two-thirds to three-quarters of the vocabulary used by adults is learned in the first 3 years of life. The ability to acquire language seems to peak at around age 3 to 4 and begins to decline steadily in subsequent years. Using sign language with children from birth until 3 years of age builds on their capacity to learn and develop language during this period. The increasing motor development of a baby's hands and his growing visual capabilities support this plan.

---

**Note from a Signing Parent**

My husband wasn't sold on the idea of signing with our son, so this is something that I did on my own with my son. One day, while at the park, our fussy 9- month-old started tapping his head with an open hand. We had no idea what was wrong with him. My husband asked me, in a frustrated tone, what sign I had been showing him that was like that. We eventually figured out that he was signing SLEEP. Our son was trying to tell us that he wanted to sleep (although it wasn't nap time) and that was the reason for his fussiness. Needless to say, my husband started to sign with our son after that, and he is now signing to our second child as well.

— Cynthia Martel, Toronto, Ontario

## Physical Prompts

The research team of Rachel Thompson, Paige McKerchar, and Kelly Dancho examined the effectiveness of specific methods used to teach babies to sign. They taught three babies and toddlers to request preferred items during play or mealtime, and concluded that "delayed physical prompting" and reinforcement were an important part of teaching independent signing.

In this study, delayed physical prompting meant showing a baby a desired object and then waiting more than 5 seconds for him to request the object by producing the sign for it. If the baby did not make the sign, caregivers would help him produce it, moving his hands together to make the sign for MORE, for example.

Physical prompts, if used, should be gentle. If a baby shows resistance to physical prompting, it should not be continued.

## Modeling

Others suggest the use of modeling in place of physical prompts. When modeling, rather than guiding your baby's hands, you use your own hands to show him how to create a sign. In my classes, I have suggested that parents focus on modeling signs for their babies and reinforcing them.

As with physical prompting, a strategy of "delayed modeling" can also be used. With delayed modeling, you show your baby a desired object and wait more than 5 seconds for him to request the object by producing the sign for it. If he does not make the sign for the item, show him the sign and say the word. For example, say "cookie" and sign COOKIE.

**cookie**

---

**Q** **I try several times a day to teach my son useful signs, but at 9 months of age he hasn't learned the signs for EAT, CHANGE, or even MOM. He *has* learned three signs (STARS, MOON, HAT) from a video we have, but these signs are not useful at his age. Am I doing something wrong?**

**A** No, you are not doing anything wrong. In fact, it's fantastic that a 9-month-old uses three signs. In your mind, separate what is useful to a 9-month-old (and his parents) and what is motivating for him. Some babies never sign CHANGE, but instead choose what interests them — STARS, MOON, and HAT in your baby's experience, or WIND, CLOUD, DOG, FISH, MORE, EAT, and TRAIN in my son's experience. Sign whatever words are most motivating for your baby.

## Incidental Learning

Thompson, McKerchar, and Dancho also recommend that parents teach their children signs during regular daily routines. This strategy, called "incidental learning," is advocated by Dr. Joseph Garcia, who points out that developing children learn most of their English vocabulary incidentally. Signs should not be formally taught to your baby, but rather shown to him in the context of activities such as eating, changing, or playing. These teaching opportunities should not be a chore for you or work for your baby. Both of you should have fun and enjoy interacting.

## Gesture Development

In their research study, Laura Namy, Linda Acredolo, and Susan Goodwyn recognized that babies, and particularly young toddlers, naturally use gestures and words early on in their development. These gestures include pointing and head shaking, as well as movements that may represent an object (two fingers hopping to represent the ears of a rabbit) or emphasize an aspect of an object, such as size (hands spread far apart to indicate a large ball). This study also looked at how parents influence toddlers' understanding by their use of both speech and gestures. Earlier research by Acredolo and Goodwyn concluded that babies learn gestures when they are taught through engaging, interactive activities.

# The Building Blocks of Communication

Several language development concepts and principles have emerged from studies on how children develop the language skills needed to communicate. Among these principles are three building blocks of language development: shared attention (joint attention), turn taking, and vocabulary growth.

## Shared Attention

Shared attention, or joint attention, refers to instances when you and your baby share interest in one object or activity. Your baby might look at something, such as a ladybug crawling up the outside of a window, and then look at you expectantly, as if he is attempting to direct your attention with his eyes.

These instances create opportunities for you to interact with your baby based on what interests him. You might notice that he is interested in the ladybug and then get down to his level to look at it with him. You can then teach him words that pertain to this fascinating new creature he has found. You might say and sign, "It's a BUG. You see a BUG. Let MOMMY see the BUG."

> **Note from a Signing Parent**
>
> When our daughter first started eating cheese, she loved it so much she kept signing "more." We had always signed PLEASE and THANK YOU to her, but didn't think she was picking it up. One night after dinner, I decided she had had enough cheese. She immediately signed PLEASE — I couldn't say no!"
>
> — Ginnie Svilans, Thunder Bay, Ontario

**bug**

## Sharing Attention

According to a study by Tricia Striano and Evelin Bertin, shared attention skills develop gradually between the ages of 5 and 10 months. A baby is able to share attention when he can:

- Look at an item of interest;

- Think about wanting to show it to someone;

- Remember who that someone is;

- Shift his attention to that someone;

- Get that someone's attention (often only with an eye gaze);

- Shift attention back to the item (which includes remembering where the item is); and

- Look back at the person to communicate, usually with a sound or gesture.

## Turn Taking

When we think of turn taking, we usually think of preschool or school-age children taking turns while playing games, but babies will take turns as well, though not in terms of board games or time on a swing. Babies take turns by imitating the sounds and movements that another person produces.

From the time he is about 4 months old, your baby may coo and goo when you coo and goo. He may move his arms to mimic big motions you make. He may open and close his mouth when you open and close your mouth. These important games help your baby understand that a conversation or communication is at least two-sided. He will learn that one person talks (or coos) and then the other responds.

*"Parents felt positive about their decision to sign and believed that the practice had improved early communication in their families."*

— Pizer, Walters and Meier, 2007

## Vocabulary Growth

What parents choose to sign to their babies differs from family to family and from child to child, based on their interests. Most families sign basic words, such as SLEEP, BATH, and CHANGE. If your baby's main interest is spending time with you and nursing, you will be signing MILK a lot. If he is interested in the people around him, frequently used signs might be DADDY, MOMMY, and GRANDMA.

Observe your child's interests and use them to help his vocabulary grow. Start with 10 to 12 signs and expand his vocabulary steadily. Be prepared for both slow times and sudden bursts of sign development.

Typically, children at 18 months will be able to use about 10 spoken words. At 18 months, my son had an expressive vocabulary of 80 words — 20 spoken words and 60 ASL signs.

# CHAPTER 3

# Signing with Your Young Baby

## 0 TO 6 MONTHS

THE MOST FREQUENTLY ASKED QUESTIONS I hear from parents are, "When should I start signing with my baby?" and "Is it too late to start signing?" Oh, the guilt and stress that comes with parenthood.

Start as early as you can, when you can. Start at day one. If your baby is 4 weeks old, start now. If your baby is 11 months old, get started. Most babies will sign back between 8 and 12 months of age. A few will sign earlier and a few will sign later.

If you start signing to a younger baby, it may be a few months before she can produce the signs you do, but you will be able to observe her growing comprehension as she learns to recognize what you sign to her. She will understand what she sees before she can make her first signs. Signing to her can help her understand her surroundings and what activities are going on or coming up next.

> *"Hearing infants with no prior sign language exposure show an interest for American Sign Language over non-linguistic pantomime."*
>
> — Krentz & Corina, 2008

### Note from a Signing Parent

When Richard was born premature, we sat in NICU and felt so helpless. We wanted to reach out to our son and comfort him. I started signing and singing "The ABC Song" and "Twinkle, Twinkle, Little Star." The nurses commented that our son was very focused on the signing. As time went on, I added new songs and signs and taught them to my husband as well. Richard seemed to follow our signs.

By 3 months of age, he began to show us that he understood simple phrases, such as "MOMMY/DADDY is going to CHANGE your DIAPER." If we just said the phrase, without signing, Richard would cry. However, if we signed and said the phrase, he would relax. It was almost as if he was telling us, "Oh, now I understand what you're doing."

By 4 months of age, Richard would lift his foot when we said and signed "SOCKS ON" or "SHOES ON." And later, the first songs he sang and signed back to us were "The ABC Song" and "Twinkle, Twinkle, Little Star."

— Joanne Davis, Brooklin, Ontario

Older babies and toddlers still benefit greatly from learning to sign. Both of my children started signing when they were between 9 and 11 months old, but it wasn't until they were toddlers that their signing skills really took off — at one point, my son was learning about one sign a day. It was remarkable to see how their little minds worked, what intrigued and interested them.

# Signing with Your Baby (0 to 3 months)

The first 3 months of your baby's life are a time of tremendous growth and development. This is also a period of strenuous adjustment for new parents. Nevertheless, you can help your child develop certain signing skills, even at this young age. Remember, every child develops at a different pace. Let your baby set the pace as you establish daily routines and create learning experiences.

These first few months with your new baby will be exciting, as well as exhausting. At times, you may feel overwhelmed, but remember that you are doing a great thing for your baby by signing with her.

## Your Baby's Developing Brain

Because the part of the brain responsible for interpreting visual stimuli develops earlier than the area responsible for analyzing auditory input, young babies get more out of your interactions when you sign and speak to them than they do from speech alone.

A young baby is more interested in you than in objects. One of your baby's favorite activities will be to gaze at your face, listen to your voice, and watch how you move. You are the star of the show, so take advantage of your celebrity!

**Note from a Signing Parent**

Every time I breastfed my daughter, I would sign MILK and say it at the same time. Very quickly, I just had to sign MILK to Olivia from across the room, and she would beam a big smile and squeal, knowing what it meant.

— Debbie-Lynn Hoste, Toronto, Ontario

## Introducing Signs to Your Baby

Signing with your little one at this early age can be a wonderful activity in the midst of feeding and bathing her, establishing routines, and trying to sleep.

## Choose Your First Signs

During these first months, you are learning your baby's behavioral patterns and body language. You are discovering that when she pulls her ear or rubs her eyes, she is telling you, "I'm tired." This is the perfect opportunity to show her the sign for SLEEP. When she starts chewing on her hand or rooting, she is sending the message "I'm hungry." Show her the sign for MILK. One fun and soothing way to reinforce these signs is to make up simple songs that emphasize the words "sleep" and "milk," allowing you to repeat the signs several times.

**sleep**

**milk**

---

### Note from a Signing Parent

Elena's first sign was for MILK. She was a very calm baby and rarely cried. One day, when we were around other children who didn't sign, I realized that she didn't have the same frustrations as the others. Elena didn't have to cry to ask for what she wanted, she just signed. She also settled down very quickly when she saw me signing, as if she recognized that I understood and MILK or a DIAPER CHANGE was coming right up. Elena's grandmother (my mom) was a non-believer in signing with babies until she noticed this behavior. Suddenly, she was so proud of her granddaughter's skills that she was telling all her friends about our signing classes.

— Vivian Likourezos, Markham, Ontario

---

## Initiate Turn-Taking Imitation Games

During quiet periods with your baby, spend time gazing at each other's faces. This is a wonderful opportunity to introduce imitation games. If your baby opens her mouth, open your mouth. If your baby coos and goos, mimic these sounds. If your baby moves or waves her arm, copy these movements.

As you imitate your baby and gaze at her, and she gazes back, you will find that you fall into a pattern of turn taking. At times, she will wait for you to stop imitating her before she makes her next sound or movement. This interactive turn taking is one of the first steps in communication development.

### ✔ SIGNING TIPS

- Make signing fun.
- Sign at your comfort level.
- Start simple and add more signs as you learn them and as your child's activities and interests grow.
- Always sign and speak at the same time.
- Speak normal sentences and phrases, but sign only key words.

### Sign Key Words

Always speak while signing with your baby, and sign only one or two key words in each phrase or sentence. Key words are usually a noun or a verb, and they carry most of the meaning in a sentence. For example, in the sentence "Do you want more milk?" the key word is "milk." If we could say only one word, "milk" said with a questioning look and intonation would get the meaning of the sentence across: "Milk?" Therefore, MILK is the word you should sign while saying the sentence.

### Sign at Your Comfort Level

When you begin signing with your baby, start at your comfort level. Signing with your baby should be fun, not stressful. If you know 3 signs, use 3 signs; if you know 20 signs, use 20 signs. Let yourself be silly and use lots of facial expression. Parentese and gesturese will help you gain your baby's attention, and once you have it, you can create opportunities for her to learn from you. Your baby will enjoy the attention — and will likely be fascinated with what you are doing with your hands.

## Language Milestones at 3 Months

Babies and toddlers reach somewhat predictable milestones in their language development, including their sign language development. The chart below presents some of the language milestones your baby will meet by the time she is 3 months old. These milestones appear in the left column. The middle column explains how you can interact with your baby when she demonstrates these behaviors. In the right-hand column is a space where you can fill in the date that your child reaches each milestone (for example, 29/11/07).

The activities in the middle column show you ways to incorporate signs into your everyday activities while playing (not working!) toward that milestone. In the course of these activities, you will create opportunities for your baby to communicate and practice her signing skills. A good way to encourage your baby to achieve a milestone behavior is to model that behavior yourself. Have fun playing games and signing songs to your baby — and enjoy making up your own games.

Every child develops somewhat differently, but if you are concerned that your baby is not meeting these language development milestones, talk with your family doctor or contact a local speech-language pathologist. To find a speech-language pathologist in the United States, contact the American Speech-Language-Hearing Association (ASHA); in Canada, contact the Canadian Association of Speech-Language Pathologists and Audiologists (CASLPA).

| Typical Speech & Language Milestones | Opportunities for Signing Interaction | Date Your Child Reached Level |
|---|---|---|
| Makes noises, such as coos or gurgles. | Imitate these sounds when your baby makes them. This will turn into a great turn-taking game for the two of you. | |
| Makes movements with her arms, hands, and mouth. | Imitate these movements when your baby makes them. Be silly, and wait to see how she responds. | |

| Typical Speech & Language Milestones | Opportunities for Signing Interaction | Date Your Child Reached Level |
|---|---|---|
| Turns toward you when you sing or speak. | Talk to your baby often, and sing and sign songs that are familiar to her, such as "The ABC Song" (page 230) or "Twinkle, Twinkle, Little Star" (page 239).<br><br>Sign and sing while you are face to face so that your baby can see your facial expressions and hands clearly. | |
| Has different cries for different needs, such as hunger, pain, or fatigue. | When your baby is hungry, show her the sign for MILK as you feed her.<br><br>When your baby seems tired, show her the sign for SLEEP as you lay her down in her crib.<br><br>When your baby needs a diaper change, show her the sign for CHANGE as you change her.<br><br>When your baby appears to be experiencing discomfort, respond to her while showing the sign for HELP or UP. | |
| Seems to recognize your voice and is calmed when you speak gently. | Talk to your baby often about what you are doing together. During these activities, sign SLEEP, PLAY, EAT, and CHANGE.<br><br>Sing and sign rhythmic songs, such as "Rock-a-bye Baby" (page 238) and "The I Love You Song" (page 234). | |
| Smiles at you and looks attentively, even expectantly, at your face. | Speak to her using parentese and sign to her using gesturese.<br><br>Sign your name as MOMMY or DADDY when she smiles at you.<br><br>Sign and say this simple chant: "Hi, I'm MOMMY [or DADDY] and I want to kiss your tummy!" | |
| Is attracted to movement and follows moving objects with her eyes. | Make lots of movement with your hands (gesturese).<br><br>Sign and sing the "Are You Sleepy?" and "Are You Hungry?" songs (pages 230–31), exaggerating your movements for the key signs in the songs. | |

Adapted by permission from *Growing with Communication: A Speech and Language Guide for Parents with Children under 5 Years of Age.* Oshawa, ON: Durham Preschool Speech and Language Program, 1999.

## Breast Milk vs. Bottle Milk

Parents who sign with their babies often worry about being specific when signing. For example, they wonder whether they should be signing MILK for cow's milk and BREAST MILK or NURSING when baby breastfeeds. Some parents choose to make the distinction by signing MILK or CUP MILK for milk from a bottle and MOTHER MILK for breast milk. Others use the sign MILK for both, but sign it over the breast to indicate breast milk. You can also combine the signs for BREAST and FEED (nourish) to sign BREASTFEED.

Regardless of how you choose to differentiate between the concepts of breast milk and milk from a bottle, be consistent with the verbal words and the signs you use. Your baby will catch on. She will likely be more focused on getting some of that white stuff than on how you label it!

### ✓ SIGNING TIPS

**Shared Attention**
- Take note of times when your baby is looking at an item and then looking at you expectantly.

- Get on the same level as your baby to see the object of interest from her point of view.

- Label the item of interest for your baby using both speech and signs.

**Note from a Signing Parent**

My daughter knew the signs for MILK and DADDY when she was 6 months old. Every time I signed MILK, she would throw herself into the nursing position.

— Laura Berg,
Toronto, Ontario

# Signing with Your Baby (4 to 6 months)

## The Building Blocks of Communication

When you are interacting and signing with your baby during playtime, bath time, or mealtime, you can focus on the three building blocks for effective communication with babies: shared attention, turn taking, and vocabulary growth.

### Shared Attention

Between 5 and 10 months of age, the development of shared attention skills is a gradual process. When you interact and play with your baby, be aware of the ways in which she is already communicating with you. She may be using her gaze and smiles as an attempt to interact. She may be reaching toward you or cooing to get your attention.

Acknowledge and build on these behaviors by showing her signs that seem appropriate to the situation. For example, if she is reaching toward you, you can respond by going to her and signing, "MOMMY? You want MOMMY? MOMMY's here." If she is looking at you and cooing, she may be requesting more of the tickles or snuggles you were giving. You can respond by playing with her more and signing, "MORE? You want MORE PLAYing? Here comes MORE!"

### Turn Taking

By the time she is about 4 months old, your baby will be developmentally ready for turn-taking or copy-cat games. When your baby makes a sound, mimic it and see how she responds. When your baby makes a movement, imitate it and see if she repeats it. See how long you can keep up these activities. You will find that for the first few weeks or months you will be doing the imitating, but it won't be long before your baby is mimicking your movements and sounds, and then your signs and words.

## Vocabulary Growth

Create a list of 10 to 12 signs you can use every day that are of interest to your family and your baby. These signs should be a combination of words for activities your baby enjoys and words for day-to-day routines. If you cannot think of 10 to 12 words, make a shorter list of 5 to 6 words. If you are comfortable with signing and come up with a list of more than 12 words, great. Sign at your comfort level and keep it fun.

Use the following table to create a vocabulary list of key words, then look up the signs for those words in the dictionary of 350 American Sign Language signs in Part 2 of this book. Share the signs with other caregivers and have them show the signs to your baby throughout the day.

| YOUR SIGN DICTIONARY | | |
|---|---|---|
| Family activities and activities your baby enjoys | | |
| | | |
| | | |
| Activities you do every day (even a few times a day) with your baby | | |
| | | |
| | | |

## Repetition

Once you've established a vocabulary list, try to sign to your baby as often as you can throughout the day. Set a daily target of signing, for example, 20 to 30 times a day. This does not mean showing 30 different signs to your baby, but rather showing her the signs from your list 30 times by the end of the day.

Show your baby these signs before, during, and after the activities you are involved in. Before your baby starts to nurse, sign MILK. While your baby is nursing, sign MILK. When your baby is finished nursing (and is still awake) sign MILK. Repetition is the key. When your baby is under 6 months old, you may be feeding her 5 to 6 times a day and changing her diapers 5 to 6 times a day (or more), so you might meet the goal of signing to her 30 times a day just by signing MILK and CHANGE before, during, and after feeding and change times.

# Language Milestones at 6 Months

Your baby will continue to develop language skills. When she is 6 months old, you can anticipate the following milestone behaviors (right column), which you can encourage with various activities (middle column). Model these milestone behaviors yourself, and have fun trying some of the suggested activities.

Remember to sign before, during, and after an activity. For example, if your baby is in her high chair and there is a set of toy keys on the table out of her reach, she may look at you, look at the keys, reach for them, and grunt. She is communicating that she wants the keys. Before you give them to her, sign KEYS. When you give them to her and while she is playing with them, sign KEYS. When she inevitably drops the keys, sign KEYS FINISH. Wait to see if she wants to play with them again; if she does, repeat the sign.

| Typical Speech & Language Milestones | Opportunities for Signing Interaction | Date Your Child Reached Level |
|---|---|---|
| Makes the sounds of various letters, including vowels and a few consonants, such as "b," "d," "m," and "n." | Imitate these sounds when your baby makes them. This will become a great imitation and turn-taking game. <br> Expand on the sounds your baby makes. For example, when she makes a "muh" sound, say the word "mama" to her and sign MOTHER. If there is a ball nearby when she makes a "buh" sound, show her the ball, say the word "ball," and show her the sign for BALL. | |
| Turns to look in the direction of new sounds (a dog barking, a visitor entering the room, the sounds of a musical toy). | Using signs and speech, tell your baby what is making the noise. When a dog barks and she looks toward it, sign and say DOG. When Grandma comes into the room, sign and say GRANDMA. When a music toy is set off, sign and say MUSIC. | |
| Makes sounds such as clicking her tongue, coughing, or blowing raspberries. | Take turns making these sounds with your baby so she can learn that communication is a two-way street. <br> During this game, stop making the sounds yourself. If your baby continues to make the sounds and pauses to look at you expectantly, sign and say, "You want MORE?" Then make the sounds again. Do not pressure her to sign MORE, just show her how to do it. She will soon catch on. | |

| Typical Speech & Language Milestones | Opportunities for Signing Interaction | Date Your Child Reached Level |
|---|---|---|
| Smiles at herself in the mirror. | Sign and say "BABY," "MOMMY," and "DADDY" (whoever is making an appearance in the mirror). Label your baby's body parts while pointing to them. | |
| Laughs aloud. | Offer more of whatever made your child giggle. If you were tickling her tummy, look expectantly at her and sign and say "MORE?" She may indicate that she wants more by wiggling or moving in some way. She is communicating! Show her the sign for MORE again and start tickling. Stop tickling, show her the sign for MORE and wait. As long as she somehow indicates that she wants more, sign and say "MORE" and then tickle-tickle-tickle. | |
| Reaches for and brings a toy to her mouth. | Tell your baby what the toy is: TOY, KEYS, BALL, BLOCK, RATTLE. | |

Adapted by permission from *Growing with Communication: A Speech and Language Guide for Parents with Children under 5 Years of Age.* Oshawa, ON: Durham Preschool Speech and Language Program, 1999.

## More Eating Activity Signs

A young baby's day is typically made up of four activities: eating, getting changed, sleeping, and playing (otherwise known as watching you). Now is a good time to introduce more signs related to eating. Even if your baby is not eating solids at this stage, you can still use the signs to describe what you are eating. And even though your baby may not be signing back at this point, you are stimulating her receptive communication abilities by using signs paired with speech.

Good resources include images of food in board books, toys representing food, and images of food on building blocks. When looking for books about food for your baby at this age, select small board books that are easy to wipe off. Books with one image (preferably a photograph) and one to two words per page are appropriate for this age. See the Resources (page 277) for a list of books recommended for this age group.

> **Note from a Signing Parent**
>
> We started signing when my oldest was 2 to 3 months old and then his brothers were newborn when we started signing with them because we were already using signs.
>
> — Isabelle Bastien, Outaouais, Quebec

## Introducing Signing to Other Family Members

New parents receive a lot of unsolicited advice when their baby comes home. Learning to deal with unwanted advice about your baby's eating, sleeping, bathing, and crying is part of becoming a new parent. If you choose to sign with your baby, you may be advised against doing so. Surround yourself as much as you can with like-minded individuals, and follow your instincts when it comes to parenting your little one. I have met many extended family members who are skeptical about signing with babies until they see their niece or grandchild signing. These converts become the proudest uncles, aunts, and grandparents you will find.

**Q** **Our extended family is criticizing our choice to sign with our baby. What should I do?**

**A** When your family sees your baby signing, most of them will be convinced and the criticism will stop. You could try teaching your extended family members one or two signs. Choose signs that may be motivating to them, such as GRANDMOTHER. Once they see a positive response, they will want to sign with your baby. For your own peace of mind, read as much as you can on the topic, get support from like-minded parents and caregivers, and enjoy the time you spend signing with your baby.

# Songs to Sign and Sing

You will find that most people have an interest in sign language and want to learn more. Children of all ages seem to be fascinated with sign language. Especially appealing are songs that can be signed. They are also a wonderful, meaningful way for older children to interact with your baby.

---

**Note from a Signing Parent**

My daughter Elena and I had been attending a WeeHands class since Elena was about 6 months old. One day after class, I picked up my nieces Kassandra (10 years) and Christina (8 years) from school. I had my WeeHands class manual in my car, and they started flipping through and found the song "On Top of Spaghetti" (to the tune of "On Top of Old Smokey"). They were asking about the signs shown in the manual and giggling all the way home (the song is funny), so I taught them how to sign the song as soon as we arrived. They loved it . . . and so did I. They kept Elena giggling all afternoon by signing and singing the song.

— Vivian Likourezos, Markham, Ontario

---

## First Songs to Sign

Below are two songs that you can sign and sing to your baby when you see that she is getting hungry or sleepy. By labeling her instinctive behaviors — pulling her ear when she is tired, rooting when she is hungry — with words and signs, you are letting her know that you understand her needs. Furthermore, you are modeling signs that she will eventually be able to use with you, before she is able to speak.

The songs are simple and have a familiar tune. Don't worry about signing all the words. Just focus on signing the key words (in small capital letters) as you sing, and keep it simple and fun.

### Are You Sleepy

Sign and sing the "Are You Sleepy?" song at your baby's nap time or bedtime, when she starts to look tired — when, for example, she is rubbing her eyes, pulling her ears, getting fussy, or putting her face into your shirt. Lay her down, place her in her swing, or hold her in your lap, then sign and sing the song. When she is in your arms, sign and sing the song as you rock. You can sign SLEEP on your face or hers.

---

**Note from a Signing Parent**

I started reading books to her and signing to her early, at 2 months. My daughter was 10 months old when she signed MOMMA LOVE YOU at nap time. Now she is a capable, smart hearing 5th grader with exceptional receptive skills.

— Lauralee Sessions Wagner, California City, California

---

**sleep**

### Are You Sleepy?

*(Sung to the tune of "Frère Jacques")*

Are you SLEEPy? Are you SLEEPy?
BABY mine. BABY mine.
Now it's time for SLEEP. Now it's time for SLEEP.
Time to SLEEP. Time to SLEEP.

### Are You Hungry?

Sign and sing the "Are You Hungry?" song when your baby is starting to look hungry — when, for example, she is rubbing or sucking on your shirt or putting toys or her fist into her mouth.

**hungry**

### Are You Hungry?

*(Sung to the tune of "Frère Jacques")*

Are you HUNGRY? Are you HUNGRY?
BABY mine. BABY mine.
Now it's time for MILK. Now it's time for MILK.
Time to EAT. Time to EAT.

## More Songs to Sign

Here are five more songs or chants that you can sign to your baby. Say or sing all the words and sign the key words (in small capital letters). With practice, this will get easier and easier to do.

If you know other signs not highlighted here, feel free to add them. Sign and sing these songs to your baby throughout the day. Be sure that you are both in comfortable positions and that she can see your face and your hands.

Additional songs to sign and sing can be found in Chapters 4 through 8 and in Part 3.

**baby**

### Rock-a-Bye Baby

Rock-a-bye BABY, in the TREEtop,
When the WIND blows, the cradle [sign BABY] will rock.
When the bough breaks, the cradle [sign BABY] will FALL,
And down will come BABY, cradle and all.

From the HIGH rooftops, DOWN to the sea [sign OCEAN],
No one's as LOVED, as BABY to me.
Wee little fingers, EYEs wide and bright,
Now sound ASLEEP, until MORNING light.

## Pat-a-Cake

Pat-a-cake, pat-a-cake, baker's man
   [clap your hands together]
Bake me a CAKE as fast as you can.
Roll it and knead it [mime rolling and kneading]
And mark it with a "B" [show the sign for the letter "B"]
And put it in the oven for BABY and ME.

## Round and Round the Garden

Round and round the GARDEN
Like a teddy BEAR;
ONE step, TWO step,
TICKLE under there! [tickle your baby]

**cake**

## The I Love You Song

I LOVE you, you LOVE me,
We're a HAPPY FAMILY.
With a great big HUG
And a KISS from me to you,
Won't you say you LOVE me too?

## My Baby Lies over the Ocean

*(Sung to the tune of "My Bonnie Lies over the Ocean")*

My BABY lies over the OCEAN.
My BABY lies over the sea [sign OCEAN].
My BABY lies over the OCEAN
O BRING back my BABY to me.

BRING back, BRING back,
O BRING back my BABY to me.
BRING back, BRING back,
O BRING back my BABY to me.

**ocean**

---

### Note from a Signing Parent

I have always sung and signed "Hush Little Baby" and *Signing Time*'s song "Goodnight Baby" to my daughters as their lullabies . . . and I still do it every night now that they are preschoolers.

— Kristen Duncan, Mississauga, Ontario

# CHAPTER 4

# Signing with Your Older Baby

## 6 TO 12 MONTHS

BY THE TIME YOUR BABY IS 6 MONTHS OLD, HE is paying more attention to you, playing with his hands, and likely making a number of sounds. He may be sitting up and may have started on solid food. His world is becoming an exciting place, and he is reacting to it with giggles, smiles, and lots of movement. You may notice him watching your hands quite a bit now. He may laugh when you sign and attempt to copy your movements. Now is a good time to show him more signs. Your baby may be ready to sign back.

## First Conversations

Between the ages of 6 and 8 months, babies typically move from cooing with one repeated sound, such as "ba-ba-ba-ba," to babbling with a variety of sounds, such as "ba-da, da-ba, ma-da." It often sounds like they are having a little conversation in phrases and sentences — we just cannot figure out what the words are.

The same thing may be happening with your baby's arm and hand movements. Movements that were repetitive may become more varied, and these combinations of movements may start to have a definite pattern. These more organized sounds and movements are your baby's way of practicing until he is ready for his first signed word and then his first spoken word.

---

**Note from a Signing Parent**

We started at 4 months. We had a family friend who signed with her boy and we just thought it was the coolest thing.

— Angela Hume-Messina, Toronto, Ontario

---

**SIGNING GAME**

Sign and say "mama" or "dada" (depending who you are!) to your baby over and over to your baby as you snuggle them in your arms.

---

**Note from a Signing Parent**

At 7 months, Olivia surprised us by signing MILK, and signed it to anyone who was holding her when she was hungry. My husband, Piet, had been quite doubtful about "this signing business" until he saw her sign back. Soon afterward, Piet became interested in taking classes with us, and we had a wonderful time in class and at home. My skeptical husband began testing me after class, and quickly caught up to me in his knowledge of signing. We also purchased the *Signing Time* videos, which all of us enjoy, and they quickly became a frequently requested treat by Olivia.

— Debbie-Lynn Hoste, Toronto, Ontario

# Teaching Signs to an Older Baby

During these months, focus on signing during typical daily activities, particularly mealtime, change time, bath time, and sleep time. Your baby may become more engaged in these activities as he begins to sleep less and play more.

Now that your baby is starting to become mobile, this is also a good time to teach him some safety signs.

## Mealtime Signs

In addition to learning about communication and language, your baby is now learning how to feed himself (though perhaps not neatly). As you offer him small bits of his first solid foods, show him the sign for each item. These may include O-SHAPED CEREAL, CRACKER, COOKIE, CARROT, BANANA, PEAR, APPLE, POTATO, PEACH, JUICE, MEAT, PASTA, PEA, CHEESE, and YOGURT. You'll also find opportunities to sign new food words at the grocery store and while reading books with food vocabulary. Add any new signs to your word list, and remember to sign the words each time you say them.

During mealtime, pause between bites and wait to see what he does to indicate that he wants more. Does he look toward you expectantly and open his mouth? Does he lean toward you and hold out his hand? Does he reach for the food item, look at it, and look at you? These are all ways that early communicators may try to get across their message, which in this case is *Feed me!* Respond to how your child is communicating now and model the correct sign for the food item.

## More

Teach the word and sign for MORE by providing your baby with many opportunities to ask for more of a small food item or a turn with a favorite toy. Between bites of a banana, or while you take a turn with your baby's train, pause and wait for a response. Your baby might open his mouth, reach toward you, or lean forward. Wait for this, show the sign MORE, and give him the item. When he has the item, sign and say, "You wanted MORE."

> ✓ **SIGNING TIPS**
> - Pause between bites at mealtime to create opportunities for your baby to sign back.
> - Never pause for a length of time that frustrates your baby.
> - If your baby does not sign back yet, keep modeling the signs and creating opportunities for him to sign back.

> ✓ **SIGNING TIPS**
> - Model food signs *before* you give a food item to your baby: "Here comes the BANANA."
> - Model food signs *during* mealtime as your baby eats: "You're EATing the BANANA. It's GOOD!"
> - Model food signs *after* the food is gone: "BANANA'S FINISHED!"

### Note from a Signing Parent

When my daughter was 10 months old, I was giving her Cheerios, but she kept signing MORE and then throwing them on the floor. I told her, "You don't want more if you are throwing them on the floor." Then she signed CHEESE. What she really wanted was cheese. It was amazing that she was able to tell me that.

— Laura Berg, Toronto, Ontario

# A Mealtime Signing Conversation

Here is an example of a conversation between Grandmother and Baby at mealtime. All the words are spoken, and key words are signed. Substitute your child's name for the word "Baby."

*Before* mealtime, Grandmother says and signs:
It's time to EAT. It's time for Baby to EAT. GRANDMA's going to get FOOD. Yummy FOOD! GRANDMA's got your FOOD. GRANDMA's going to get WATER. Here's your WATER.

*During* mealtime, Grandmother says and signs:
Oh my, Baby is HUNGRY! EAT it up! Here comes MORE FOOD. Baby's eating FOOD. Is it GOOD? Here's a DRINK of WATER. Baby's DRINKing. Here's MORE FOOD. MORE FOOD!

*After* mealtime, Grandmother says and signs:
Baby was HUNGRY! The FOOD's all FINISHED. Baby's WATER is all FINISHED too! Baby's FINISHED EATing!

In this example, Grandmother has signed before, during, and after the meal. She has signed 30 times, using nine signs, for EAT, GRANDMA, FOOD, WATER, HUNGRY, MORE, GOOD, DRINK, and FINISHED. Other signs can be substituted into this script, including signs for food that your baby is eating or drinking. You can also sign and sing the "Are You Hungry?" song (see page 230) to add more signs and fun to mealtime.

**eat**

## Diaper Change Time Signs

Provide opportunities for your baby to communicate when you're changing his diaper by showing him the signs for words related to change time, such as DIAPER, CHANGE, FULL, DIRTY, WET, CLEAN, and FINISHED. You can also introduce other signs, such as TOY, if your baby needs something to keep him occupied while you're cleaning him up.

### Note from a Signing Parent

We didn't bring my daughter home from Russia until she was $10\frac{1}{2}$ months old. My husband is Deaf, so we naturally started signing with her. After being in a strange new world for only a month, she started signing back to us. MORE was her first word. She had more than 10 ear infections before the doctor put her tubes in, but even when she couldn't hear, she wasn't missing language. Recently, at age 3, she had a language evaluation and scored 3 years, 9 months. We are the poster family for signing with a baby!

— Cara Senterfeit, Lexington, South Carolina

# A Diaper Change Time Conversation

Here is an example of a conversation between Daddy and Baby at diaper change time. All the words are spoken, and key words are signed. Substitute your child's name for the word "Baby."

*Before* diaper change time, Daddy says and signs:
It's time to CHANGE your DIAPER. Let's get a DIAPER. Let's get Baby CLEAN. DADDY's going to CHANGE Baby's DIAPER.

*During* diaper change time, Daddy says and signs:
DADDY's CHANGE-ing Baby's DIAPER! Let's get you all CLEAN. Do you WANT a TOY? Here's a TOY. Do you WANT MUSIC?

*After* diaper change time, Daddy says and signs:
Baby's all CLEAN! We're FINISHED! CHANGE-ing is FINISHED!

In this example, Daddy has signed before, during, and after the diaper change. He has signed 20 times, using eight signs, for CHANGE, DIAPER, CLEAN, DADDY, WANT, TOY, MUSIC, and FINISHED. You can substitute other signs that work for your family. Add fun by singing and signing "It Is Time to Change Your Diaper."

## A Diaper Change Time Song

The following song, sung to the tune of "She'll Be Coming 'Round the Mountain," may help keep a squirming baby occupied while you change him. You can also sing and sign the song just before change time to let your baby know what's going to happen. If your baby is very squirmy, just sign what you can during the diaper change.

### Change Your Diaper Song
*(Sung to the tune of "She'll Be Coming 'Round the Mountain")*

It is time to CHANGE your DIAPER 'cause it's WET.
Oh, it's time to CHANGE your DIAPER 'cause it's WET.
Yes, it's time to CHANGE your DIAPER,
It is time to CHANGE your DIAPER,
Oh, it's time to CHANGE your DIAPER 'cause it's WET.

It is time to CHANGE your DIAPER 'cause it's FULL.
Oh, it's time to CHANGE your DIAPER 'cause it's FULL.
Yes, it's time to CHANGE your DIAPER,
It is time to CHANGE your DIAPER,
Oh, it's time to CHANGE your DIAPER 'cause it's FULL.

**diaper**

### Bath Time Signs

The signs for BATH , WATER, BUBBLE, WASH, SOAP, and MORE will be useful during bath time with your baby. You may have a BALL or DUCK in the tub, as well as waterproof bath books that you can sign and read.

## A Bath Time Conversation

Here is an example of a conversation between Mommy and Baby at bath time. All the words are spoken, and key words are signed. Substitute your child's name for the word "Baby."

*Before* bath time, Mommy says and signs:
It's time for your BATH. Time for Baby's BATH. Let's put the WATER in the tub. Let's put the BUBBLES in the tub. Let's put your DUCK in the tub. Now we'll get your DIAPER off. It's time for your BATH.

*During* bath time, Mommy says and signs:
Let's get you CLEAN. MOMMY's WASHing Baby. Here comes the SOAP. Do you WANT a TOY? Here's a TOY. Do you WANT MUSIC? Do you need MORE SOAP? Let's play with the BUBBLES! Here's your BALL! Let's find the DUCK.

*After* bath time, Mommy says and signs:
Baby's all CLEAN! We're FINISHED! BATH time is FINISHED. The WATER's all gone [sign FINISHED]. The BUBBLES are all gone [sign FINISHED]!

  In this example, Mommy has signed before, during, and after bath time. She has signed 29 times, using 15 signs, for BATH, WATER, BUBBLES, DUCK, DIAPER, CLEAN, MOMMY, WASH, SOAP, WANT, TOY, MUSIC, MORE, BALL, and FINISHED. Feel free to substitute other signs into this script. Add fun by singing and signing "Wash, Wash" or other favorite songs.

**bath**

### A Bath Time Song

Bath time is a great time for all your signing songs. Here's one specifically for bath time that uses the signs for WASH and WATER and involves naming different body parts. It is sung to the tune of "Row, Row Your Boat."

### Wash, Wash
*(Sung to the tune of "Row, Row Your Boat")*

WASH, WASH, WASH your _____ [fill in the blank].
WASH your little _____.
Pour the WATER on your _____.
And WASH your little _____.

## Bedtime Signs

Useful signs at bedtime and nap times include BED, BOOK, MUSIC, I LOVE YOU, LIGHTS OFF, and SLEEP.

## A Bedtime Conversation

Here is an example of a conversation between Daddy and Baby at bedtime. All the words are spoken, and key words are signed. Substitute your child's name for the word "Baby."

*At bedtime*, Daddy says and signs:
It's time for BED. Time for Baby to go to SLEEP. Let's put on your PAJAMAS. Let's READ a BOOK and sing a SONG. It's time for BED.

*After* Daddy reads and signs a favorite book and sings and signs a favorite song, he says and signs:
It's time for BED. Time for Baby to go to SLEEP. The BOOK is FINISHED. The SONG is FINISHED. Time to SLEEP. LIGHTS OFF. I LOVE YOU.

In this example, Daddy has signed 16 times, using nine signs, for BED, SLEEP, PAJAMAS, READ, BOOK, SONG, FINISHED, LIGHTS OFF, and I LOVE YOU, plus any signs he used while reading and singing. The bedtime routine you use with your baby may vary from this example. Every family does something slightly different at bedtime, based on what suits their schedule and their baby's temperament. Just be consistent with your routine — it will help your baby understand what is happening and may make for smoother bedtimes.

## Safety Signs for Curious Movers

Now that your baby is crawling and is on the verge of walking, you'll need to childproof your home, if you have not already done so. You can also use sign language to help ensure your baby's safety. If you teach him signs such as NO-TOUCH-NO, CAREFUL, HOT, and DOWN while he is safe, you will be able to warn him at times when a situation threatens to become unsafe.

- NO-TOUCH-NO: The signed phrase NO-TOUCH-NO uses English word order and repeats the most important word in the safety phrase as the last word your baby will see and hear. Accompany the signed phrase with an appropriate facial expression and say, "Don't touch."

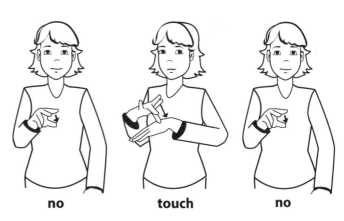

no        touch        no

- CAREFUL: Practice using this sign when helping your little one come down the stairs or off a bed. Always be with your baby during these times.
- HOT: Use this sign when you are cooking, when boiling the kettle, and when you have a hot cup of tea. From a safe distance, show your baby that steam and the stove are HOT using the appropriate sign and show a hurt look on your face.
- DOWN: Practice using this sign when you are coming down stairs with your baby and when you are getting him down from his high chair.

careful      hot      down

# The Building Blocks of Communication

The same building blocks of communication that you used when your baby was younger will help his development when he is between 6 and 12 months of age. During this time, you will see many of his abilities progress.

### Shared Attention

To encourage shared attention at this age, make sure that your baby sees the signs you make. Read books and tell stories that have repetitive language. Repetition helps the brain reinforce existing neural connections and make new ones.

### Turn Taking

Your baby is now learning that good conversations go back and forth. He is taking turns more and more during interactions. Imitation games that involve sounds will help with his speech development, while imitation games with movements will help him develop signing skills.

---

✓ **SIGNING TIPS**

- Sign words within your baby's range of vision.
- Sign between your baby and the object you are naming.
- Sign on your child (for example, tap the sign for DADDY on your baby's forehead).
- Sign on objects (for example, make the sign for BALL around your baby's favorite ball).

---

## Vocabulary Growth

So far, you have focused on signs for daily activities, such as eating, bathing, and diaper changing. Now you can introduce more signs related to your baby's interests.

Think of at least 10 to 12 activities or items he finds motivating, and start to use these signs throughout the day. As you get comfortable, you can add more and more signs to the list. We do not limit our speech when we communicate with babies, and you do not have to limit the number of signs you use. Say each word while you are signing it to give your little learner both auditory and visual input regarding the concepts you are teaching him. Sign the words in your list before, during, and after their related activities.

You can use these lists to track your baby's interests over time. Share this list of words and signs with all caregivers who interact with your baby.

| YOUR SIGN DICTIONARY | | |
|---|---|---|
| Family activities and activities your baby enjoys | | |
| | | |
| | | |
| Activities you do every day (even a few times a day) with your baby | | |
| | | |
| | | |

## Light On/Light Off

Your baby may be fascinated by light switches and overhead lights, so it may be helpful to know the signs for the phrases LIGHT ON and LIGHT OFF. He might not be able to turn lights off and on yet, but he'll love to watch you do it while you hold him in your arms.

**To sign LIGHT ON:**

- **Hand Shape:** Make a flat "O" shape with your dominant hand. Your palm will be facing the floor.
- **Body Space:** Depends on where the lights are in the room. For a table lamp, make the sign at shoulder level. For overhead lights, make the sign over your head.
- **Movement:** Open the "O" shape into a "5" shape, showing the light shining out.

**light on**

**light off**

**To sign LIGHT OFF:**

- **Hand Shape:** Make a "5" shape with your dominant hand. Your palm will be facing the floor.
- **Body Space:** Depends on where the lights are in the room. For a table lamp, make the sign at shoulder level. For overhead lights, make the sign over your head.
- **Movement:** Close the "5" shape into a flat "O" shape, as if the light is going out.

---

### Note from a Signing Parent

I always say, never limit what you sign with your baby, because you never know what he will be interested in. At 7 months of age, our son learned the signs for FAN, LIGHTS ON, and LIGHTS OFF. When in the stroller, Richard often had a different view of things than we did. He would tell us about unique ceiling fans and lights he saw. By giving Richard the signs early on, we were able to enhance our communication with our son — and see many beautiful fixtures at the same time.

— Joanne Davis, Brooklin, Ontario

---

**fan**

### Ceiling Fans

You may have noticed that one of your baby's favorite things to watch is a ceiling fan. Here's how to sign FAN, as in ceiling fan:

- **Hand Shape:** Make a "1" shape, pointed up, with your right hand.
- **Body Space:** Hold your hand at head or shoulder level.
- **Movement:** Move your hand in a circular motion (imitating one blade of the fan).

### Animal Signs

Children love animals, so you'll want to add lots of animal signs to your signs list. You'll find many opportunities to use these signs in day-to-day life, even if you don't have pets. Your baby likely has at least a few stuffed animals, and animals are popular characters in board books. When you go for a walk outside, your baby will see birds, squirrels, and cats, and you're bound to come across a dog or two. Depending on where you live, you might even meet horses, cows, or rabbits.

Whenever you are signing about animals, whether you are talking about the family pet or an orangutan at the zoo, pair the animal sound with the sign and imitate the gestures and sounds the animal makes, whenever appropriate.

Animal signs are likely to be some of the first ones your child attempts. In many cases, two-thirds of a toddler's vocabulary is related to animals.

**ZOO**

## Your Baby's First Signs

Between 8 and 12 months of age, your baby's babbling sounds become more conversational. The words may not be clear, but it almost sounds as if he is babbling in sentences. At this age, your baby may also begin to sign back to you. As his movements became more and more patterned, it will start to look like he is imitating your signs. Most likely, he is.

During regular routines in your baby's day, such as when he is eating or looking at a favorite board book, keep an eye out for these patterns of movement. If your baby is making a gesture that you think might be an attempt at a sign, take note of the body space and movement of his gesture and compare them to signs you have been using regularly in the context of the activity he is involved in. Chances are he is trying to mimic the signs you have shown him and is getting the body space and movement right but can't quite achieve the hand shape. Show him the item you think he might be signing, and model the correct sign. It may take a few tries before you pinpoint the item he is referring to, but when you do, you will be well on your way to your first real conversation with your baby!

**Q** Why is my baby not signing even though I have been using signs for a while?

**A** Every child develops at his own pace. Remember that your purpose in signing with your baby is not just about getting him to produce signs, it is also about helping him understand the signs you show him. Does he react to the signs you show him? Does he seem to relax when you sign FOOD? Does he get excited when you sign BATH? Your baby may be taking in everything you sign and say to him; he simply might not be ready to start making the signs himself.

Don't give up, he'll be signing soon. My son signed FISH at 9 months, and my daughter signed NO, MORE, and EAT at 11 months — not all together but at different times in the same week.

Put together a list of 5 to 6 signs that represent items or activities your little one finds motivating. To this list, add 5 to 6 more signs for activities that occur every day, a few times a day. He may not be as motivated by these signs, but they represent activities he is involved in often. Once you have this list, try signing each of these words, before, during, and after related activities. This way, you are showing him the sign quite a few times during the day. The repetition will help him absorb the meaning of the sign and reinforce the movements necessary to produce the sign.

# Language Milestones at 12 Months

The table below presents typical speech and language milestones that are met by most 12-month-old babies. To encourage these behaviors, model them yourself. But keep in mind that every child develops at his own pace; don't get anxious if your baby does not meet all of these milestones by the time he is 12 months old. Don't push him, just encourage him — and be sure to make learning fun! Play games and sign songs to your baby at every opportunity.

| Typical Speech & Language Milestones | Opportunities for Signing Interaction | Date Your Child Reached Level |
|---|---|---|
| Recognizes his own name. | Just for fun, practice fingerspelling your little one's name to him. | |
| Understands "mama," "daddy," and a few other simple words, such as "bye-bye," "more," and "up." | Sign the words he understands to show him how he can express these words before he is able to speak them. | |
| Says "mama" or "dada." | Applaud his spoken words and show him how to expand on them using both speech and sign language. Use phrases such as "Yes, MOMMY's here. You WANT MOMMY?" | |
| Has a 2- to 10-word spoken vocabulary. | Model 2-word phrases that use the words he can say. For example, sign and say, "DADDY HOME" and "MOMMY TICKLE" (and tickle him). | |
| Imitates sounds such as "oh, oh" and familiar words (but not always clearly — he might say "buh" for "ball," for example). | Repeat these sounds and words back to him to give him more practice. | |
| Follows simple instructions, such as "Stand up," "Sit down," or "Don't touch." | To encourage understanding, pair these instructions with signs: "STAND up," "SIT down," or "NO-TOUCH-NO" (for "Don't touch"). | |
| Understands "no." | When using this word yourself, continue to pair the verbal "no" with the sign for NO. | |
| Tries to sing and dance along with music. | Sing and dance with him! Before you join him, sign and say "MUSIC" or "DANCE." While you are dancing, show him these signs again. When he is finished dancing or the music ends, say and sign, "DANCE FINISHED." | |

| Typical Speech & Language Milestones | Opportunities for Signing Interaction | Date Your Child Reached Level |
|---|---|---|
| Imitates actions such as stirring with a spoon or banging on a drum. | Get on the floor and take turns stirring or banging with him. Gently take the spoon or drumsticks from him, signing and saying "MOMMY's TURN." Stir or drum for a few seconds, then sign and say "YOUR TURN" and give the spoon or drumsticks back. Keep your turns short so you don't frustrate him. | |
| Waves "hi" or "bye-bye." | Model these gestures back to him. Expand on them by saying and signing, "BYE-BYE, MOMMY," "BYE-BYE, GRANDMA," or "HI, DADDY." | |
| Shakes his head to mean "no." | Accept this way of saying "no," model the spoken word, and sign NO to him. | |
| Reaches for an object or points to it with interest. | Label the object using spoken words and signs. If you don't know the sign for the object, make a note of it so that you can look it up in the ASL dictionary in this book when it's convenient. | |
| Uses speech or non-crying sounds to get attention. | Acknowledge any positive way of getting your attention and show him the sign for MOMMY or DADDY. | |
| Anticipates events. For example, knows that a drink is coming when he sees a cup or bottle. | When you see him getting excited about an upcoming event, show him the sign for the event, such as BATH, DRINK, or a food. Make note of his preferred activities and objects so that you can show him these signs throughout the day. | |

Adapted by permission from *Growing with Communication: A Speech and Language Guide for Parents with Children under 5 Years of Age.* Oshawa, ON: Durham Preschool Speech and Language Program, 1999.

 **SIGNING TIPS**

Once you have the right books, here's how you can get and keep your baby's attention:

- Sign and say "LOOK" with an expectant and excited tone. Once your baby looks at you, use the sign to show him where to look.
- Use signs that, with their movement, will help your baby focus on the pictures.

# Reading and Signing

You can now introduce more and more vocabulary to your baby using board books and bath books. Parents often say that it is hard to read a book to a baby, let alone sign it. It's true: it *is* sometimes difficult to get babies to concentrate on pictures (they may have more fun chewing on a book than reading it).

## Choosing Books

The key lies in choosing the right type of book for this age range:
- Choose sturdy board books or washable bath books.
- Choose books with one concept and one or two words per page.
- Choose books with illustrations that are simple, yet bright and colorful.
- Choose books you know, so the flow of reading and signing is natural.

## How to Read and Sign

When you're sharing a book with your child, it's important to keep both the book and your signs visible. But you've only got two hands, so how is that possible?

- When sitting on the bed with your child in your lap, put the book on a pillow so that he can see the book and your signs. Most board books for small children will stay open.

- Use a cookbook stand to hold the book up and open.

- Sit side by side on the couch or on the floor and make your signs right on the book itself.

- When your baby is in his high chair, if you do not mind reading upside down, put the book on his tray and share the story with him.

- Read in front of a mirror so your child can see your facial expression as well.

- Choose books with repetitive language and familiar vocabulary. Soon, you won't even have to look at the words because you will have them memorized.

(Adapted by permission from www.babyhearing.org)

## Food Books

Try reading books (particularly those about food) to your baby at mealtime. When he was between 7 and 11 months, my son needed lots of entertaining during meals, so I made up songs and played games. Once, in desperation, I put a load of laundry in so that he could watch the water and bubbles swish around in our front-loading washing machine — just to get him to eat! I also read many board books to him during mealtimes to keep him interested in the activity. Your baby may not be eating all the foods shown in a board book, but reading books about food creates opportunities to say and sign words such as BERRY, ORANGE, and SANDWICH.

> **Note from a Signing Parent**
>
> All my babies in my childcare were taught MORE, PLEASE, and THANK YOU. Most had it down before speech ... at 10 to 12 months of age.
>
> — Deborah Dial, Lubbock, Texas

## Animal Books

Choose books about topics your baby is interested in. In addition to basic food signs, animal signs may be some of the first signs your child will attempt. Often, two-thirds of a toddler's vocabulary is related to animals. Animals are fascinating to our children whether you are talking about the family cat or a monkey at the zoo. Whenever you are signing about animals, say the word for the animal or pair the animal sound with the sign.

Animal books that are ideal for reading and signing include:

- *Brown Bear, Brown Bear, What Do You See?* by Bill Martin and Eric Carle
- *Good Night, Gorilla* by Peggy Rathmann
- *Dear Zoo: A Lift-the-Flap Book* by Rod Campbell
- *Peek-a-Moo!* by Marie Torres Cimarusti
- *Moo, Baa, La La La!* by Sandra Boynton

**cat**

**dog**

## Repetition

Over the course of the next few years, you will find yourself reading many books over and over again. Repetition is a comfort to your child, and the most requested books are often the ones with a repetitive, chant-like vocabulary. The repetition will help your child learn the vocabulary and phrasing used in the book — and it will also help you! You will soon know the words by heart and will be able to concentrate on making the signs. I cannot count how many times I have read and signed Margaret Wise Brown's *Goodnight Moon*. I am now so familiar with the text of this classic book that I need only glance at it from time to time. I can balance the book in my lap, positioned so that the child I am reading to can see the pictures, and my hands are free to sign.

# Signing Games

Play lots of signing games with your baby and encourage other people to do the same. Some examples of fun signing games follow, but enjoy making up your own games too!

### Attention Games

These games teach your baby appropriate ways to get someone's attention. For example, have Grandma (or any family member) pretend to read a book. Approach her with your baby and sign and say "GRANDMA!" Be sure that your baby can see you sign.

Grandma can act surprised, saying and signing, "GRANDMA! You want GRANDMA. GRANDMA's here!" Then Grandma can play with the baby for a little while. Repeat this game for as long as all three participants have the energy.

## Pause and Wait Games
Interactive games that allow you to pause and wait for your baby to respond are a great way for your 6- to 12-month-old to learn signing and spoken language skills.

### Hide and Seek
Have Daddy hide around the corner, then sign and say, "WHERE is DADDY?" Daddy can then run into the room, signing and saying, "DADDY, DADDY, DADDY" and give your baby hugs and kisses. Take turns doing this with different family members.

**where**

### Peek-a-boo
Peek-a-boo is a nice continuation of the hide-and-seek game. Choose a favorite stuffed animal, such as a teddy bear, and, when your baby is watching, cover it with a blanket. Sign and say, "WHERE is your BEAR?" Wait to see if your baby will look or point toward the blanket and then look at you. Then you or your baby can uncover the bear and sign and say, "Here's your BEAR." Take turns with your baby, hiding different toys.

### Up Games
Sign and say "UP" each time you take a step upstairs with your baby in your arms. Sign and say "UP" and the name of the toy when you throw a ball, a toy airplane, or a balloon into the air. When blowing bubbles, sign and say, "LOOK . . . UP!"

**bear**

### Photograph Games
Look through photo albums with pictures of family members. Point to the individuals in the photos, then sign and say their names to your baby.

## Songs to Sign and Sing

Here are five more songs or chants you can sign with your baby — including one you will be eager to learn as his first birthday approaches! Feel free to adapt other songs you know and even make songs up. It's okay to make mistakes — just have fun.

Keep in mind that, while you will be singing all the words, you will be signing only the key words. We do this for two reasons: because there is no direct word-for-word translation of ASL to English, and because we want to emphasize to our early language learners the information-carrying words in our speech.

> **Note from a Signing Parent**
>
> Julia's first sign at 9 months of age was CHANGE.
>
> — Angela Hume-Messina,
> Toronto, Ontario

**rain**

### Rain, Rain, Go Away
RAIN, RAIN, go away [sign FINISH].
Come again some other DAY.
We want to go OUTSIDE and PLAY.
So RAIN, RAIN, go away [sign FINISH].

### This Little Piggy Went to Market
This little PIGgy went to market [sign STORE].
This little PIGgy stayed HOME.
This little PIGgy had roast beef [sign MEAT].
This little PIGgy had NONE [sign NO].
And this little PIGgy cried [sign CRY], "Wee! Wee! Wee!"
    all the way HOME.

**dance**

### Baby's Fingers
BABY's fingers UP
And BABY's fingers DOWN.
BABY's fingers DANCE-ing
All around the TOWN.
DANCE-ing on your shoulders,
DANCE-ing on your head,
DANCE-ing on your knees,
then tuck them into BED.

*[repeat with MOMMY's or DADDY's fingers]*

### Zoom, Zoom, Zoom
Zoom, zoom, zoom [sign FAST],
We're going to the MOON.
Zoom, zoom, zoom [sign FAST],
We're going to the MOON.
If you want to take a TRIP,
Climb aboard my ROCKET ship.
Zoom, zoom, zoom [sign FAST],
We're going to the MOON.
5, 4, 3, 2, 1, blast off! [sign ROCKET]

**fast**

### Happy Birthday
HAPPY BIRTHDAY to you [point to your child].
HAPPY BIRTHDAY to you [point to your child].
HAPPY BIRTHDAY, DEAR [use the sign for
    LOVE and fill in your child's name]
HAPPY BIRTHDAY to you [point to your child].

# CHAPTER 5

# Signing with Your Young Toddler

## 12 TO 18 MONTHS

MANY PARENTS COMPARE NOTES ON THEIR baby's milestones and "firsts." Is your baby sitting up yet? Has she started eating solid food? Has she started to walk? Is she sleeping through the night? The answers for every baby will be different. The same holds true for the questions "Is she talking yet?" and "Is she signing yet?" The ability to communicate develops differently for every child.

---

**Note from a Signing Parent**

Each stage of development is a new joy. Our insight into our son's world began when he signed MILK for the first time, at 5 months of age. By the time he was 1 year old, he was developing his own personality and view of the world and was able to communicate, using American Sign Language, with his Deaf aunt. He was also able to clarify his words through his signs. For example, when he said "Nana," we never knew if we should pick up the phone to call his grandmother or hand him a banana to eat, but then he would sign either GRANDMA or BANANA to help us out. He described his grandparents' in-ground swimming pool by signing WATER BATH. After having a good chuckle about what a big bathtub that would be, we explained the difference and showed him the sign for SWIMMING (the breaststroke). From that point on, he had fun practicing the sign, and he is on his way to becoming a wonderful swimmer.

— Joanne Davis, Brooklin, Ontario

---

## Communication Development

At 1 year of age, your child understands more words and signs than she is able to express. She finds the world a fascinating place and is curious about almost everything. She may be imitating your sounds, your movements, and even your verbal words. She is likely paying attention for longer periods and is learning new things daily.

---

**Note from a Signing Parent**

My daughter was around 7 months (I think!) when she first signed MILK.

— Amanda Lutty, Carleton, California

You may want to start keeping an informal record of the signs and words your child is using to express herself. Don't stop there, though — record the signs and words she understands as well. Over the course of the next few weeks, you will be amazed at what she is learning.

## Name Recognition

At 12 months, your child will likely be able to recognize her spoken name, particularly when it is paired with a sign name. In the Deaf community, sign names are often given to people based on their personality and positive characteristics. When I was given my sign name by a member of the Deaf community, I had long, curly hair. My sign name uses the ASL letter "S" (for Sara) and, starting at the side of the head, moves downward in wavy movements (to indicate my hair).

Consider getting involved with the Deaf community in your area, especially baby sign language workshops or Deaf playgroups or family events. These will provide great opportunities for you and your toddler to practice your signing skills.

## Self-Expression

Your baby may now be able to express herself in a number of ways, using sounds, gestures, eye gaze, and even a 2- to 10-word vocabulary of signs or spoken words. For example, she may:

- Say "Mama" or "Dada."
- Wave "bye-bye."
- Shake her head to mean "no."
- Reach or point to an object of interest.
- Use speech or non-crying vocal sounds to get attention.

## Understanding Milestones

Your baby may now understand a number of key concepts:

- "Mommy," "Daddy," and a few simple words such as "bye-bye," "more," and "up."
- Simple commands such as "Stand up," "Sit down," and "Don't touch."
- "No."

She may also be able to anticipate events — for instance, knowing that a drink is coming when she sees a cup or bottle.

> **Note from a Signing Parent**
>
> It was comforting to know that when our son Richard had an "owie," he could tell us through his signs that he had hurt himself and how it had happened. I remember him signing PAIN (on his head) + DOOR + THERE (pointing to the door) on more than one occasion. After Richard explained what had happened, he would give us a hug and slow down his sobs. It was quite soothing for Richard to be able to express himself. One day, when he was in his playpen, he let out the biggest scream I had ever heard. Worried that he was hurt, I asked him what had happened. He signed BALL and pointed under the couch. His ball had rolled under the couch. He was so relieved when I explained to him that the couch had not eaten his ball and we could get it back.
>
> — Joanne Davis, Brooklin, Ontario

> **Note from a Signing Parent**
>
> One morning, I went to get my 11 month old daughter out of her crib, she signed EAT. Usually, I would take her out of her crib and then go around cleaning and making all the beds, but because she knew sign language and was able to tell me that she was hungry, we went right downstairs to eat breakfast.
>
> — Angela Messina, Stouffville, Ontario

## Playing with Language

Once children learn to use a sign in one way, they may practice and play with that sign to see how it works and what they can do with it. Along with playing interactive, turn-taking games, your child may now begin to play with language, specifically with sounds, movements, and word beginnings. Children at this age typically imitate sounds such as "oh-oh" and familiar words such as "ball," though they don't always say the words clearly. They may also try to sing along to music. Encourage these advances by mimicking the sounds and movements your child is making.

These language activities are not just random acts of play; they are very purposeful. Babies are built to learn language, whether it is spoken or signed. They are not intimidated by the challenge, as an adult learner may be. Adults whose first language is English may be nervous about having others watch and listen while they practice words in Italian, for example, but a baby has no fears when it comes to practicing. This is what babbling is all about, whether it is with sounds or with fingers.

Children learn language, spoken or signed, not just by imitating those around them, but by using language with a purpose and by making mistakes. Mistakes create opportunities for parents to model corrections.

> **SIGNING GAME**
>
> Signing and playing rhyming, clapping and singing games with your baby will help them to develop social skills. Your baby is learning that playing with others is fun!

# The Building Blocks of Communication

Continue to work on the three building blocks of communication with your young toddler.

**my turn**

## Shared Attention

Be aware of where your child is looking and pointing, especially when she looks back at you while she is doing this. She may be trying to direct your attention to something she wants to share with you. Take note of what she is interested in, and label these people, animals, or objects, using words and signs.

## Turn Taking

One-year-olds love to interact with you, and they enjoy playing games that involve you. This is a great time to continue working on turn-taking skills. You can take turns rolling a ball back and forth, filling and dumping out cups, and banging on pots and pans. Each time you take a turn, say and sign, "MY TURN." When your turn is done, while your young toddler waits for her turn, sign and say, "YOUR TURN."

**your turn**

## Vocabulary Growth

Continue to show your child signs for items and activities that motivate her. As she gets more active, her interests will grow. Take note of these interests, as well as any new activities that you are involved in daily.

Your personal sign dictionary will help you decide what new signs to show your toddler. Share these signs with other caregivers and have them show the signs to your baby throughout the day. Remember to sign the words in this list before, during, and after related activities.

| YOUR SIGN DICTIONARY | | |
|---|---|---|
| Family activities and activities your baby enjoys | | |
| | | |
| | | |
| Activities you do every day (even a few times a day) with your baby | | |
| | | |
| | | |

# Teaching New Signs at 12 to 18 Months

At every stage in your child's development, there are opportunities to introduce new signs. From 12 to 18 months, try focusing on everyday activities and new contexts.

## New Everyday Activity Signs

Help your child learn more signs about her daily routine by talking about what you are doing as you are doing it, using short phrases while signing key words.

## Clothing Signs

Learning the signs for items of clothing will help your toddler understand her daily routine. While getting your child dressed, sign and say, "SHIRT ON," "SOCKS ON," "HAT ON," and so on. While helping her get undressed, sign and say, "HAT OFF," "SOCKS OFF," "SHIRT OFF." When you're getting ready to go for a walk, sign and say, "SHOES ON." This sign will help you down the road, when you want to tell your 6-year-old that it is time to leave an indoor playground. It is much easier to sign, SHOES ON, we're GOING HOME NOW, than to shout loudly across a noisy room.

## More Food Signs

By this time, your child likely understands many words for food items. Now you can add some verbs and adjectives to her sign vocabulary to increase her understanding of the properties of different foods and her relationship to them. At lunchtime, you might say and sign, "WANT JUICE?" as you pull a sippy cup out of the refrigerator. When you pull a bag of frozen peas out of the freezer, let your child touch it while you sign and say, "COLD PEAS."

*"Using signs for emotions with your toddler may help them to express themselves & to help them understand the feelings of others."*

— Claire Vallotton,
Michigan State University

## New Contexts

Once you start showing your child how to sign, you will see her use signs in a number of novel contexts. I showed my son the sign for HOT when and where I thought it be most important to use it. Anytime we were near the stove, I signed HOT. When I had a cup of tea in my mug, I signed HOT. When a pot boiled on the stove, I showed him the steam from a safe distance and signed HOT. He did not show the sign back in any of these instances, as far as I can recall. I did not expect him to. I was not trying to teach him the sign for or concept of "hot" so that he could use the word, but so that he would understand that these items could be dangerous to him.

One cold day, I was surprised when I saw him looking out our front window and signing HOT as each car drove by. I sat with him at the window and asked him, "WHAT do you SEE?" When the next car went by, he looked at the back of it and signed HOT again. He was pointing to the muffler and labeling the exhaust with the sign for HOT. Who would have thought that I could have a discussion with a 15-month-old about muffler exhaust fumes?

Joshua had learned the sign for HOT in one instance and applied it to another. He did the same thing for COLD. I taught him the sign for COLD when taking cold items out of the freezer. Joshua signed COLD while we were walking through the freezer section of a grocery store one day.

# New Teaching Strategies

There are a number of teaching strategies you can employ at this age, including communicative temptations and teachable moments.

## Communicative Temptations (Delayed Modeling)

When my daughter was about 13 months old, she loved to play with balls and used the sign BALL frequently throughout the day. That year, we often sat by the Christmas tree for up to 20 minutes at a time because Sabrina wanted to sign BALL for just about every ornament on the tree. In January, I was making fruit salad and there was an orange on the counter. I had not yet introduced Sabrina to citrus fruit, so she was not quite aware of what you did with an orange. She pointed at it, looked at me, and signed BALL. This was my cue to teach her a new word. I picked up the orange and shook my head, saying and signing, "This is not a BALL. It's an ORANGE." She appeared puzzled, looked at the orange then back at me, and signed very firmly BALL. I smiled, then said and signed, "NO, it's an ORANGE." Of course, she signed BALL right back to me!

To this day, Sabrina will let you know what she wants and will tell you that you are wrong without hesitation. That was my first glimpse of her developing personality.

I stopped debating with her, peeled the orange, cut it into small pieces, and started feeding it to her. She loved it. I continued to feed her small pieces, showing her the sign for ORANGE before and after giving her a piece to eat. After I had shown her the sign a few times, I held up a piece in one hand and showed her the sign for ORANGE with the other — and then waited. She signed MORE. After eating about 30 small pieces, she could produce the sign for ORANGE without any prompting from me. She now understood a new sign and knew that an orange was different from a ball.

This is an example of a delayed modeling approach called communicative temptations. Communicative temptations are strategies that tempt your child to communicate in a new way, without frustrating her. Sabrina was communicating her desire by reaching toward the piece of orange, but I encouraged her to communicate in a way that was more sophisticated and symbolic: with a new sign.

> ### ✓ SIGNING TIP
>
> Rather than anticipating your young toddler's needs, give her a reason to communicate:
>
> - Give her a cracker in a closed but clear container. Your child can see the cracker, but needs your help to get it. When she looks at the container, looks at you, and indicates that she wants the cracker, say and sign, "You want the CRACKER?" and help her get it. Then put a new cracker in the container. After a few repetitions of this game, pause and wait for her to sign CRACKER before helping her open the container. Never wait so long that she gets frustrated, however.

## Teachable Moments

Every day, you will have many opportunities to teach your child new signs. The following strategies will help you turn everyday activities into teachable moments:

- Talk and sign about what you are doing as you are doing it, using short phrases. Throughout your daily activities with your child, sign and say, for example, "WANT MILK?" "HOT CUP," or "GENTLE CAT."

- Say and sign the names for pieces of clothing and body parts as you dress your toddler. Repetitive phrases, such as "SOCK ON," "SHOE ON," and "HAT ON," will help your toddler learn the words and signs.

- Teach the sign for MORE by giving your child many opportunities to ask for something, such as more food or more turns at an activity. Pause in what you're doing and wait for a response, which could be a movement or a sound.

- Clarify your child's approximations of words and signs by modeling the correct word or sign. For example, if your toddler says "daw" for "dog," sign and say, "Yes, DOG! There's a DOG outside!" If she uses the incorrect hand shape for WATER, sign and say "Yes, you want WATER," modeling the correct hand shape.

### ✓ SIGNING TIPS

Rather than anticipating your young toddler's needs, give her a reason to communicate:

- Eat a food that your child likes, such as cereal, in front of her and wait for her to indicate that she wants it. She may look at you and reach for the cereal or indicate in some other way that she wants it. When she does, give her a small amount and sign and say, "Here's the CEREAL!"

- Activate a wind-up toy and see how she responds to it. When it runs down, wait to see if she will ask for it to be wound up again. She might look at you and smile, for example. When she indicates that she wants to see it move again, sign and say, "You want MORE?" then activate the toy.

**Q** **My daughter signs MORE for everything! What can I do to introduce other signs?**

**A** For beginners, words may do double duty (or more). All men become, embarrassingly at times, DADA. All four-legged creatures are DOG. To move beyond this stage, keep showing her a variety of signs for objects and activities she is interested in.

When she signs MORE, acknowledge her request and show her how to expand on the sign. Show her, for example, MORE MILK when it looks like she wants more milk. Show her MORE BUBBLES when she wants you to blow more bubbles.

Offering her a choice may also encourage her to produce a more specific sign. When you are feeding her applesauce and she signs MORE, show her the applesauce and sign APPLE. Then bring out a cracker and sign CRACKER. Sign and say, "Do you want MORE CRACKER or MORE APPLE?" Wait and see what she does. If she signs MORE and reaches for the applesauce, show her how the two words can be signed together. Give her some applesauce and sign and say, "Oh, you want MORE APPLE. You're eating APPLE."

For a while, I thought Richard was fascinated with hats, but he really just loved his daddy. DADDY is signed at the front of the head, and HAT is signed on top of the head. Richard's placement of signs was a little off at times. One day I heard the commuter train and saw Richard excitedly signing TRAIN and HAT, and I finally clued in. Richard was trying to sign DADDY. He wanted to go for a stroller ride to see his daddy get off the train.

— Joanne Davis, Brooklin, Ontario

# Language Milestones at 18 Months

Encourage your baby to meet milestone behaviors by modeling them yourself. Take your time and have fun making up games and playing with your toddler.

| Typical Speech & Language Milestones | Opportunities for Signing Interaction | Date Your Child Reached Level |
|---|---|---|
| Says "no!" | Whenever you say "no," sign it. | |
| Asks for something by pointing to an object and saying "uh-uh!" | Acknowledge his gesture, show him the sign for the object, and say its name: "Yes, it's a FAN." | |
| Is aware that objects exist even when they're out of sight. For example, he will help find Mom's glasses or the television remote when they're lost. | Play hiding games with familiar objects. For example, hide a book behind a pillow and then sign and say, "WHERE's the BOOK?" Ask for help by saying and signing, "I'm SEEKing the BOOK. HELP MOMMY. WHERE's the BOOK?" | |
| Follows simple instructions, such as "Find Daddy" or "Get your shoes." | Model signs that are often used in directions for toddlers, such as FIND, BRING, PUT ON, or GET. The added visual input (the signs paired with speech) will help your toddler understand and remember your instruction. | |
| Understands the names of common objects, such as toys or articles of clothing, and family members' names. | Label common items by playing a simplified game of I Spy. While sitting in the living room, sign and say "LOOK, a BALL" and wait for your toddler to find it. After a few seconds, point more specifically toward the ball, using the signs for LOOK and BALL again. You can also play this game while at the park, while looking at family photo albums, and while reading picture books. | |

| Typical Speech & Language Milestones | Opportunities for Signing Interaction | Date Your Child Reached Level |
|---|---|---|
| Although her words might not be very clear, your toddler uses many different sounds, including "b," "p," "w," "n," "t," and "d," at the beginning of words. | If you know what word she is trying to say, repeat the word correctly and show her the sign for it. For example, if she points to a dog and says "tog," model the correct spoken word while signing DOG. This way, in addition to teaching her the right way to say the word, you are giving her another way to communicate the concept of a four-legged furry pet. | |
| Points and gestures to call attention to an event or to indicate a need or want. | Point to objects that you know interest your toddler and sign their names. For example, while in a grocery store, point out all the ceiling fans, signing and saying, "There's a FAN. There's another FAN." While you are feeding ducks at the park, sign and say, "There's a DUCK. There's a big DUCK." | |
| Turns the pages of a book. | Model the sign TURN as she turns a page. | |
| Imitates chores you do, such as wiping up spills or setting the table. | Positively reinforce this helpful behavior by saying and signing, "THANK YOU for HELPing." | |
| Hums or sings simple tunes. | Play music and dance with your little one often. Sign DANCE and MUSIC before you put the music on and while you are listening to it. When it's over, sign and say, "MUSIC FINISHED." | |

Adapted by permission from *Growing with Communication: A Speech and Language Guide for Parents with Children under 5 Years of Age*. Oshawa, ON: Durham Preschool Speech and Language Program, 1999.

## Signing Games

Each day, your child is trying harder to understand language, sounds, and gestures. Her motor skills have increased, as well as her ability to concentrate. She seems to have limitless energy, compelling her to take part in interactive games like pat-a-cake and peek-a-boo. Continue to play these games with her. She will be able to participate more in them now and will likely request them.

Interactive games that allow you to pause and wait for your child to respond are great at this age. You can tempt her to request a game she loves by stopping the game and waiting for her to indicate that she wants more. When she does this by reaching toward you, vocalizing, or attempting a word or sign, you can respond by signing and saying, "MORE PLAY?" and then quickly continue to play the game with her. You are motivating her to communicate a feeling (that she loves the game), you are creating an opportunity for her to communicate (by pausing and waiting), and you are enhancing the way she communicates (by responding to her attempt to communicate and showing her how to do so in a more advanced way).

## Hide the Object

Let your toddler watch you when you hide a favorite object, then ask her, using speech and signs, where it is. When she gets good at playing the game this way, try partially hiding the object (so that part of it is still visible) while your toddler is not looking. Use common objects, saying their names and showing the signs for them as you play.

## Ball Rolling

Roll a ball back and forth with your child, modeling the signs for WANT, MY TURN, YOUR TURN, and BALL. When she is used to rolling a ball, surprise her by instead rolling a car or train to her, modeling the sign for CAR or TRAIN. Watch for her joyous reaction when she looks at you and the new toy.

**ball**

# Songs to Sign and Sing

"Ring Around the Rosie" and "Row, Row Your Boat" are traditionally great action songs, so why not sign them? Songs that have an anticipatory component ("Here comes a tickle") are also lots of fun for this age group (as long as the tickling is gentle). Sign and say "MUSIC" before you start to sing, and at the end sign and say, "MORE MUSIC?"

### Ring Around the Rosie
Ring around the rosie [sign FLOWER],
A pocketful of posies [sign FLOWER],
Husha, husha [sign SNEEZE],
We all FALL DOWN.

*Join hands and recite the chant again while skipping in one direction (it's okay — you can't sign while holding hands). When you fall down, sign and say "MORE?" If your child indicates in some way that she wants more, play the game again.*

**flower**

### Row, Row Your Boat
ROW, ROW, ROW your BOAT
Gently down the STREAM.
Merrily, merrily, merrily, merrily [sign HAPPY],
Life is but a DREAM.

**bus**

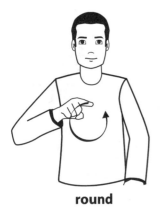

**round**

## The Wheels on the Bus

*(I've included just a few lyrics here, but you can add as many as you like. To sign WHEEL or ROUND, draw a circle in the air.)*

The WHEELS on the BUS go ROUND and ROUND,
ROUND and ROUND, ROUND and ROUND.
The WHEELS on the BUS go ROUND and ROUND,
All through the TOWN.

The DOOR on the BUS goes OPEN and CLOSE,
OPEN and CLOSE, OPEN and CLOSE.
The DOOR on the BUS goes OPEN and CLOSE,
All through the TOWN.

The BABY on the BUS goes wah, wah, wah [sign CRY],
Wah, wah, wah [sign CRY], wah, wah, wah [sign CRY].
The BABY on the BUS goes wah, wah, wah [sign CRY],
All through the TOWN.

The MOMMY on the BUS goes sh, sh, sh [sign QUIET],
Sh, sh, sh [sign QUIET], sh, sh, sh [sign QUIET].
The MOMMY on the BUS goes sh, sh, sh [sign QUIET],
All through the TOWN.

### Note from a Signing Parent

A 14 month old that just started at my daycare about a month ago signed MILK almost immediately. Having never been signed to before I was surprised she caught on so quickly. Her signs now are COW, HORSE, and DOG. She really loves animals!

— Carolina Alvarez, Regina, Saskatchewan

### Note from a Signing Parent

We have been teaching my youngest baby sign language since he was about 8 or 9 months old. He knows how to sign: PLEASE, MORE, EAT, and PUPPY. Now that he is older (15 months old) and becoming more vocal he doesn't sign as much. I am trying to get my older daughter to teach him more sign language. She was born deaf. Sign language is a great way for kids to learn a second language and help improve their vocabulary at a young age. It doesn't interfere with their language skills; in fact, I think it enhances their receptive and expressive language skills.

— Christy Garrett, Willow Park, Texas

# CHAPTER 6

# Signing with Your Older Toddler

## 18 TO 24 MONTHS

YOUR BABY IS OFFICIALLY A TODDLER WHEN he turns 18 months old. You may think he is trying to turn into a miniature you as he watches you more closely now, imitating your actions, signs, and spoken words.

You will be able to understand only about 25% of what he says, so even though he is becoming verbal, it is still important to sign with him and expect him to sign back. The 75% of his words that are unclear can lead to misunderstandings and frustrations for your child and his caregivers. For some toddlers, this is the start of what is often referred to as the "terrible two's."

## Developing Understanding

Children are becoming more and more aware of their world at 18 months, and their memories are rapidly improving.

### Memory
Children at this age are aware that an object exists even when it is out of sight. For example, if a ball rolls behind a couch, an 18-month-old will typically point toward the object, remember where it is, and attempt to sign and say "BALL."

### Following Instructions
Your 18-month-old is learning to follow simple instructions. He understands more and more of what you say to him. If you sign and say, "Go get your SHOES" or "Show me the BOOK," he will understand what you say and what you sign. Pairing the sign for the key word with your spoken words in these instructions provides information both visually and aurally.

### Recognition
Children at this age are able to recognize familiar objects and family members, whether they are physically present or in

---

✔ **SIGNING TIPS**

The challenging behaviors a child may show at this age are often motivated by wanting something, wanting to escape a situation, or wanting attention. By signing, you can show your child different ways to express his needs.

- Teach him the signs for his favorite items or activities, as well as the signs for MORE and WANT.

- Show him signs he can use to escape a situation, such as NO and FINISHed.

- Demonstrate signs that will help him get attention appropriately, such as LOOK, MOMMY, and DADDY.

pictures. Take time to study photographs with your child and browse through family photo albums, speaking the words and making signs for various objects and people.

### Imitation

Your child may begin to imitate your household chores, wiping up spills, pretending to cook, and setting the table. These are all indications that he is learning and remembering.

---

**Note from a Signing Parent**

Griffin has different signs for each member of the family. DADDY and GRANDPA started out the same, but he soon started pulling his hand away from his head for GRANDPA and GRANDMA. With seven grandparents (because of remarriages), you would think he'd get confused. But I have made a point of showing him pictures of each of the grandparents who live far away, using the appropriate signs, especially just before they come to visit. By the end of each visit, he is referring to each grandparent with the appropriate sign.

— Laurinda Reddig, Camas, Washington

---

## Self-Expression

At this stage in your child's development, he will continue to develop a sense of his own self — and express it.

### Saying or Signing "No"

Children at 18 months of age can often communicate the word "no" using speech or sign, but again, all children are different. My son never used the sign and first said the word very clearly at 22 months after an 8-hour flight to Italy. He had had enough. My daughter, on the other hand, signed NO when she was 11 months old.

**SIGNING GAME**

Gather animal toys or pictures, and make silly animal sounds, while naming the animals, e.g., "The dog says, "Bow wow." The cow say, "Moo moo.""

### Pointing and Grunting

Typically, 18-month-old children will make requests for preferred items or activities by pointing at the object and saying "da" or "uh, uh!" They will often be looking at you when they do this. We can translate this "point and grunt" to mean, "See that thing? I would like it please!" When you see your child doing this, you definitely want to acknowledge and respond to his attempts at communication. This is one of those moments of joint or shared attention — a wonderful teaching moment. While you are responding to his simple way of communicating, you can model a more sophisticated way by showing him the sign for the item he wants.

## Naming

An 18-month-old may be able to sign or say the names of his favorite toys, foods, pets, and family members. His spoken words may not be very clear, so continue to pair signs with speech to help him communicate.

## Calling Attention

Toddlers at 18 months of age typically call attention to items or people to demonstrate a need or a want. I remember Joshua calling me one day when he was this age, saying "b ___, b __." I could not figure out what he was trying to tell me: did he want a book, or had a bug flown into the house? With desperation in his eyes, he repeated, "Mama, b __!" Finally, when he realized I just wasn't getting it, he signed BALL. His ball had rolled under a chair. Not only did he remember where his ball was, but he was using a two-word phrase to request help in retrieving it. Plus, once he recognized that I couldn't understand what he was asking me for, he solved the problem by clarifying his request.

## Playing with Language

Toddlers often begin to narrate their activities to an audience, real or imaginary. Watch closely. While your child is turning pages in his favorite books, perhaps a few pages at a time, you may see and hear him "reading" the book, using words, sounds, and signs.

By now, your toddler likely has a love of music, and you may find him humming, signing, or singing simple tunes as he plays with language on his own. I recall hearing a noise in Sabrina's room early one morning when she was 18 months old. I peeked in and saw the outlines of her hands signing TWINKLE, TWINKLE, LITTLE STAR as she hummed along. I smiled and went back to bed.

> ### Note from a Signing Parent
>
> My youngest daughter, Jaimie, is almost 2 years old and immediately does the sign for CHANGE now when she fills her diaper. She then proceeds up the stairs to grab a new diaper, her wipes, and cream. She also signs COOKIE every time she hears cellophane being opened.
>
> — Kristen Duncan, Mississauga, Ontario

---

> *"Sharing a book provides all sorts of opportunity for talking. You can read the words on the page, talk about the pictures, or make up new parts to the printed story."*
>
> — Topping, Dekhinet, & Zeedyk (2011)

**Q** **What if my childcare provider doesn't use signs?**

**A** Ask if she would be willing to start! The three childcare providers who have cared for my kids all embraced signing with them. They enjoyed having fun with the signs and songs. I was amazed at the number of signs my daughter learned by 24 months that I did not teach her. If your childcare provider is hesitant, tell her that childcare centers that use sign language with infants and toddlers have experienced fewer incidents of hitting and biting from the children in their care.

# Teaching New Signs at 18 to 24 Months

When your toddler is about a year and a half old, you may only be able to understand 25% of what he is saying. Sign language will help augment his verbal speech, lessening frustrations for a little one who is learning at an enormous speed.

## New Communication Strategies

You can encourage your toddler's communication abilities with the following four strategies:

### 1. Try to figure out what lies behind his attempt to communicate.
For example, if he is calling to you and attempting to say a word you do not understand, look around his environment and at the activity he is involved in to try to discover what might be motivating him. Does he want something? Is he directing your attention to something? Does he want attention? Does he need help? Is he protesting something?

### 2. Respond immediately and consistently to his attempts to communicate, whether he has used sign language or speech.
For example, get down on your child's level and say and sign, "Tell MOMMY what you WANT." This is not a time to test your little one or to put his communication skills on display, as tempting as that might be.

### 3. Tailor your response to his reason for communicating.
For example, if he seems to be hungry, say and sign, "Are you HUNGRY? Do you WANT a COOKIE?" If he is pointing to a chair, sign and say, "Do you need HELP? Is there something under the CHAIR?"

### 4. Expand on what he is communicating.
For example, if his ball rolled under the chair, you could sign and say, "Oh, you're LOOKing for your BALL! You WANT your RED BALL."

---

### Note from a Signing Parent

I adopted my daughter from China when she was 19 months old. She was able to make only two sounds, as reported in her documents and verified by the orphanage staff. She had no words at all and few sounds to combine into words. I used key word signs along with spoken words with my daughter from the moment she was put into my arms. What really surprised me was that I had her using the sign and the word together for quite a few items within a week.

— Doris Bauer, speech-language pathologist, Toronto, Ontario

## Routines

Routines for eating, getting dressed, and bedtime help life run more smoothly — for both toddlers and parents. Knowing what comes next in a routine is also very reassuring. Bedtime routines — such as taking a bath, putting on pajamas, brushing teeth, and reading a story — teach toddlers a sequence of behaviors and may help everyone wind down from a busy day. These routines are particularly reassuring for toddlers who are phasing out an afternoon nap.

## Reading and Signing

Encourage your child to sign along with you as you point to pictures of objects in books and show him the signs for these items. Once he learns to make the signs himself, point to the pictures and sign and say, "WHAT's that?" with an expectant look on your face. Children love to pretend they are reading and will proudly name the pictures you point out.

Slow down and emphasize the main concepts in books so he can "read" the books himself. As you turn to each new page of his favorite books, pause to see what he will do when you come to key words and familiar lines of text. He may finish sentences for you if you pause before the key word or last word.

You and your baby may have a favorite place to sit and read. Wherever you choose to read to him, be sure he can see your face, the signs, and the book.

You may come across sign language board books that contain regional signs you do not know. You may also find books that claim they are ASL-based, but contain little ASL vocabulary. For a list of recommended sign language books for children, see the Resources on page 241.

# The Building Blocks of Communication

Keep building your child's communications skills, block by block, using the strategies of shared attention, turn taking, and, especially at this age, vocabulary growth.

## Vocabulary Growth

Your toddler's vocabulary is growing daily now. Continue to keep track of new items and activities he likes. Complete the sign list on page 84 and compare it to your earlier lists. It is interesting to see how his interests and abilities have grown and changed. Share the signs for these items with other caregivers and ask them to show these signs to your toddler throughout the day. Sign the words in this list before, during, and after their related activities.

> ### ✓ SIGNING TIPS
>
> - Routines reinforce learning by repetition. How many times have you read *Goodnight Moon* at bedtime? You and your child may by now be able to recite the book in sign without looking at the pictures.
>
> - Routines are very reassuring to your toddler. He knows what to expect from hour to hour, day to day. If he needs a reminder about what comes next in a routine, you may be able to prompt him with just a sign.
>
> - Routines are an early literacy skill. Showing your child visually what activities come first, second, and third in a routine will help him with later reading skills.

## YOUR SIGN DICTIONARY

| Family activities and activities your baby enjoys | | |
| --- | --- | --- |
| | | |
| | | |
| **Activities you do every day (even a few times a day) with your baby** | | |
| | | |
| | | |

**sorry**

### Good Manners Signs

Introduce the signs PLEASE, SORRY, and THANK YOU. I have been impressed by how early children can actually use these signs. If we expect our children to use them, they will. I have found it helpful to ask a young toddler to sign SORRY instead of saying it when he is too upset to get the word out verbally.

It is also nice that we can quietly cue them to use the words later in their lives. We do not have to remind them verbally to say thank you to Grandma; we can just get their attention quietly and show them the sign with an expectant look. Grandma will be so impressed.

---

### Note from a Signing Parent

We ride on the bus and subway a lot because I don't drive. My daughter has noticed that some people sleep on the subway. She finds it fascinating to watch these sleeping people. At one point, she tried to wake them up by hollering to them. I quickly got her to stop this by speaking quietly, shaking my head, and signing NO WAKE UP. He is SLEEPing. Now she points or nods at them with her head and signs SLEEP while looking at me. This is a nice private "game" we can play to pass the time. I don't think it harms anyone, since the people we are signing about are asleep! We don't sign anything about them except that they are sleeping.

— Susan Fearnley, Toronto, Ontario

---

### Note from a Signing Parent

My son loves to large building blocks apart and put them back together. One day, he was having a hard time doing this and he gave two pieces to me that were stuck together. He then signed and said, HELP, PLEASE!

— Lori Motluck, Cape Coral, Florida

# Language Milestones at 2 Years

Here are typical speech and language milestones met by most 2-year-olds. You may notice that your 2-year-old signs certain words and says others.

| Typical Speech & Language Milestones | Opportunities for Signing Interaction | Date Your Child Reached Level |
|---|---|---|
| When asked, points to body parts and familiar objects. | Play hide-and-seek games with familiar objects around the house. Pretend to forget where something is hidden and ask for help, saying and signing, "WHERE'S the BEAR?"<br><br>Label body parts while your child is in the bath and is getting dressed. Point to each body part, tell him what it's called, and show him the sign for it.<br><br>Sign and sing "Head and Shoulders" (see page 233). | |
| Makes animal sounds, such as "moo" for a cow or "grrr" for a bear. | Sign and sing "Old MacDonald" (see page 235). | |
| Consistently uses two-word phrases, such as "Go bye-bye," "Where doggy?" "No sock," or "Me go." | Once your child is consistently signing one word at a time, start signing to him at a two-word level. For example, if he signs "MILK" to request a drink, sign "You WANT MILK?" You are showing him a model just above his language level and encouraging him to enhance his language skills without frustrating him.<br><br>Do not try to force him to sign at a two-word level — getting a glass of milk should not be contingent on his ability to sign a two-word phrase. Always respond to his initial attempt to communicate, then provide him with an enhanced model. | |
| Uses descriptive words, such as "hot" or "cold," "big" or "small." | Use these signs yourself and make a point of showing them to your child.<br><br>Create opportunities to show your child the sign for COLD by opening the freezer and allowing him to touch the food you take out, such as a bag of peas or blueberries. Even eating these can be a different treat for your 2-year-old.<br><br>Sign HOT whenever you're around steamy things — just keep your child a safe distance away.<br><br>Sign and say "HOT" and "COLD" while playing at a play kitchen with your child.<br><br>Show him the signs for BIG and SMALL when you're cutting up food items. For example, sign and say, "Do you WANT the BIG piece of BANANA or the SMALL piece of BANANA? BIG or SMALL?"<br><br>Have a fun game of trading shoes. Talk and sign about Mommy's "BIG" shoes and his "SMALL" shoes. | |

| Typical Speech & Language Milestones | Opportunities for Signing Interaction | Date Your Child Reached Level |
|---|---|---|
| Carries on conversations with himself and with toys. | Strike up conversations with your child's bear or doll. Model conversations during pretend picnics and ball games. | |
| Refers to himself by name, for example, "me, Joshua." | Continue to show your toddler how to fingerspell his name. | |
| Names pictures of familiar objects. | Look through family photo albums and favorite picture books together. | |
| When asked, points to the correct pictures in a book. | Continue signing and reading picture books together. For very familiar books, sign and read as usual, but stop before the last word. For example, when reading *Brown Bear*, read and sign, "BROWN BEAR, BROWN BEAR, what do you . . . ?" Wait to see if your little one will finish the sentence with a sign or word. For *Goodnight Moon*, you can do this with every line; the rhymes will help your child figure out what word is needed to fill in the blank. Read and sign, "GOOD NIGHT MITTENS, GOOD NIGHT . . ." and wait for him to fill in "KITTENS." | |
| Listens attentively to stories. | Continue to read and sign with your 2-year-old, modeling the signs BOOK, MORE, TURN, and FINISHED with each book. Team up with your child to read and sign his favorite books to other caregivers. Use key word signing to highlight the main nouns and verbs on every page. See the Resources on page 243 for a list of suggested books for toddlers. | |
| Listens attentively to songs and rhymes. | Listen to CDs of both traditional and non-traditional music. Sign MUSIC and DANCE before the music starts, while it's playing, and after it ends. Sing along with the music. Encourage your child to join in by signing, "YOU sing [sign MUSIC]." | |

Adapted by permission from *Growing with Communication: A Speech and Language Guide for Parents with Children under 5 Years of Age.* Oshawa, ON: Durham Preschool Speech and Language Program, 1999.

# Signing Games

## Containers, Containers, Containers

Put objects, water, or sand in plastic containers, cups, and bowls to create opportunities to sign and say "IN," "OUT," "MORE," and "WHERE." It's also fun to stack these containers.

## Imaginative Play

Provide your child with toys that will allow him to safely imitate the activities he sees you doing. Play with him in toy kitchens or on toy workbenches, providing him with language he can use during these activities. Examples of signs to use include WORK, CLEAN, COOK, FIX, HOT, and CAREFUL.

## I Look

Play this simplified version of I Spy while you're out on a walk with your toddler. Point to items and sign and say their names: "TREE," "BIRD," "SWINGS," and "SQUIRREL," for example. Sign and say, "I see [sign LOOK] with my little EYE . . . a BIRD."

**play**

---

### Note from a Signing Parent

When Jacob was around 24 months old, he would often point to objects and sign the wrong signs on purpose. He would point to a ball and sign APPLE or point to a piece of bread and sign CRACKER. He would smirk, laugh, and wait for me to correct him. I thought it was amazing that, at 24 months old, he was showing me his personality and telling a joke in his own way. Signing gave us insight into his fun-loving personality and his desire to make people laugh. Now that he is almost 4, he still plays these types of games and laughs at how funny he thinks he is!

— Tammy Clanton, Sacshe, Texas

---

# Songs to Sign and Sing

### You Are My Sunshine

You are my SUNshine, my only SUNshine,
You make me HAPPY when SKIES are GRAY.
You'll never [shake your head to indicate negation]
    KNOW, DEAR,
How much I LOVE YOU.
Please don't [shake your head to indicate negation]
    take my SUNshine away.

**sun**

**ant**

### The Ants Go Marching

The ANTs go marching ONE by ONE, hurrah, hurrah
    [sign WONDERFUL]
The ANTs go marching ONE by ONE, hurrah, hurrah
    [sign WONDERFUL]
The ANTs go marching ONE by ONE,
And the little [sign SMALL] ONE stops to suck his THUMB,
And they all go MARCHing down to the ground
To get out of the RAIN, boom! boom! boom! [sign LOUD]

TWO by TWO . . . to tie his SHOE.
THREE by THREE . . . to climb a TREE.
FOUR by FOUR . . . to shut the DOOR.
FIVE by FIVE . . . to take a dive [sign SWIM].

**bird**

### Two Little Blackbirds

TWO little blackBIRDs sat on a HILL,
ONE named Jack and ONE named Jill.
FLY away, Jack; FLY away, Jill.
COME back, Jack; COME back, Jill.
TWO little blackBIRDs sat on a HILL,
ONE named Jack and ONE named Jill.

### Five Little Frogs

FIVE little FROGs sat on a shore.
ONE went for a SWIM, and then there were FOUR.

FOUR little FROGs LOOKed out to sea [sign OCEAN].
Another went SWIMming, and then there were THREE.

THREE little FROGs said, "WHAT can we do?"
ONE JUMPed in the WATER, and then there were TWO.

TWO little FROGs sat in the SUN.
Another SWAM off, and then there was ONE.

ONE little FROG said, "This is NO FUN!"
He dove in the WATER, and then there were none
    [sign FINISH].

**frog**

# CHAPTER 7

# Signing with Your Young Preschooler

## 2 TO 2½ YEARS

W HERE, OH WHERE DID YOUR BABY GO? This little person is no longer a baby and is barely a toddler. Your young preschooler is becoming more and more independent and has an attention span that grows almost daily. Many children at this age start to play more on their own, but they also love games that involve taking turns. Most 2-year-olds don't like to sit still — running, jumping, and chasing are favorite sports.

When you ask your child where certain body parts are, she will be able, very proudly, to point out them out. Games such as "WHERE's your belly?" and "WHERE's your nose?" are fun when your child is this age. Use the signs for WHERE and WONDERFUL while playing this game, with lots of expression and enthusiasm.

## Teaching New Signs at 2 Years

As your child develops and as you both continue to learn, you can add the strategies of parallel talk, self-talk, expansion, and providing choices to your parenting toolkit.

### Parallel Talk

While your child is playing, talk and sign to her about what she is doing. For example, if she is playing with trains, sign and say, "You're PLAYing with the TRAIN. There's a BLUE TRAIN and there's a RED one. The RED one looks FAST!" Speech-language pathologists call this strategy parallel talk. You can adapt this strategy by using parallel talk with parallel sign. When you tell your child a story about her activities, you provide her with great models of main words (signed and spoken) she can use later.

### Self-Talk

Another strategy recommended by speech-language pathologists is self-talk. It is similar to parallel talk in that you narrate a

> **Note from a Signing Parent**
>
> I started teaching my daughter sign language at 6 months and at 8 months she signed her first word. By 18 months, she was consistently signing 35 words and verbally spoke 10 words. I noticed consistent warning signs of low muscle tone when she was 22 months. After having her evaluated, I was told she had low oral, core, and leg muscles and qualified for occupational and speech therapy. After the evaluation, the first question several people asked me was "Did teaching sign language cause her to be speech delayed?" No! She was speech delayed because of the low muscle tone. Sign language gave her a way to communicate and eliminated any frustration.
>
> — Kali Burch,
> Lafayette, Indiana

**red**

**truck**

situation for your child, but in this case you describe what *you* are doing. For example, while preparing a snack, you can sign and say, "MOMMY's getting the MILK. Oh, and I need TWO CUPs. One CUP for MOMMY, one CUP for YOU. Here they are. Now I'll get the COOKIEs. Let's have 1, 2, 3 . . . . 4 COOKIEs. TWO for MOMMY and TWO for BABY."

## Expansion

When your child uses spoken or signed words that relate to specific topics, such as animals, toys, food, body parts, or clothing, add more content or expand on her words or phrases. If she signs one word, such as TRUCK, show her how to expand on this by signing and saying, "RED TRUCK!" If your child signs a two-word phrase, such as CAR GO, expand on this by signing and saying, "Yes, the CAR GOes FAST!"

## Providing Choices

Provide your toddler with choices when you can. Sign and say, "Do you want a BANANA or a COOKIE?" or "Do want the BLUE cup or the RED cup?" This strategy is especially useful if your child uses the same sign for many different items (for example, she signs PLEASE for everything). Asking her to make a choice will make her stop and think about what she wants and will encourage her to be more specific — and it will give her a feeling of control over a situation. Wait until you see the delight on your child's face when you give her the opportunity to choose what she wants!

---

### SIGNING GAME

Help your child to notice familiar sounds, by signing and talking about the chirping "bird", a "car" as it drives by, "dogs" as they bark, "airplanes" flying overhead. Label the sounds with signs and speech and have fun trying to imitate the sounds!

---

### Note from a Signing Parent

My daughter, Olivia, loves books and is very interested in the letters of the alphabet. Around her second birthday or shortly thereafter, she could say every letter when we pointed to it. She quickly became interested in the signing of each letter. Now she can sign every letter we ask her to sign, and she recognizes every letter we sign to her. Needless to say, we are very proud parents! I thoroughly believe that signing helped Olivia become so interested in communication and the written word.

— Debbie-Lynn Hoste, Toronto, Ontario

### Note from a Signing Parent

My daughter is 19 months old and one day when my husband was leaving for work, she signed and said, DADDY GO and then adding the sign for SAD as well! So sweet!

— Stacy MacInnes, Detroit, Michigan

# The Building Blocks of Communication

Keep building your child's communications skills, block by block, using the strategies of shared attention, turn taking, and, especially at this age, vocabulary growth.

## Vocabulary Growth

Continue to keep track of your child's preferences and activities as your list of signs grows and grows. Share the signs for these words with other caregivers and have them show the signs to your preschooler throughout the day. Sign the words in this list before, during, and after their related activities.

| YOUR SIGN DICTIONARY | | |
| --- | --- | --- |
| Family activities and activities your baby enjoys | | |
| | | |
| | | |
| Activities you do every day (even a few times a day) with your baby | | |
| | | |
| | | |

### Note from a Signing Parent

Olivia is now 2½, and she loves to sign to her twin brothers, who are 10 months old. The boys understand the sign for MILK and will sign it back. FOOD, DRINK, NICE/GENTLE, and various other signs words are now understood by the whole family. Olivia still requests her signing videos on a daily basis, and the boys light up at the sound of the *Signing Time* song. These videos have been a huge help now that we have three children under 3 years old. Clear communication is extremely important.

— Debbie-Lynn Hoste, Toronto, Ontario

# Language Milestones at 2½ Years

Here are a few typical speech and language milestones met by most children this age. You may notice that your child signs certain words and says others.

| Typical Speech & Language Milestones | Opportunities for Signing Interaction | Date Your Child Reached Level |
|---|---|---|
| When asked, offers her first name, but usually refers to herself as "me," such as "Me want it." | Sign and say, "MY NAME is MOMMY" or "MY NAME is DADDY." Then model "YOUR NAME is _____." Take turns playing the name game with your preschooler.<br><br>Continue to practice fingerspelling your child's name. | |
| Begins using plural word endings, such as "big dogs" and "small cats." | Using the ASL numbers 1 to 10, practice counting objects. For example, sign and say, "1 BALL, 2 BALLS, 3 BALLS." Verbally emphasize the "s" at the end of each word. | |
| Begins using -ing verb forms, such as "kicking ball." | Read books that emphasize these verbs and model the signs as you read: "SLEEPing, EATing, WALKing, JUMPing, SWINGing." See the Resources on page 244 for a list of activity books and CDs for preschoolers.<br><br>Play pretend games with dolls or toys that may be sleeping, eating, dancing, walking, sitting, swimming, singing, running, jumping, or swinging.<br><br>Model action verbs by playing a modified Simon Says game. For example, sign and say, "Sarah is . . . JUMPing." Take turns picking the action verb.<br><br>Sign and sing, "It's RAINing, It's POURing" (see page 234) with your little one. | |
| Uses short sentences to announce what she will do or what she has done, such as "Me do it" or "Want more milk." | When your child uses a single word, expand on what she has said using a two-word phrase. For example, if she says or signs "MILK," respond by giving her milk and saying and signing, "WANT MILK?"<br><br>When your child uses a two-word phrase, expand on what she has said using a longer sentence. If she signs or says "MORE MILK," give her more milk and say and sign, "You WANT MORE MILK? Sarah WANTs MORE MILK."<br><br>When she attempts short sentences, echo them back to her while signing key words: "You WANT MORE MILK? Here's MORE MILK" or "YOU do it? YES, YOU do it!" | |
| Follows simple one-step directions, such as "Clean up your toys" or "Hang up your coat." | Pair your one-step instructions with appropriate signs, such as CLEAN, TOYS, and COAT. | |

| Typical Speech & Language Milestones | Opportunities for Signing Interaction | Date Your Child Reached Level |
|---|---|---|
| Answers what, which, where, and yes/no questions if they are about the present. | Model the signs for WHAT, WHICH, and WHERE when asking your child questions.<br><br>Model the signs for YES and NO when answering questions.<br><br>Take turns hiding favorite toys and asking, "WHERE's the TRAIN?"<br><br>Give your child a choice between two items, signing and saying, "WHICH do you WANT?" For example, when offering a drink, say and sign, "WHICH do you WANT? MILK or JUICE?" | |
| Asks where and what questions, such as "What's this?" "Where doggy?" or "Where my toy?" | Model asking these types of questions, signing and saying WHAT and WHERE.<br><br>Play more hiding games. Place two items in front of you and ask your child to cover her eyes — no peeking! Hide one of the items close by, under your leg or under a pillow. When she opens her eyes, encourage her to sign and say, "WHERE's the _____?" | |

Adapted by permission from *Growing with Communication: A Speech and Language Guide for Parents with Children under 5 Years of Age.* Oshawa, ON: Durham Preschool Speech and Language Program, 1999.

# Songs to Sign and Sing

**Ten in the Bed**
There were TEN in a BED
And the little ONE said [sign SAY],
"ROLL over, ROLL over."
So they all ROLLed over
And one fell out [sign FALL].

*Continue to sign and sing for each number down to 1.*

There was ONE in the BED
And the little ONE said [sign SAY]
"GOOD NIGHT"!

**bed**

**music**

### Head and Shoulders
*This is a classic song/chant, and children love it. Point to each of the body parts. You can sign during this song by stopping in the middle and asking your toddler, "WANT MORE?" At the end of the song, sign and say, "FINISHED! NO? You WANT MORE? MORE MUSIC!" You can even use ASL numbers to count up to the song, signing and saying, "MORE MUSIC? READY, 1, 2, 3 . . ." Then start the song again.*

Head, shoulders, knees and toes,
Knees and toes.
Head, shoulders, knees and toes,
Knees and toes.

And eyes and ears and mouth and nose,
Head, shoulders, knees and toes.

**doll**

### Miss Polly Had a Dolly
Miss Polly had a DOLLy
Who was SICK, SICK, SICK,
So she called for the DOCTOR
To be quick, quick, quick [sign FAST, FAST, FAST].
The DOCTOR came
With his bag and his HAT,
And he knocked at the DOOR
With a rat-a-tat-tat [mime knocking].

He looked at the DOLLy and he shook his head,
And he said, "Miss Polly, put her straight to BED."
He wrote out a PAPER
For a pill, pill, pill [sign MEDICINE].
"That'll make her better, YES it will, will, will!"

*"Effective parent–child language interaction in the first 3 years is a key determinant of a child's future progress in language and other areas."*

— Topping, Dekhinet & Zeedyk (2011)

### Note from a Signing Parent

My daughter, Gaby, and I did baby sign language as a bonding activity when she was 7 to 12 months old. Once she started daycare, however, she became verbal very quickly and took to using her words vs. her signs. It wasn't until our son was born that I truly realized the impact it had on both of us. If our son fell asleep downstairs, I could sign to 2-year old Gaby, PLEASE BE QUIET, COLSEN IS SLEEPING. She understood immediately what I was 'talking' about and all was quiet. My son also did baby sign language toward the end of his first year, and uses MORE and PLEASE all the time.

— Tracy Nickleford, Brooklin, Ontario

# CHAPTER 8

# Signing with Your Older Preschooler

## 2½ TO 3 YEARS

IT SEEMS LIKE ONLY YESTERDAY THAT YOU WERE counting your child's age in weeks or months, not years. Your 30-month-old (that's 2½ years) is likely now a very active communicator. Around this time, you will find yourself able to have back-and-forth conversations with your child. Should you continue to sign? You are reading this chapter, so the only answer to that question is a wholehearted yes!

Families are motivated to continue signing with their preschool children for a number of reasons: they might have another baby on the way, a family member who is Deaf, a child with special needs, or a love of sign language. Another completely legitimate reason to continue is simply that signing is fun!

---

### Note from a Signing Parent

My daughter, Carmen, is now 33 months old, and her baby brother is 9 months. We signed a lot with Carmen when she was a baby, and she signed back at 9 months and communicated with us from then on. She spoke early and quite a lot. After she started talking well, I let up on the signing some, although she never completely stopped. When Connor came along, we got some *Signing Times* DVDs to get her back to signing, and she is now signing a lot. She loves those DVDs! The best thing is that she is helping me teach her brother to sign. It has really helped them to bond. She loves being the big sister teaching her baby brother. It makes her feel so good. We can't wait for him to sign back! How neat will it be for her to know that *she* taught him?

— Jen Dillman, Springfield, Illinois

**pasta**

---

*"When choosing toys (for Christmas or birthdays or any day), buy those that give lots of opportunities for talking and pretend play— puppets, building blocks, puzzles, dolls, tea sets."*

— Topping, Dekhinet, & Zeedyk (2011)

# Bridging Two Spoken Languages

Sign language can be useful when two languages are spoken in a family. A child may hear the word "milk" from one parent and "*latte*" from another parent. If both parents use the American Sign Language sign for MILK, this sign will act as a visual bridge between the two spoken words. A child may think, "Mommy says 'milk' and she signs MILK. Daddy signs '*latte*' and he signs MILK. They must mean the same thing!"

My family traveled to Italy when Joshua was 16 months old. We quickly taught my husband's family the signs that Joshua used most often, such as MORE, COOKIE, MILK, and PASTA (of course). They signed to him using these ASL signs and spoke Italian. Joshua had no problem understanding them. In fact, I think sign language helped me the most during our vacation! Joshua used his first three-word phrase while we were there: "MORE PASTA, Z*ia*!" He signed the word MORE, signed and said the word "PASTA," and said the word "Z*ia*," the Italian word for aunt. The Italian side of our family, especially Zia, was thrilled.

# Teaching Signs at 2½ to 3 Years

In *How to Talk to Your Baby*, speech-language pathologist Dorothy Dougherty describes five basic strategies for teaching language: naming, describing, comparing, explaining, and giving directions. Combine these strategies with others you are currently using to sign with your child.

### Naming

Most 2½-year-olds are able to tell you their name when they are asked, but they often refer to themselves, in speech and sign, as "ME." Many children at this age turn into little helpers, so you may hear the phrase "Me do it" quite often. This is a great time to model the signs for MY TURN and YOUR TURN.

Continue to name objects, using both spoken words and signs to allow your child to experience the words with two senses, hearing and vision. For example, as you put on his hat, sign and say, "This is your HAT." As you put on your hat, sign and say, "This is DADDY's HAT." By using signs to label items, you place emphasis on the name of the object.

## Describing

Continue to use parallel talk to sign about what your child is doing and self-talk to sign about what you are doing. You can further describe objects of interest to your child by listing their qualities, such as color (RED APPLES), size (BIG CAR), texture (SOFT CAT), and quantity (FIVE GRAPES).

## Comparing

By comparing objects, you will be helping your child learn how things are the same or different. Signs can help a child visually discriminate between items, so it is helpful to use sign language when making comparisons. When signing BIG, your hands make the opposite movement to SMALL. When signing OPEN, your hands make the opposite movement to CLOSE. When signing COME, your hands make the opposite movement to GO.

## Explaining

When you explain the activities you and your child are involved in, it helps him understand daily routines and learn how things work. You can explain a sequence — "FIRST we'll READ, and THEN it's time to SLEEP" — or the use of familiar objects: "We wear a HAT because it's RAINing." Understanding how and why things work is the first step in learning to problem-solve.

## Giving Directions

Who doesn't wind up using their hands when giving directions! Using sign language to give directions to your child will help draw his attention to the instruction. You cannot give someone a direction unless you have his attention. Because of their visual component, signs also help a child understand the direction. Helpful signs include UP, DOWN, ON, OFF, IN, OUT, UNDER, and OVER.

---

### ✔️ SIGNING TIPS

Here are some good books for preschoolers about opposites:

- *Opposites* by Sandra Boynton
- *Oh My Oh My Oh Dinosaurs!* by Sandra Boynton
- *Wet Pet, Dry Pet, Your Pet, My Pet* by Dr. Seuss
- *Big Dog . . . Little Dog: A Bedtime Story* by P.D. Eastman
- *Olivia's Opposites* by Ian Falconer

---

### SIGNING GAME

Pretend to cook and add humor to the recipe, e.g., say "I know what this CEREAL needs...a cup of SPAGHETTI! or "I'm making PIZZA, please pass the CHOCOLATE SPRINKLES! Show the signs for the silly ingredients!

---

*"Symbol skills, including both gestures and words, predict the development of children's social skills."*

— Vallotton & Ayoub, (2010)

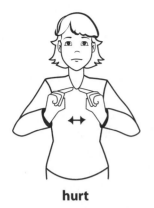

hurt

# The Building Blocks of Communication

Keep building your child's communications skills, block by block, using the strategies of shared attention, turn taking, and, especially at this age, vocabulary growth.

## Vocabulary Growth

Continue to keep track of your child's favorite items and activities, and teach him signs that will help him communicate his thoughts and feelings about these preferences. Share these signs with other caregivers and have them show the signs to your preschooler throughout the day. Using phrases, sign the words in this list before, during, and after their related activities.

| YOUR SIGN DICTIONARY | | |
| --- | --- | --- |
| Family activities and activities your baby enjoys | | |
|  |  |  |
|  |  |  |
| Activities you do every day (even a few times a day) with your baby | | |
|  |  |  |
|  |  |  |

### Potty Time!

Around this age, children are typically being toilet trained. Relevant signs, such as TOILET, WASH, NOW, FINISHED, and PROUD, will prove helpful — and once your child has learned them, you'll be able to use them silently in public.

# Language Milestones at 3 Years

Here are a few typical speech and language milestones that are met by most 3-year-olds. Encourage your child to meet milestone behaviors by modeling them yourself. Take your time and have fun making up games and playing with your child.

| Typical Speech & Language Milestones | Opportunities for Signing Interaction | Date Your Child Reached Level |
|---|---|---|
| When asked, can put a toy "on," "in," or "under" something. | Say and sign the words "ON," "IN," and "UNDER" when you are playing with cups, blocks, and other toys. Use phrases such as "Put the BALL IN the CUP," "The BLOCK is UNDER the CUP," and "The BLOCK is ON the BEAR." Use the words "ON" and "IN" when your child is getting dressed. For example, sign and say, "SOCK ON, FOOT IN, SHOE ON." | |
| Follows two-step directions, such as "Pick up your spoon and put it on the table." | Say and sign the words "FIRST" and "THEN" when you give directions. This will help your child understand that there are two parts to the instruction and figure out which direction is first and which is next. Sign the key words in both parts of the direction to add visual information and increase understanding. For example, sign and say, "FIRST, pick up your SPOON and THEN put it ON the TABLE." | |
| Asks and answers why, where, who, and what questions, such as "What is mommy doing?" | Model these types of questions for your child, using signs and speech. Use the signs for WHY, WHERE, WHO, and WHAT when asking your own questions. | |
| Uses three or more words in a sentence. | Continue to encourage your child to use more words. If he is communicating at a one-word level, sign and speak to him at a two-word level. If he is expressing himself at a two-word level, sign and speak to him at a three-word level. | |

| Typical Speech & Language Milestones | Opportunities for Signing Interaction | Date Your Child Reached Level |
|---|---|---|
| Clearly makes the "p," "b," "m," "n," and "w" sounds in words. | Continue to sign words that your preschooler has difficulty with. | |
| Can name colors and understands what the words mean. | Label the colors of your child's clothing: "RED SHIRT," "BLUE PANTS," "WHITE SOCKS." Sign and say the colors of fruit and veggies at home and at the grocery store. Read and sign board books with color vocabulary, such as *Brown Bear, Brown Bear, What Do You See?* by Bill Martin and Eric Carle, and *Blue Hat, Green Hat* by Sandra Boynton. | |
| Understands what objects are used for. For example, he can answer the questions, "What do you eat with?" or "What do you wash with?" | Be silly in front of your child and make mistakes using common objects: try to eat soup with a fork, or leave the cap on when trying to put toothpaste on a toothbrush. Encourage your child to point out your mistakes and help him explain why it's a mistake. | |

Adapted by permission from *Growing with Communication: A Speech and Language Guide for Parents with Children under 5 Years of Age.* Oshawa, ON: Durham Preschool Speech and Language Program, 1999.

### Note from a Signing Parent

Riley is 4 years old but will turn 5 in 3 months. We are working on table manners because she was talking while eating — and spraying food everywhere! I reminded her not to talk with her mouth full, and she continued her story in sign. Later the same night, she was brushing her teeth and trying to talk at the same time. As I started to remind her, saying, "Riley, we don't talk . . . ," she signed OOPS! FORGOT . . . SORRY. Too cute!

— Karen Horvath, ASL interpreter, South Bend, Indiana

# The Benefits of Long-Term Signing

When you stop signing with your little one is up to you, but there are many advantages to continuing to sign into his school years.

### 1. Teaching Siblings

He can help you teach signs to his siblings. My son was 27 months old when my daughter was born. He was the first to sign to her, and he often signed on her behalf. When she was crying in her bassinet, he would look at her, sign MILK, and then run over to me and sign MILK again. He was problem-solving for his little sister already.

## 2. Learning the Alphabet

Fingerspelling will help him learn the alphabet and acquire new spoken words. When Joshua started kindergarten, we placed a stronger emphasis on signing the alphabet to help him learn his letters. As the school year progressed, we continued to play with the alphabet and fingerspell the words he was learning at school. While he was doing his homework, if he needed a hint for any of his practice words, I would fingerspell the word and he would get it right away.

## 3. Second Language Learning

Fingerspelling can help him learn other spoken languages. As I write this, Joshua is in a grade one French immersion program, so we are now practicing his sight words in ASL and in French! As he prepares for his dictation test, we practice words that are more difficult by both writing them out and fingerspelling them. I am convinced that both seeing and feeling how a word is spelled is helping him learn new words.

## 4. Life-Long Learning

Sign language enhances life-long learning. A local center for the Deaf in our community offers children's camps that teach ASL. Joshua and Sabrina will be attending these camps next year as part of our life-long interest in using sign language. Learning any language opens doors. You never know when a skill will be useful. As long as an activity is still fun, why not continue with it?

## 5. Silent Communication

The ability to use signs with my speaking and hearing children has paid off in so many ways. Joshua was misbehaving at a play center one day when he was 4 years old. All I had to do was call his name and sign, STOP, DOWN NOW. He immediately stopped what he was doing and sheepishly came over to me. I was very happy that I did not have to embarrass him by using a loud mommy voice across a playground.

You will find signing useful in typically quiet places (for example, at church or the library) and when distance or location makes speech impossible or difficult. I have signed with my children through our backyard window, through a parents' viewing window at a local gymnastics club, and through Plexiglas barriers during hockey practice. Seeing my son try to sign back with hockey gloves on was one of our funniest signing experiences! I also remember signing I LOVE YOU to him across the schoolyard just before he went into class.

> **Note from a Signing Parent**
>
> My son Noah stopped looking at a picture book that he loves just before his 3rd birthday and asked me with the cutest face, MOMMY, this is BOOK. What's the sign for READ I showed him and he signed I READING BOOK back to me!
>
> — Terry Brown, Oakville, Ontario

**stop**

**I love you**

## Songs to Sign and Sing

**rainbow**

**color**

### The Rainbow Song
*(Sung to the tune of "Hush Little Baby")*

RAINBOW PURPLE
RAINBOW BLUE
RAINBOW GREEN
And YELLOW too
RAINBOW ORANGE
and RAINBOW RED
RAINBOW shining overhead.

COME and count
The COLORS with me
How many COLORS
Do you SEE?
1-2-3 on down to GREEN
4-5-6 COLORS can be seen.

RAINBOW PURPLE
RAINBOW BLUE
RAINBOW GREEN
And YELLOW too
RAINBOW ORANGE
and RAINBOW RED
RAINBOW shining overhead.

## On Top of Spaghetti
*(Sung to the tune of "On Top of Old Smokey")*

On top of spaghetti [sign PASTA]
All covered with CHEESE,
I lost my poor meatball
When somebody SNEEZEd.

It rolled off the TABLE
And onto the FLOOR,
And then my poor meatball
Rolled out of the DOOR.

It rolled in the GARDEN
And under a bush [sign TREE],
And then my poor meatball
Was nothing but mush [sign WET/SOFT].

## It's Raining, It's Pouring
It's RAINing, it's pouring,
The old MAN is SNORE-ing.
He went to BED
And he bumped [sign HURT] his HEAD
And he couldn't get UP in the MORNING.

**cheese**

**snore**

---

### Note from a Signing Parent

I love that my daughter can "read" and sign her favorite books to her baby brother. I'm not sure that she's actually reading the text because she has the books memorized by now but she's so proud that she's 'teaching' him the signs!

— Rebecca Ward, Harvey, Louisiana

---

**SIGNING GAME**

Talk about and pretend to be your child's favorite animals and imitate the animal's movements. As you move around the room, sign and talk about what the animal, you, are doing and feeling.

# CHAPTER 9

# Signing with Your Child with Special Needs

CHILDREN WITH DOWN SYNDROME, AUTISM, or other global developmental delays may have trouble learning to speak or may be unable to speak for a number of reasons. Even though a person with special needs may be 10 or 16 years of age, she may still be a beginning communicator, just like a toddler or preschooler. Speech therapists and educators often recommend sign language as a way for special needs children, adolescents, and even adults to communicate.

Other communication strategies used with special needs children include pictures, communication boards, and voice output communication aids. The advantage to sign language is that it requires no additional equipment — you always have your hands with you, whereas pictures or communication books may be lost or forgotten. The disadvantage to sign language is that most people don't understand signs. As more and more children learn sign language, however, this drawback will be mitigated.

**Did You Know?**

For children who are having difficulty learning to speak, sign language is often an effective bridge to verbal speech. For children with limited speech, signing can augment their communication skills.

**Note from a Signing Parent**

I used American Sign Language with the students who are non-verbal that I worked with as an Educational Assistant. I had seen frustration levels go down immediately with these students.

— Rebecca Skean, Thunder Bay, Ontario

**Note from a Speech Pathologist**

I started signing with a young boy I was working with who had been diagnosed with autism. I diagnosed him with auditory processing and dyspraxia. I recommended that he attend a school for the Deaf that accepted hearing children. The school demanded no verbal until he learned sign language and used it fluently. He had a difficult time with this, but we supported it, and he now is verbal and reads well. He has returned to the public school system, and his teachers report that his skills are well above those of other children. He still has some of the difficulties with social skills typical of autism, but that is changing quickly. It is so exciting!

— Kathleen Davis, speech-language pathologist, Norwood, Massachusetts

# Visual Communication

Sign language may help children with special needs express themselves in a way they cannot with speech. For some special needs children, the motor skills needed for speech may not develop normally or may not develop at all. Signing allows them to communicate in visual signs, if not in spoken words.

Sign language may also enhance a special needs child's ability to process information. She may have difficulty understanding what is said to her, but when information is presented visually, she may be able to understand it. In addition, signs can be held for longer periods than spoken words, which may help someone who has understanding or memory difficulties. Spoken words are transient — once they are said, they are gone. If you did not catch them or understand them, you may have difficulty remembering them.

# Challenging Behaviors

Learning to sign may help children with special needs avoid challenging behaviors. Many children with special needs are motivated to communicate but are unable to do so in a way that is clear and understandable. This is a grave source of frustration, which may manifest as behavior problems or inappropriate ways of communicating.

The child with special needs may want to say, "I want that" or "I'm tired of this activity" or "I want to spend time with you," but may not have an appropriate way of communicating these concepts. To indicate that she wants something, the child may hit someone to get their attention. But this behavior rarely results in her needs being met, and to get out of this frustrating situation she may drop to the floor and refuse to get up. She may even try to hurt herself. These challenging behaviors are all motivated by her desire to communicate. Learning to sign allows her to communicate effectively and appropriately, thus circumventing challenging behavior.

# Approximations

Children with a wide range of abilities can sign, but we have to learn to recognize their approximations if they have difficulty with fine motor skills. For example, a child with fused fingers or difficulty with fine motor skills may produce a sign with the correct body space and movement, but her hand shape will not be exact. Respond to the sign as if it is made correctly. You can model the correct sign, just to be sure you understand what she is communicating. Some children may learn to produce the sign correctly over time by watching how you model it.

**SIGNING GAME**

Narrate your child's world through signs and spoken words. Use signs and words to talk about what you are both doing, feeling and seeing. Point out family objects and tell your child what they are using both speech and signs.

## Note from a Signing Parent

I worked in a preschool classroom with children aged three to five from lower income families, including bilingual and some with special needs. My assistant asked if I had any objections to teaching the children sign language, and I said no. I also wanted to learn. We began teaching the children one to five signs a day, starting with PLEASE, THANK YOU, MORE and built up to colors, numbers, animals, and the alphabet. There was a little boy in our class who would not speak and he kept hitting the other children, so we showed the children how to sign to him STOP, NO HIT. It gave the other children confidence to stand up for themselves and he understood those signs. The children really embraced learning sign. Sign language offered us the opportunity to connect with the children in our classroom.

— Mari Ewell-Torres, Lake Station, Indiana

# PART 2

# Baby Sign Dictionary

# How to Use This Dictionary

ALL THE SIGNS PRESENTED HERE ARE STANDARD American Sign Language. These signs were chosen based on words that are developmentally appropriate for young children and that we have found are important to families of babies and toddlers.

When learning signs from a two-dimensional picture, keep these guidelines in mind:

## Hand Choice

Sign with your dominant hand. If you are right-handed, your right hand will do most of the movement. If you are left-handed, your left hand will do most of the movement. For simplicity, we have presented the signs here, for the most part, as if signed by a right-handed person.

## Male and Female Signs

Traditionally, male signs are made in the forehead area (think of a man wearing a top hat in the 1800s, when sign language was developed) and female signs are made in the mouth or chin area (think of a woman in the 1800s wearing a bonnet with a big bow below the chin). This helps when you're learning certain male or female signs, such as FATHER (made at the forehead), MOTHER (made at the chin), BROTHER (starting at the forehead), and SISTER (starting at the chin). The male area of the face is above the nose, and the female area of the face is below the nose.

## Fingerspelling

Certain signs, such as BUS and CARROT, are sometimes fingerspelled. English words, such as KIWI, that do not have an ASL sign equivalent are always fingerspelled. It is okay to fingerspell with young children. They may not be able to make the exact hand shapes until they are older, but they may imitate your finger movements in general.

## Dialects

You may find that a sign shown here is different from the way you have learned to sign that word elsewhere. There is often more than one way to sign a concept or idea, and different geographical regions may use different signs for the same concept. This type of regional and dialectic variation is found in all languages.

## Emotions

When showing signs for words related to emotions, such as CRY and ANGRY, it is very important that your facial expression match the sign.

## Nouns and Verbs

In ASL, a single movement often depicts verbs, while a double or repeated movement depicts nouns. For example, the signs for CHAIR and SIT are the same, except that the movement for SIT (the verb) is a single movement, while the movement for CHAIR (the noun) is repeated. Another ASL verb-and-noun pair is the signs for EAT and FOOD. The movement for EAT is a single movement, while the movement for FOOD is a double movement.

## Resources

It can be difficult to learn signs from a printed resource. When in doubt about a sign, visit www.weehands.com to view an online sign language dictionary for parents and caregivers. You can also join the WeeHands online discussion group to talk about signs you'd like to learn. Seek out ASL classes and events in your community, and befriend community members who might be willing to teach you the signs your family needs to know.

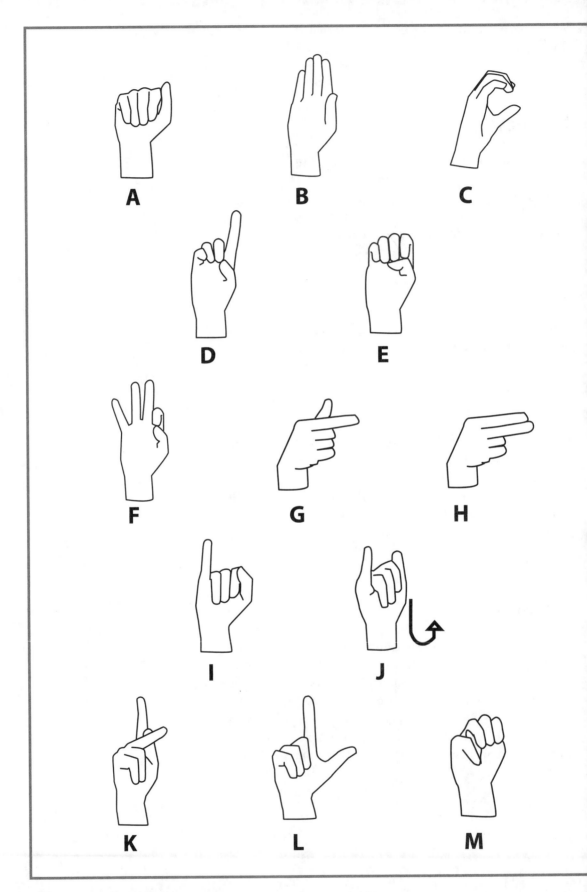

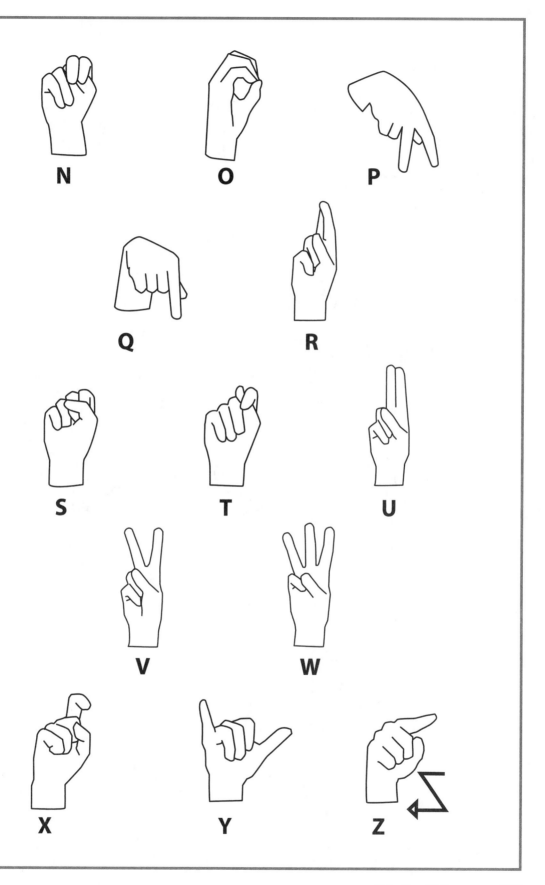

N        O        P

Q        R

S        T        U

V        W

X        Y        Z

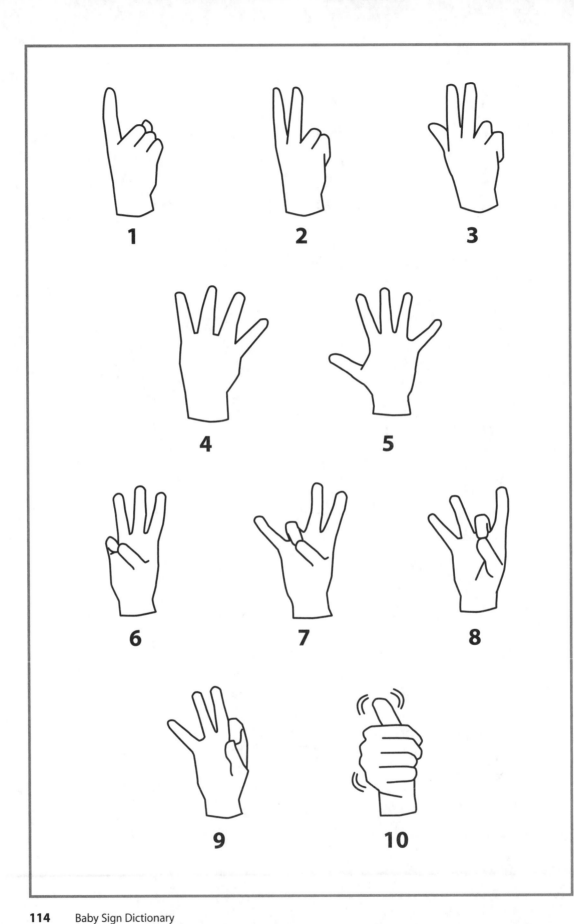

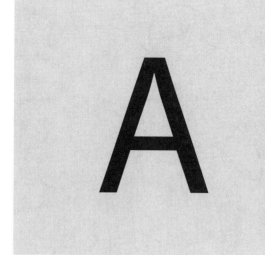

## accident

**Hand Shape:** "5" shapes both hands, ending in "A" shapes

**Body Space:** at chest level

**Movement:** hands change shape and move together quickly

**Memory Aid:** Looks like two objects crashing together. Use an animated facial expression as well!

**Date Introduced:** _____

**Date Produced:** _____

## again

**Hand Shape:** Bent "B" shape right hand and an open "B" shape for your left hand

**Body Space:** at chest level

**Movement:** move your right hand's fingertips onto your left hand's palm

**Memory Aid:** shows something going into your palm again

**Date Introduced:** _____

**Date Produced:** _____

# airplane

**Hand Shape:** "Y" shape with right hand, index finger extended, palm outward (same as I LOVE YOU sign)

**Body Space:** at shoulder level

**Movement:** move forward twice

**Memory Aid:** as if you are flying an airplane forward; sounds are optional but encouraged!

Date Introduced: _____

Date Produced: _____

# all

**Hand Shape:** "B" shapes both hands

**Body Space:** at chest level with right hand palm facing out; left hand palm facing your body

**Movement:** flip right hand toward your chest ending with fingers resting on fingers of other hand

**Memory Aid:** as if you are putting all of something in your left hand

Date Introduced: _____

Date Produced: _____

# all done

**Hand Shape:** "5" shapes, both hands, palms facing chest

**Body Space:** at chest level

**Movement:** hands twist and flick forward, ending with palms facing forward

**Memory Aid:** as if waving something that you are all done with away. This is also the sign for FINISHED

Date Introduced: _____

Date Produced: _____

# alligator

**Hand Shape:** claw shapes both hands, hands on top of each other, palm facing palm

**Body Space:** at chest level

**Movement:** move your hands up and down

**Memory Aid:** your hands move like the jaws of an alligator

**Date Introduced:** _____

**Date Produced:** _____

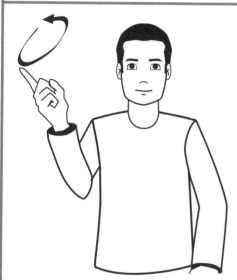

# always

**Hand Shape:** "1" shape or your pointer finger

**Body Space:** at shoulder level

**Movement:** move your upper arm in two large circles

**Memory Aid:** as if you are pointing to indicate "all the time"

**Date Introduced:** _____

**Date Produced:** _____

# angry

**Hand Shape:** claw shape in your right hand

**Body Space:** starts at your chin

**Movement:** moves upward and outward sharply

**Memory Aid:** as if the anger is coming out of you. Match your facial expression to the emotion

**Date Introduced:** _____

**Date Produced:** _____

# ant

**Hand Shape:** "A" shape with both hands

**Body Space:** at chest level

**Movement:** slide right-hand thumb on left-hand thumb twice

**Memory Aid:** thumbs represent ants working; an ant-size version of the sign for WORK

Date Introduced: _____

Date Produced: _____

# apple

**Hand Shape:** "X" shape with right hand

**Body Space:** at cheek

**Movement:** twist back and forth twice

**Memory Aid:** as if twisting an apple stem at the "apple" of your cheek

Date Introduced: _____

Date Produced: _____

# art

**Hand Shape:** "I" shape, right hand. "B" shape, left hand, fingertips forward

**Body Space:** at chest level

**Movement:** fingertip of pinkie finger moves like a pencil across left hand

**Memory Aid:** as if creating art on a piece of paper

Date Introduced: _____

Date Produced: _____

# aunt

**Hand Shape:** "A" shape with right hand, palm facing out

**Body Space:** at jaw or cheek level (the female area of the face)

**Movement:** move up and down in small movements several times

**Memory Aid:** "A" is for aunt

**Date Introduced:** _____

**Date Produced:** _____

# avocado

**Hand Shape:** "A" shapes both hands

**Body Space:** at your chest level

**Movement:** your left hand stays still, while your right hand moves back towards your body in short movements a few times

**Memory Aid:** as if one hand is slicing a piece of avocado, the other hand

**Date Introduced:** _____

**Date Produced:** _____

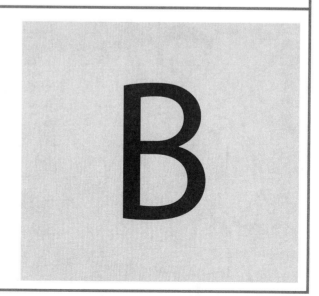

# baby

**Hand Shape:** "B" shape with both hands

**Body Space:** between chest and stomach level

**Movement:** with arms overlapping, rock back and forth

**Memory Aid:** as if rocking a baby back and forth

Date Introduced: _____

Date Produced: _____

# backpack

**Hand Shape:** slightly bent "B" shape, right hand

**Body Space:** over shoulder and backward

**Movement:** hand moves backward twice

**Memory Aid:** as if you were patting where your backpack is

Date Introduced: _____

Date Produced: _____

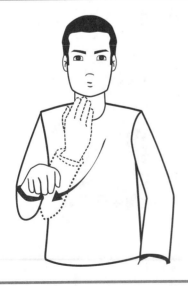

# bad

**Hand Shape:** "B" shape, palm toward your mouth

**Body Space:** starts at your mouth

**Movement:** moves outward and down sharply, ending with your palm down

**Memory Aid:** as if moving something that tastes "bad" away from your mouth

Date Introduced: _____

Date Produced: _____

# ball

**Hand Shape:** spread "C" shapes with both hands

**Body Space:** at chest level

**Movement:** tap fingertips together

**Memory Aid:** as if outlining the shape of a ball

Date Introduced: _____

Date Produced: _____

# balloon

**Hand Shape:** "S" shape with both hands

**Body Space:** at mouth

**Movement:** move hands outward and spread open

**Memory Aid:** as if outlining the shape of a balloon being blown up

Date Introduced: _____

Date Produced: _____

# banana

**Hand Shape:** "1" shape with left hand, "O" shape with right hand

**Body Space:** at chest level

**Movement:** move dominant fingertips of flat "O" up and down "1" shape

**Memory Aid:** as if peeling a banana

Date Introduced: _____

Date Produced: _____

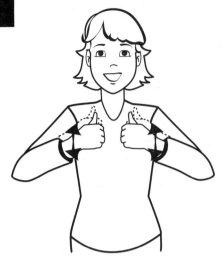

# bath

**Hand Shape:** "A" shape with both hands

**Body Space:** at chest level

**Movement:** move fingers up and down at the same time

**Memory Aid:** as if scrubbing your chest during a bath

Date Introduced: _____

Date Produced: _____

# bear

**Hand Shape:** clawed "5" shape with both hands

**Body Space:** arms crossed with hands just below shoulders

**Movement:** move fingers downward and upward

**Memory Aid:** imitating a bear scratching; sounds are optional but encouraged!

Date Introduced: _____

Date Produced: _____

# beautiful

**Hand Shape:** A flat "5" shape moves into flat O shape, and then opens into another "5" shape

**Body Space:** starts at one side of the face and moves to the other side

**Movement:** your hand moves around your face and then upward

**Memory Aid:** your hand moves around your face and then opens up, like a flower opening

Date Introduced: _____

Date Produced: _____

# bed

**Hand Shape:** "B" shape with right hand

**Body Space:** hand held against side of face

**Movement:** tilt head slightly down

**Memory Aid:** as if laying your head on a bed

Date Introduced: _____

Date Produced: _____

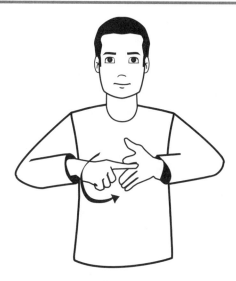

# bee

**Hand Shape:** use an "F" shape and then an open "B" shape

**Body Space:** at your cheek, then forward

**Movement:** move your hand quickly from your cheek and forward

**Memory Aid:** as if swatting at a bee that's stung your cheek

Date Introduced: _____

Date Produced: _____

# begin

**Hand Shape:** "1" shape right hand, fits between the pointer and middle (or touch) fingers of the left hand

**Body Space:** at chest level

**Movement:** twist your right hand toward your body

**Memory Aid:** as if you are turning a key to begin driving

Date Introduced: _____

Date Produced: _____

# bell

**Hand Shape:** "S" shape with right hand, "B" shape with left hand

**Body Space:** at chest level

**Movement:** strike right hand against palm of left hand

**Memory Aid:** as if holding a bell in right hand and striking it against the left hand to ring it

**Date Introduced:** _____

**Date Produced:** _____

# berry

**Hand Shape:** "O" shape with right hand, "I" shape with left hand

**Body Space:** at chest level

**Movement:** twist little finger on left hand with right hand

**Memory Aid:** as if picking a berry off a vine; signs vary considerably by region

**Date Introduced:** _____

**Date Produced:** _____

# big

**Hand Shape:** "B" shape with both hands

**Body Space:** at chest level (first position is shown in dotted line)

**Movement:** palms facing, move away from each other

**Memory Aid:** as if indicating a really big fish

**Date Introduced:** _____

**Date Produced:** _____

# bike

**Hand Shape:** "S" shape with both hands, palms down

**Body Space:** at chest level

**Movement:** alternate moving hands up and down

**Memory Aid:** as if moving the pedals on a bicycle

Date Introduced: _____

Date Produced: _____

# bird

**Hand Shape:** "G" shape with right hand

**Body Space:** at mouth

**Movement:** open and close index finger and thumb twice

**Memory Aid:** indicating the beak of a bird

Date Introduced: _____

Date Produced: _____

# birthday (version 1)

BIRTH: **Hand Shape:** open "B" shape with both hands, right palm toward body, left palm up

**Body Space:** starts close to lower chest level, little finger and right hand touching body (first position is shown with dotted line)

**Movement:** move right hand up and back, and lay right hand on left palm

**Memory Aid:** a combination of the signs for BIRTH and DAY; signs vary considerably by region

DAY: **Hand Shape:** "1" shape with right hand held vertically on tips of "B"-shaped left hand

**Body Space:** at lower chest level

**Movement:** move right forearm down until right hand is at left elbow

Date Introduced: _____

Date Produced: _____

# birthday (version 2)

**Hand Shape:** "5" shape right hand

**Body Space:** middle (or touch) finger touches chin

**Movement:** move hand downward so that middle (or touch) finger touches the middle of your chest

**Memory Aid:** this is one way to sign BIRTHDAY

Date Introduced: _____

Date Produced: _____

# birthday (version 3)

**Hand Shape:** "3" shape right hand

**Body Space:** at the side of your cheek

**Movement:** brush your "3" shape forward along your jaw line twice

**Memory Aid:** think about blowing out 3 candles on your birthday cake when you make this version of the word, BIRTHDAY

Date Introduced: _____

Date Produced: _____

# bite

**Hand Shape:** "B" shape left hand; "C" shape right hand

**Body Space:** at chest level

**Movement:** your "C" hand moves toward your left hand and closes on it

**Memory Aid:** as if one hand is biting the other

Date Introduced: _____

Date Produced: _____

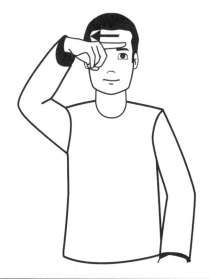

# black

**Hand Shape:** "1" shape

**Body Space:** at your eyebrow level

**Movement:** move your hand across your forehead, from your non-dominant side to your dominant side

**Memory Aid:** as if outlining black eyebrows

Date Introduced: _____

Date Produced: _____

# blanket

**Hand Shape:** "B" shape both hands, palms facing body

**Body Space:** starts at lower chest level (first position is shown with dotted line)

**Movement:** draw both hands upward at the same time so that fingertips touch upper chest

**Memory Aid:** as if you are pulling up the bed covers

Date Introduced: _____

Date Produced: _____

# block (building)

**Hand Shape:** wide "G" shape with right hand

**Body Space:** at shoulder level

**Movement:** twist hand from wrist, indicating the sides of a block

**Memory Aid:** as if you are outlining the top and bottom of a block and then the sides of a block

Date Introduced: _____

Date Produced: _____

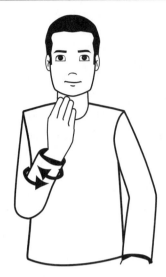

# blue

**Hand Shape:** "B" shape with right hand

**Body Space:** at shoulder level

**Movement:** twist at the wrist several times

**Memory Aid:** "B" sign is used for blue; resembles a royal or "blue blood" wave

Date Introduced: _____

Date Produced: _____

# boat

**Hand Shape:** cupped "B" shape with both hands

**Body Space:** at chest level

**Movement:** move up and down

**Memory Aid:** indicating the hull of a boat bobbing in the water

Date Introduced: _____

Date Produced: _____

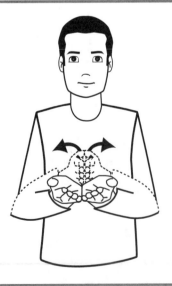

# book

**Hand Shape:** "B" shape with both hands, palms touching

**Body Space:** at chest level

**Movement:** open palms to end, facing upward

**Memory Aid:** as if opening a book

Date Introduced: _____

Date Produced: _____

# boots

**Hand Shape:** "B" shapes both hands

**Body Space:** just below chest level

**Movement:** tap your hands, at the thumbs, together twice

**Memory Aid:** "B" is for BOOTS! This is the same movement as the sign for SHOES

Date Introduced: _____

Date Produced: _____

# bottle

**Hand Shape:** "B" shape left hand, palm upward. "C" shape left hand

**Body Space:** at or just below chest level

**Movement:** move your right hand upward, closing to an "S" shape

**Memory Aid:** as if you are outlining the shape of a bottle

Date Introduced: _____

Date Produced: _____

# bowl

**Hand Shape:** cupped "B" shape with both hands, little fingers touching

**Body Space:** at chest level

**Movement:** move hands apart and upward

**Memory Aid:** as if outlining the shape of a bowl

Date Introduced: _____

Date Produced: _____

# boy

**Hand Shape:** flattened "C" shape with right hand

**Body Space:** at forehead

**Movement:** open and close hand twice

**Memory Aid:** indicating the brim of a boy's cap

**Date Introduced:** _____

**Date Produced:** _____

# bread

**Hand Shape:** clawed "5" shape with right hand in front of "B"-shaped left hand

**Body Space:** at chest level

**Movement:** move right hand down back of left hand twice

**Memory Aid:** as if slicing a loaf of bread

**Date Introduced:** _____

**Date Produced:** _____

# break (noun)

**Hand Shape:** "4" shape left hand, palm facing chest. "B" shape right hand, palm facing downward

**Body Space:** at chest level

**Movement:** slide right hand's fingers between middle (or touch) and ring finger of left hand

**Memory Aid:** one hand is separating the fingers of the other. This is also the sign for INTERMISSION or INTERLUDE

**Date Introduced:** _____

**Date Produced:** _____

# breast

**Hand Shape:** Bent "B" shape, right hand

**Body Space:** at chest level. Fingertips to chest

**Movement:** above fingertips from right breast to your left breast

**Memory Aid:** you're simply indicated where your breasts are. Pair with the sign for FEED/NOURISH to create a version of the sign for BREASTFEEDING

Date Introduced: _____

Date Produced: _____

# bring

**Hand Shape:** "B" shape with both hands, palms up

**Body Space:** at chest level

**Movement:** arc both hands to the right

**Memory Aid:** as if bringing or moving an object in the direction that your hands move

Date Introduced: _____

Date Produced: _____

# brother

**Hand Shape:** "L" shape with both hands

**Body Space:** right hand at forehead, left hand at chest level

**Movement:** move right hand down on top of left hand

**Memory Aid:** starts at the male area of the face and ends in a modified version of the sign CARE — your brother is a male you care about

Date Introduced: _____

Date Produced: _____

# brush

**Hand Shape:** "A" shape, right hand

**Body Space:** at the side of your head

**Movement:** move hand downward in small motions, twice

**Memory Aid:** as if brushing your hair

Date Introduced: _____

Date Produced: _____

# bubble

**Hand Shape:** "F" shape with both hands

**Body Space:** at chest level

**Movement:** float hands upward

**Memory Aid:** as if showing bubbles (small circles) floating in the air

Date Introduced: _____

Date Produced: _____

# bug

**Hand Shape:** "3" shape with right hand

**Body Space:** thumb placed at nose

**Movement:** move two fingers up and down

**Memory Aid:** imitating a bug's antennae twitching

Date Introduced: _____

Date Produced: _____

# bunny (rabbit)

**Hand Shape:** bent "U" shapes with both hands, hands held one in front of the other

**Body Space:** at chest level

**Movement:** bend extended fingers up and down at the same time

**Memory Aid:** imitating a bunny's or rabbit's ears twitching up and down

Date Introduced: _____

Date Produced: _____

# bus

**Hand Shape:** "S" shapes with both hands, palms down

**Body Space:** at chest level

**Movement:** move hands and upper body back and forth

**Memory Aid:** imitating holding and steering the wider steering wheel of a bus; may also be fingerspelled

Date Introduced: _____

Date Produced: _____

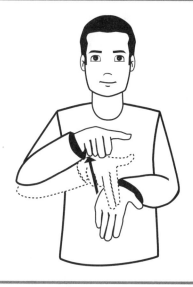

# butter

**Hand Shape:** "H" shape right hand, palm facing down. "B" shape left hand, palm facing up

**Body Space:** just below chest level

**Movement:** brush your fingertips across the palm of your left hand

**Memory Aid:** as if you are buttering a slice of bread

Date Introduced: _____

Date Produced: _____

# butterfly

**Hand Shape:** "B" shape with both hands, thumbs hooked, palms facing you

**Body Space:** at chest level

**Movement:** bend fingers of both hands back and forth toward you twice

**Memory Aid:** imitating the wings of a butterfly flying

Date Introduced: _____

Date Produced: _____

# cake

**Hand Shape:** clawed "C" shape with right hand on palm of "B"-shaped left hand

**Body Space:** at chest level

**Movement:** slide right hand down palm of left hand

**Memory Aid:** as if cutting and moving a slice of cake

Date Introduced: _____

Date Produced: _____

## call

**Hand Shape:** "Y" shape with your right hand

**Body Space:** at your ear

**Movement:** move right hand up to your right ear

**Memory Aid:** as if you are pretending to call someone on the phone

Date Introduced: _____

Date Produced: _____

## car

**Hand Shape:** "S" shape with both hands, palms facing you

**Body Space:** at chest level

**Movement:** move hands up and down alternately

**Memory Aid:** as if holding and steering a steering wheel of a car

Date Introduced: _____

Date Produced: _____

## careful

**Hand Shape:** "K" shape with both hands, right hand resting on left hand

**Body Space:** at chest level

**Movement:** move hands together up and down in a circular motion

**Memory Aid:** accompany with a concerned facial expression

Date Introduced: _____

Date Produced: _____

## carrot

**Hand Shape:** "S" shape with right hand

**Body Space:** at side of mouth

**Movement:** twist hand forward and down

**Memory Aid:** as if biting a carrot; may also be fingerspelled

Date Introduced: _____

Date Produced: _____

## cat

**Hand Shape:** "F" shape with right hand

**Body Space:** at side of mouth

**Movement:** move hand outward several times

**Memory Aid:** indicating the whiskers of a cat

Date Introduced: _____

Date Produced: _____

## catch

**Hand Shape:** claw shapes both hands, palms facing

**Body Space:** just in front of face

**Movement:** move hands toward body and downward

**Memory Aid:** as if catching a ball

Date Introduced: _____

Date Produced: _____

# cereal

**Hand Shape:** "X" shape with right hand, "B" shape with left hand, palm up

**Body Space:** at chest level

**Movement:** brush "X" shape toward elbow of left arm twice

**Memory Aid:** as if cutting grain for your cereal; sign may vary by region

Date Introduced: _____

Date Produced: _____

# chair

**Hand Shape:** "H" shapes both hands

**Body Space:** at chest level

**Movement:** "H" shape of right hand taps "H" shape of left hand twice

**Memory Aid:** as if the fingers of one hand are sitting on the other hand

Date Introduced: _____

Date Produced: _____

# change

**Hand Shape:** "A" shape with both hands, palms facing each other

**Body Space:** at chest level

**Movement:** twist hands and reverse position

**Memory Aid:** indicating your hands changing position

Date Introduced: _____

Date Produced: _____

# cheese

**Hand Shape:** heel of right hand in a "C" shape on heel of left hand

**Body Space:** just below chest level

**Movement:** twist right hand back and forth several times

**Memory Aid:** as if you are squeezing the whey from curds to make cheese

**Date Introduced:** _____

**Date Produced:** _____

# chew

**Hand Shape:** "A" shape with both hands, palms facing each other

**Body Space:** at chest level

**Movement:** rub hands together in circles in opposite directions

**Memory Aid:** imitating teeth grinding up food

**Date Introduced:** _____

**Date Produced:** _____

# chicken

**Hand Shape:** "G" shape with right hand, "B" shape with left hand, palm up

**Body Space:** "G" shape at mouth, "B" shape at chest level

**Movement:** open and close "G" shape and move down to left hand

**Memory Aid:** imitating a bird eating grain

**Date Introduced:** _____

**Date Produced:** _____

## clean

**Hand Shape:** "B" shape with both hands, palms facing

**Body Space:** at chest level

**Movement:** move right hand across left hand

**Memory Aid:** as if wiping a table clean; also used as the sign for NICE

Date Introduced: _____

Date Produced: _____

## close

**Hand Shape:** "B" shape with both hands, palms up and slightly apart

**Body Space:** at chest level

**Movement:** turn both hands over and move together

**Memory Aid:** as if closing the lid of a box

Date Introduced: _____

Date Produced: _____

## clothes

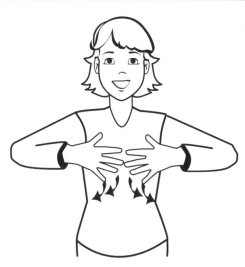

**Hand Shape:** "B" shape with both hands, palms facing

**Body Space:** at chest level

**Movement:** move right hand across left hand

**Memory Aid:** as if wiping a table clean; also used as the sign for NICE

Date Introduced: _____

Date Produced: _____

# cloud

**Hand Shape:** clawed "5" shape with both hands, held apart, palms facing

**Body Space:** above face level

**Movement:** bounce hands gently to the side

**Memory Aid:** as if outlining the shape of a cloud

Date Introduced: _____

Date Produced: _____

# coat

**Hand Shape:** "A" shape with both hands, held apart, palms facing

**Body Space:** at chest level

**Movement:** move hands down chest a short distance

**Memory Aid:** as if shrugging on a coat or jacket

Date Introduced: _____

Date Produced: _____

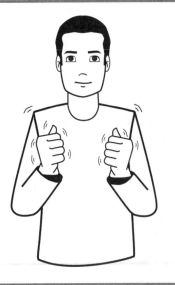

# cold

**Hand Shape:** "A" shape with both hands, held apart, palms facing

**Body Space:** at chest level

**Movement:** shake hands back and forth

**Memory Aid:** as if shivering, with facial expression matching sign

Date Introduced: _____

Date Produced: _____

# color

**Hand Shape:** "5" shape with right hand

**Body Space:** at chin

**Movement:** wiggle fingertips

**Memory Aid:** as if waving a colorful flag at your chin

**Date Introduced:** _____

**Date Produced:** _____

# comb

**Hand Shape:** clawed "5" shape with right hand

**Body Space:** at side of head

**Movement:** move downward twice

**Memory Aid:** as if combing your hair with your fingers

**Date Introduced:** _____

**Date Produced:** _____

# come

**Hand Shape:** "1" shape with right hand, fingertip upward, palm facing body (may be done with two hands)

**Body Space:** at shoulder level

**Movement:** move arm while arcing finger toward body

**Memory Aid:** pointing as if asking someone to come to you

**Date Introduced:** _____

**Date Produced:** _____

# container

**Hand Shape:** "C" shape with right hand, palm left; "B" shape with left hand, palm up

**Body Space:** at chest level

**Movement:** move right hand upward

**Memory Aid:** as if outlining the sides and size of a container

Date Introduced: _____

Date Produced: _____

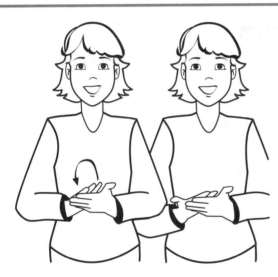

# cook

**Hand Shape:** "B" shape with both hands, left hand palm up, palms touching

**Body Space:** at chest level

**Movement:** flip right hand over from palm down to palm up

**Memory Aid:** as if flipping a hamburger or pancake

Date Introduced: _____

Date Produced: _____

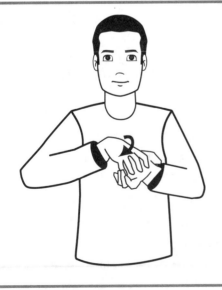

# cookie

**Hand Shape:** "B" shape with left hand, palm up, clawed "5" shape with right hand

**Body Space:** at chest level

**Movement:** touch fingertips of right hand to left palm and twist

**Memory Aid:** as if using a cookie cutter

Date Introduced: _____

Date Produced: _____

# corn

**Hand Shape:** "1" shape, right hand

**Body Space:** at your mouth

**Movement:** twist your hand, at the wrist, forward twice

**Memory Aid:** your finger represents an ear of corn that you are eating

Date Introduced: _____

Date Produced: _____

# count

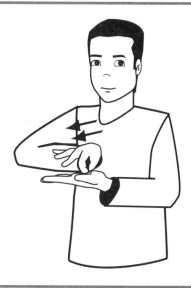

**Hand Shape:** "F" shape right hand, open "B" shape left hand

**Body Space:** just below chest level

**Movement:** "F" hand slides forward on palm of other hand twice

**Memory Aid:** as if you are counting coins out of your hand

Date Introduced: _____

Date Produced: _____

# cousin (female)

**Hand Shape:** "C" shape with right hand

**Body Space:** at side of chin (female area of face)

**Movement:** move hand back and forth in a small circular motion

**Memory Aid:** a family member title that starts with a "C"

Date Introduced: _____

Date Produced: _____

# cousin (male)

**Hand Shape:** "C" shape with right hand

**Body Space:** at side of temple (male area of face)

**Movement:** move hand back and forth in a small circular motion

**Memory Aid:** a family member title that starts with a "C"

Date Introduced: _____

Date Produced: _____

# cow

**Hand Shape:** "Y" shape with right hand, palm down

**Body Space:** at temple

**Movement:** twist hand upward

**Memory Aid:** indicating the horns of a cow; mooing is optional but encouraged!

Date Introduced: _____

Date Produced: _____

# cracker

**Hand Shape:** "A" shape with right hand

**Body Space:** at left elbow

**Movement:** tap twice

**Memory Aid:** imitating a baker cracking sheets of biscuits on the edge of a table

Date Introduced: _____

Date Produced: _____

# cry

**Hand Shape:** "1" shape with both hands, palms facing you

**Body Space:** just below your eyes

**Movement:** move fingers down face repeatedly

**Memory Aid:** imitating tears coming down face; accompanying facial expression matches sign

**Date Introduced:** _____

**Date Produced:** _____

# cup

**Hand Shape:** "C" shape with right hand, "B" shape with left hand, palm up

**Body Space:** at chest level

**Movement:** move right hand up and down twice on palm of left hand

**Memory Aid:** as if outlining the shape of a cup on a saucer

**Date Introduced:** _____

**Date Produced:** _____

# cupcake

**Hand Shape:** small claw shape, right hand, palm downward. "B" shape left hand, palm facing upward

**Body Space:** at chest level

**Movement:** move small claw shape into palm of left hand

**Memory Aid:** as if outline the shape of a cupcake. This is also the sign for MUFFIN

**Date Introduced:** _____

**Date Produced:** _____

## cute

**Hand Shape:** "U" shape

**Body Space:** at your chin

**Movement:** brush your fingertips down your chin once or twice

**Memory Aid:** this is also the sign for SWEET; imagine sweet syrup on your chin

**Date Introduced:** _____

**Date Produced:** _____

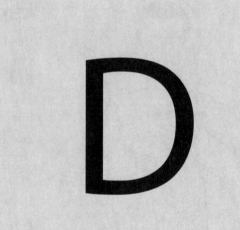

## daddy (father)

**Hand Shape:** "5" shape with right hand

**Body Space:** at forehead (male area of face)

**Movement:** tap twice

**Memory Aid:** sign for father and daddy

**Date Introduced:** _____

**Date Produced:** _____

# dance

**Hand Shape:** "V" shape with right hand, "B" shape with left hand, palm up

**Body Space:** at chest level

**Movement:** move right hand back and forth across upturned palm of left hand

**Memory Aid:** imitating someone dancing on a dance floor

Date Introduced: _____

Date Produced: _____

# danger

**Hand Shape:** "A" shape with both hands

**Body Space:** at chest level

**Movement:** move right hand up quickly and past left hand, striking it on the way up

**Memory Aid:** as if hands almost hitting; accompany with appropriate facial expression

Date Introduced: _____

Date Produced: _____

# daughter

**Hand Shape:** "B" shape, right hand

**Body Space:** starts at the side of your chin

**Movement:** move your hand into the crook of your other forearm

**Memory Aid:** this sign evolved from the signs for GIRL and BABY

Date Introduced: _____

Date Produced: _____

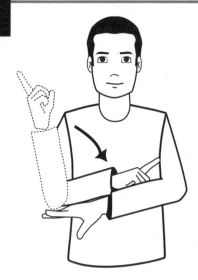

# day

**Hand Shape:** "1" shape with right hand, "B" shape with left hand, palm down

**Body Space:** right elbow on top of left hand at chest level

**Movement:** move right hand downward toward left elbow

**Memory Aid:** left forearm indicating the horizon, and right hand indicating the sun during a day

Date Introduced: _____

Date Produced: _____

# dear (beloved)

**Hand Shape:** "A" shape with both hands, crossed at wrist, palms facing body

**Body Space:** at chest level

**Movement:** press hands against chest

**Memory Aid:** as if hugging someone dear or beloved; accompany with appropriate facial expression

Date Introduced: _____

Date Produced: _____

# delicious

**Hand Shape:** "8" shape, right hand

**Body Space:** at your lips

**Movement:** move your hand upward

**Memory Aid:** as if the food is so good you need to kiss your fingertips!

Date Introduced: _____

Date Produced: _____

# diamond

**Hand Shape:** "D" shape with right hand, left hand palm down

**Body Space:** at chest level

**Movement:** brush thumb and middle finger of right hand down base of ring finger on left hand twice

**Memory Aid:** indicating where a diamond ring would be placed on a finger

Date Introduced: _____

Date Produced: _____

# diaper

**Hand Shape:** "H" shape with both hands, palms facing body

**Body Space:** at waist

**Movement:** snap index and thumb together twice

**Memory Aid:** indicating the placement of diaper pins

Date Introduced: _____

Date Produced: _____

# different

**Hand Shape:** "1" shape with both hands, forefingers crossed, palms facing outward

**Body Space:** at chest level

**Movement:** move hands apart and outward

**Memory Aid:** indicating two items moving apart from each other

Date Introduced: _____

Date Produced: _____

# dinosaur (version 1)

**Hand Shape:** bent "V" shape with both hands, palms facing

**Body Space:** at chest level

**Movement:** alternate hands moving up and down in small circles

**Memory Aid:** imitating the small arms of a T. rex; sounds are optional but encouraged!

Date Introduced: _____

Date Produced: _____

# dinosaur (version 2)

**Hand Shape:** flat "O" shape with right hand

**Body Space:** at shoulder level

**Movement:** bounce hand up and down to the left in small movements

**Memory Aid:** imitating the head of a dinosaur as it walks; sounds are optional but encouraged!

Date Introduced: _____

Date Produced: _____

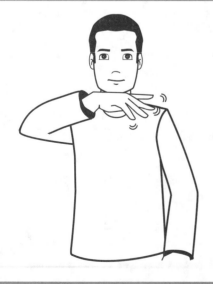

# dirty

**Hand Shape:** "5" shape with right hand, palm down

**Body Space:** under chin

**Movement:** wiggle fingers

**Memory Aid:** as if you were lying on the ground and your chin might get dirty; or think of crumbs falling off a dirty face

Date Introduced: _____

Date Produced: _____

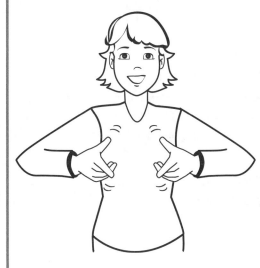

# dish

**Hand Shape:** curved "L" shapes both hands

**Body Space:** at chest level

**Movement:** move

**Memory Aid:** as is outlining the sides of a dish

Date Introduced: _____

Date Produced: _____

# doctor

**Hand Shape:** "M" shape with right hand

**Body Space:** at left wrist

**Movement:** tap wrist twice with fingertips of right hand

**Memory Aid:** as if a doctor was using a medical procedure to take your pulse

Date Introduced: _____

Date Produced: _____

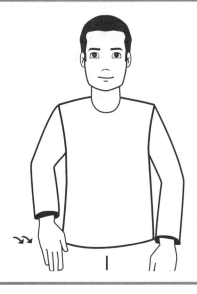

# dog

**Hand Shape:** "B" shape with right hand, palm facing body

**Body Space:** at right thigh

**Movement:** tap thigh a few times

**Memory Aid:** as if calling a dog to you with this gesture; can add a finger snap to the end of this sign

Date Introduced: _____

Date Produced: _____

# doll

**Hand Shape:** "X" shape with right hand, palm facing left

**Body Space:** at tip of nose

**Movement:** tap nose twice with right bent forefinger in a downward motion

**Memory Aid:** indicating the cute nose of a doll

**Date Introduced:** _____

**Date Produced:** _____

# donkey

**Hand Shape:** "B" shape right hand, thumb on side of head

**Body Space:** thumb touching your temple

**Movement:** bend fingers of hand down twice

**Memory Aid:** imitates the ear of a donkey; may also be used with two hands

**Date Introduced:** _____

**Date Produced:** _____

# door

**Hand Shape:** "B" shape with both hands, palms facing outward

**Body Space:** at chest level, thumbs of both hands touching

**Movement:** twist right hand backward so that palm is facing you

**Memory Aid:** as if one side of a set of French doors is opening

**Date Introduced:** _____

**Date Produced:** _____

# down

**Hand Shape:** "1" shape with right hand

**Body Space:** at chest level

**Movement:** point hand and move downward

**Memory Aid:** indicating the direction of down

**Date Introduced:** _____

**Date Produced:** _____

# dragon

**Hand Shape:** "O" shape with right hand, palm outward

**Body Space:** back of hand at mouth

**Movement:** move hand forward with force while opening to a claw shape

**Memory Aid:** imitating a dragon breathing fire; accompany with appropriate facial expression

**Date Introduced:** _____

**Date Produced:** _____

# draw

**Hand Shape:** "I" shape right hand; B shape left hand

**Body Space:** at chest level

**Movement:** fingertip of pinkie finger, an "I" shape, moves like a pencil across left hand

**Memory:** as if creating art on a piece of paper

**Date Introduced:** _____

**Date Produced:** _____

# dream

**Hand Shape:** "1" shape with right hand

**Body Space:** at temple

**Movement:** move hand gently outward and upward, alternately changing from "1" shape to an "X" shape

**Memory Aid:** as if dreams are floating out of your head

Date Introduced: _____

Date Produced: _____

# dress

**Hand Shape:** "5" shapes both hands, palms facing body

**Body Space:** starts at chest level and moves downward to your hips

**Movement:** move your hands downward

**Memory Aid:** as if you are outline the shape of a dress you are wearing

Date Introduced: _____

Date Produced: _____

# drink

**Hand Shape:** "C" shape with right hand, palm facing left

**Body Space:** at mouth

**Movement:** tilt hand upward

**Memory Aid:** as if taking a drink from a cup

Date Introduced: _____

Date Produced: _____

# drop

**Hand Shape:** "S" shapes both hands

**Body Space:** at chest level

**Movement:** open hands into "5" shapes while moving downward slightly

**Memory Aid:** as if drop a block out of your hand. May also be signed with one hand

**Date Introduced:** _____

**Date Produced:** _____

# dry

**Hand Shape:** "X" shape with right hand, palm down

**Body Space:** at chin

**Movement:** move hand across chin from left to right

**Memory Aid:** as if wiping something wet off your chin

**Date Introduced:** _____

**Date Produced:** _____

# duck

**Hand Shape:** Bent "3" shape with right hand, palm facing outward

**Body Space:** at mouth

**Movement:** open and close "3" shape a few times

**Memory Aid:** indicating the bill of a duck opening and closing; quacking is optional but encouraged!

**Date Introduced:** _____

**Date Produced:** _____

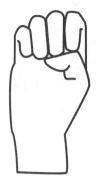

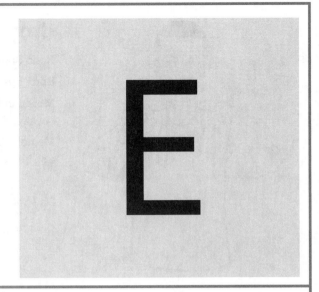

## earth

**Hand Shape:** "S" shape left hand, palm down. Thumb of "F" shape right hand on back of left hand

**Body Space:** at chest level

**Movement:** "F" shape rocks back and forth

**Memory Aid:** imitates the earth moving on its axis

Date Introduced: _____

Date Produced: _____

## eat

**Hand Shape:** "O" shape with right hand, palm facing you

**Body Space:** at mouth

**Movement:** tap mouth once with fingertips; tap twice for noun FOOD

**Memory Aid:** as if bringing food to your mouth

Date Introduced: _____

Date Produced: _____

# egg

**Hand Shape:** "U" shape with right hand on top of "U" shape with left hand, palms facing you

**Body Space:** at chest level

**Movement:** curve hands downward quickly so that fingertips point out

**Memory Aid:** as if cracking an egg in two

**Date Introduced:** _____

**Date Produced:** _____

# elephant

**Hand Shape:** "C" shape with right hand, palm facing left, or "B" shape

**Body Space:** at nose

**Movement:** move right hand down and forward

**Memory Aid:** as if you are outlining an elephant's trunk; sounds are optional but encouraged!

**Date Introduced:** _____

**Date Produced:** _____

# everybody

**Hand Shape:** "1" shape, right hand

**Body Space:** at your dominant shoulder

**Movement:** move your hand in an arc, away from your body and then toward your other shoulder

**Memory Aid:** as if you were pointing, in a sweeping motion, to everybody

**Date Introduced:** _____

**Date Produced:** _____

# everyone

**Hand Shape:** "A" shapes both hands, ending with a "1" shape, right hand

**Body Space:** at your chest level

**Movement:** brush the knuckles of your right hand against the knuckles of the other and then make a "1" shape with your right hand

**Memory Aid:** last shape indicates the word ONE

Date Introduced: _____

Date Produced: _____

# excited

**Hand Shape:** "5" shapes both hands, palms toward you

**Body Space:** at chest level

**Movement:** move your hands toward your chest in circular motions several times, brushing your middle (or touch) finger against your chest

**Memory Aid:** as if the feelings are coming out of you, excitedly!

Date Introduced: _____

Date Produced: _____

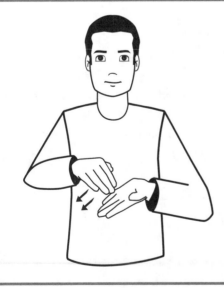

# excuse me

**Hand Shape:** "B" shape, left hand, palm facing upward. Bent "B" shape right hand, fingertips touching palm of left hand

**Body Space:** at chest level

**Movement:** brush your right hand, forward twice

**Memory Aid:** brush your fingers lightly as if whispering "'excuse me"

Date Introduced: _____

Date Produced: _____

# eye

**Hand Shape:** "1" shape with right hand

**Body Space:** just under your right eye

**Movement:** move tip of finger toward eye

**Memory Aid:** pointing, gently, to your eye

**Date Introduced:** _____

**Date Produced:** _____

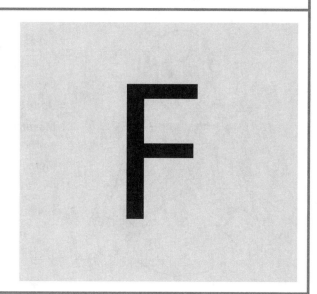

**F**

# face

**Hand Shape:** "1" shape with right hand

**Body Space:** at right temple

**Movement:** move in a circle around face

**Memory Aid:** as if outlining the shape of your face

**Date Introduced:** _____

**Date Produced:** _____

# fall (verb)

**Hand Shape:** "V" shape with right hand, B shape with left hand, palm up

**Body Space:** at chest level

**Movement:** stand right fingertips on left palm, and move right hand up slightly and downward

**Memory Aid:** imitating a person standing and then falling down; accompanying facial expression shows concern or relevant emotion

**Date Introduced:** _____

**Date Produced:** _____

# family

**Hand Shape:** "F" shape with both hands, tips of thumbs touching

**Body Space:** at chest level

**Movement:** move both hands outward in a circle, ending with little fingers touching

**Memory Aid:** indicating your family circle

**Date Introduced:** _____

**Date Produced:** _____

# fan

**Hand Shape:** "1" shape with right hand, palm facing left

**Body Space:** at shoulder level

**Movement:** move right forearm in small circles

**Memory Aid:** indicating the motion of blades in a ceiling fan

**Date Introduced:** _____

**Date Produced:** _____

# farm

**Hand Shape:** "5" shape with right hand, palm down

**Body Space:** thumb touches left side of chin

**Movement:** sweep thumb across chin to the right

**Memory Aid:** indicating fields being plowed with outstretched fingers

Date Introduced: _____

Date Produced: _____

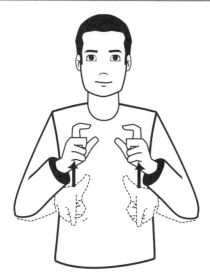

# fast

**Hand Shape:** "L" shape with both hands

**Body Space:** just below chest level

**Movement:** pull both hands back together quickly into "X" shapes

**Memory Aid:** indicating very quick or fast movement

Date Introduced: _____

Date Produced: _____

# father

**Hand Shape:** "5" shape, right hand

**Body Space:** thumb touches the middle of your forehead

**Movement:** hold your hand at your forehead or tap your hand twice against your forehead

**Memory Aid:** use a "5 shape and "five" starts with an "f" just as "father" does

Date Introduced: _____

Date Produced: _____

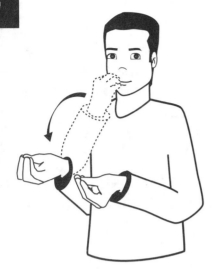

# feed (nourish)

**Hand Shape:** flat "O" shapes both hands

**Body Space:** your right hand is at your mouth, while your left hand is just below your chest

**Movement:** move your right hand forward, from your mouth, and down

**Memory Aid:** this sign starts with the sign for FOOD and then moves outward. Use this sign after the sign for BREAST to indicate "breastfeeding"

**Date Introduced:** _____

**Date Produced:** _____

# feelings

**Hand Shape:** "5" shape, right hand

**Body Space:** at your chest

**Movement:** brush the middle (or touch) finger of your "5" shape upward against your chest twice

**Memory Aid:** as if your feelings are coming out of you

**Date Introduced:** _____

**Date Produced:** _____

# fiddle

**Hand Shape:** F shape, right hand; "8" shape, left hand

**Body Space:** at shoulder level

**Movement:** move your right hand back and forth towards your non-dominant arm

**Memory Aid:** as if moving the bow of a fiddle you are holding

**Date Introduced:** _____

**Date Produced:** _____

# fine

**Hand Shape:** "5" shape, right hand

**Body Space:** at your chest

**Movement:** tap your thumb against your chest once or twice

**Memory Aid:** remember, you use a "5" shape to sign FINE

Date Introduced: _____

Date Produced: _____

# finish

**Hand Shape:** "5" shape with both hands, palms facing you

**Body Space:** at chest level

**Movement:** turn hands over and away from body, and end with palms facing outward

**Memory Aid:** as if dropping something you are finished with

Date Introduced: _____

Date Produced: _____

# fire

**Hand Shape:** "5" shapes both hands

**Body Space:** at chest level

**Movement:** wiggle your fingers and alternate your hands moving up and down

**Memory Aid:** as if imitating the flames of a fire with your fingers

Date Introduced: _____

Date Produced: _____

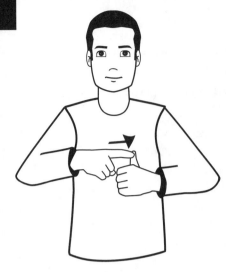

# first

**Hand Shape:** "A" shape with left hand, palm facing right, "1" shape with right hand

**Body Space:** at chest level

**Movement:** tap "1" shape of right hand on thumb of left "A" shape once

**Memory Aid:** as in "FIRST, put on your socks."

Date Introduced: _____

Date Produced: _____

# fish

**Hand Shape:** "B" shape with right hand, palm facing left

**Body Space:** at chest level

**Movement:** move right hand to the side while bending wrist left and right

**Memory Aid:** imitating the tail of a fish swimming

Date Introduced: _____

Date Produced: _____

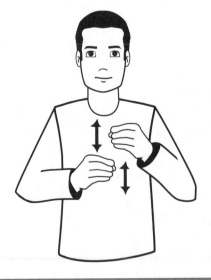

# fix

**Hand Shape:** "O" shape with both hands, palms facing

**Body Space:** at chest level

**Movement:** brush fingertips together in an up and down motion

**Memory Aid:** indicating work being done on something that needs fixing

Date Introduced: _____

Date Produced: _____

# floor

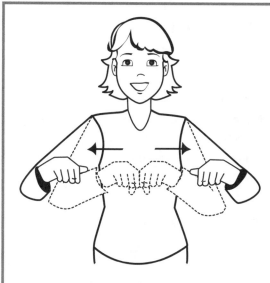

**Hand Shape:** "B" shape with both hands, palms down, index fingers touching

**Body Space:** at chest level

**Movement:** move hands apart at the same time

**Memory Aid:** as if your hands are moving across a flat floor

Date Introduced: _____

Date Produced: _____

# flower

**Hand Shape:** "O" shape with right hand

**Body Space:** at right side of nose

**Movement:** move hand to left side of nose

**Memory Aid:** as if you are holding and smelling a flower

Date Introduced: _____

Date Produced: _____

# fly (noun)

**Hand Shape:** "S" shape, left hand, palm down; open "5" shape right hand

**Body Space:** at chest level

**Movement:** move your right hand quickly over your left hand closing it into an "S" shape

**Memory Aid:** as if catching a fly on the back of your hand

Date Introduced: _____

Date Produced: _____

# fly (verb)

**Hand Shape:** "B" shape with both hands, palms down

**Body Space:** at shoulder level

**Movement:** flap forearms up and down at the same time

**Memory Aid:** imitating the movement of a bird's wings

**Date Introduced:** _____

**Date Produced:** _____

# food

**Hand Shape:** "O" shape with right hand, palm facing you

**Body Space:** at mouth

**Movement:** fingertips tap mouth twice; tap once for verb EAT

**Memory Aid:** as if putting food in your mouth

**Date Introduced:** _____

**Date Produced:** _____

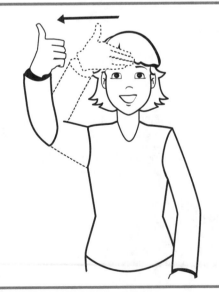

# forget

**Hand Shape:** "B" shape right hand

**Body Space:** at your forehead

**Movement:** move your hand across your forehead and close it into an "A" shape

**Memory Aid:** as is something has been wiped from your memory

**Date Introduced:** _____

**Date Produced:** _____

# fork

**Hand Shape:** "V" shape, right hand; "B" shape, left hand, palm upward

**Body Space:** at chest level

**Movement:** move the V shape into the palm of your other hand a few times

**Memory Aid:** as if poking your palm with a fork

**Date Introduced:** _____

**Date Produced:** _____

# Friday

**Hand Shape:** "F" shape, right hand, palm may face you or face outward

**Body Space:** at shoulder level

**Movement:** circle your hand in the air

**Memory Aid:** "F" is for Friday!

**Date Introduced:** _____

**Date Produced:** _____

# friend

**Hand Shape:** "X" shape with left hand, palm up; "X" shape with right hand palm down, forefingers linked

**Body Space:** at chest level

**Movement:** rotate wrists so hands change position

**Memory Aid:** indicating how friends are linked together

**Date Introduced:** _____

**Date Produced:** _____

# frog

**Hand Shape:** "V" shape with right hand, palm down

**Body Space:** under chin

**Movement:** bend and straighten fingers repeatedly

**Memory Aid:** imitating the throat of a bullfrog moving in and out; sounds are optional but encouraged!

Date Introduced: _____

Date Produced: _____

# fruit

**Hand Shape:** "F" shape with right hand, palm facing right

**Body Space:** thumb and forefinger touch cheek

**Movement:** twist wrist forward once

**Memory Aid:** as if you are twisting the stem of a fruit

Date Introduced: _____

Date Produced: _____

# full

**Hand Shape:** "B" shape with right hand, palm down; "S" shape with left hand, palm facing right

**Body Space:** at chest level

**Movement:** sweep right hand across top of left hand

**Memory Aid:** indicating a full cup

Date Introduced: _____

Date Produced: _____

# fun

**Hand Shape:** "H" shape both hands

**Body Space:** starts at your nose and moves to just below chest level

**Movement:** the fingertips of your right hand brush against your nose and moves onto the fingertips of your other hand

**Memory Aid:** something "funny" as your nose moves onto your other hand

**Date Introduced:** _____

**Date Produced:** _____

# funny

**Hand Shape:** "U" shape with right hand, palm toward your face

**Body Space:** fingertips at nose

**Movement:** brush nose with tips of fingers twice

**Memory Aid:** as if brushing something funny off your nose; accompany with appropriate facial expression

**Date Introduced:** _____

**Date Produced:** _____

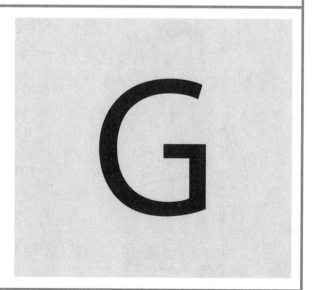

# game

**Hand Shape:** "A" shapes both hands

**Body Space:** at chest level

**Movement:** move hands together quickly so that knuckles touch, make contact twice

**Memory Aid:** as if two dice are hitting against each other

Date Introduced: _____

Date Produced: _____

# garden (version 1)

**Hand Shape:** "O" shape with right hand, palm up; "C" shape with left hand, palm facing you

**Body Space:** at chest level

**Movement:** move "O" shape of right hand upward through "C" shape of left hand, and then circle over left forearm

**Memory Aid:** combining signs for PLANT and AREA; sign may vary by region

Date Introduced: _____

Date Produced: _____

# garden (version 2)

**Hand Shape:** flat "O" shape, right hand; "C" shape left hand

**Body Space:** just below chest level

**Movement:** move your right hand up through your other hand and open it into a "5" shape. Shift your arms to the left slightly and repeat

**Memory Aid:** this shows more than one plant growing beside another. This is the sign for "plant" with just one movement

Date Introduced: _____

Date Produced: _____

# gate

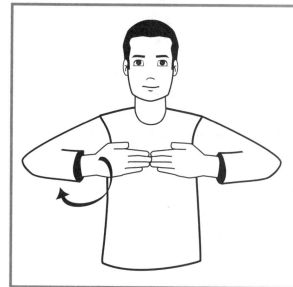

**Hand Shape:** "B" shape with both hands, palms facing you, fingertips touching

**Body Space:** at chest level

**Movement:** swing right hand outward and back from wrist

**Memory Aid:** imitating the opening and closing of a gate

Date Introduced: _____

Date Produced: _____

# gentle

**Hand Shape:** "B" shape with both hands, palms down

**Body Space:** at chest level

**Movement:** move right hand up back of left hand a few times

**Memory Aid:** As in "Be GENTLE with the cat." Similar to sign for PET

Date Introduced: _____

Date Produced: _____

# get (version 1)

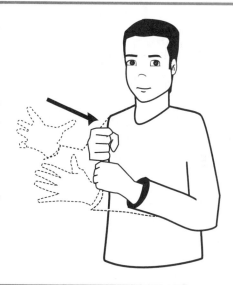

**Hand Shape:** clawed "C" shape with both hands, right hand on top of left hand

**Body Space:** at chest level

**Movement:** move hands toward you at the same time, closing into "S" shapes

**Memory Aid:** as if you are grabbing something and bringing it toward you

Date Introduced: _____

Date Produced: _____

# get (version 2)

**Hand Shape:** "5" shapes both hands, then move into "S" shapes both hands

**Body Space:** at chest level, one wrist on the other, away from the body at first

**Movement:** move hands together, towards the body, closing into "S" shapes

**Memory Aid:** as if getting something and bringing it towards you

**Date Introduced:** _____

**Date Produced:** _____

# giraffe

**Hand Shape:** "C" shape with right hand, palm facing you

**Body Space:** at your neck

**Movement:** move "C" shape upward to above your head

**Memory Aid:** indicating a long neck

**Date Introduced:** _____

**Date Produced:** _____

# girl

**Hand Shape:** "A" shape with right hand, palm toward face

**Body Space:** at your cheek (female area of face)

**Movement:** stroke hand forward and down twice

**Memory Aid:** indicating the area just above where the ribbons of a girl's bonnet would be tied

**Date Introduced:** _____

**Date Produced:** _____

# glasses

**Hand Shape:** crooked "G" shape with both hands, palms facing each other

**Body Space:** at sides of eyes

**Movement:** move hands outward and inward a few times

**Memory Aid:** as if outlining the rims of a pair of glasses

Date Introduced: _____

Date Produced: _____

# gloves

**Hand Shape:** "5" shapes both hands

**Body Space:** at chest level

**Movement:** one hand on top of the other, slides backwards toward your body

**Memory Aid:** as if you are pulling on a pair of gloves

Date Introduced: _____

Date Produced: _____

# glue

**Hand Shape:** "G" shape, right hand

**Body Space:** in front of your mouth

**Movement:** move your hand across your mouth while opening and closing your fingers

**Memory Aid:** as if you are "gluing" your lips together!

Date Introduced: _____

Date Produced: _____

# go

**Hand Shape:** "1" shape with both hands, palms facing forward (only one hand may be used)

**Body Space:** at chest level

**Movement:** move wrists forward and down so that palms are facing downward

**Memory Aid:** as if moving in the direction that you are going

Date Introduced: _____

Date Produced: _____

# goat

**Hand Shape:** bent "V" shape, right hand

**Body Space:** at your chin and then at your forehead

**Movement:** touch your hand to your chin and flick your fingers up to make a V; repeat the same motion at your forehead

**Memory aid:** think of imitating a goat's beard and horns

Date Introduced: _____

Date Produced: _____

# gold

**Hand Shape:** "1" shape, right hands; moves in to a "Y" shape

**Body Space:** starts at your ear and moves down to shoulder level

**Movement:** move your hand from your earlobe outward, stop at shoulder level, shake the "Y" shape slightly

**Memory Aid:** thinking of pointing first to where a gold earring would be that is made of "yellow" gold

Date Introduced: _____

Date Produced: _____

# good

**Hand Shape:** "B" shape with right hand, fingertips at mouth; "B" shape with left hand, palm up

**Body Space:** right hand at mouth, left hand at chest level

**Movement:** move right hand onto left hand

**Memory Aid:** indicating something that tastes good; you want to keep or share it with others

Date Introduced: _____

Date Produced: _____

# goodbye

**Hand Shape:** "B" shape, dominant

**Body Space:** at head level

**Movement:** bend your fingers up and down

**Memory Aid:** as if waving "bye-bye"

Date Introduced: _____

Date Produced: _____

# grandfather

**Hand Shape:** "5" shape with right hand, palm facing left

**Body Space:** thumb touches forehead (male area of face)

**Movement:** move hand forward, making two small bounces

**Memory Aid:** indicating another generation

Date Introduced: _____

Date Produced: _____

# grandmother

**Hand Shape:** "5" shape with right hand, palm facing left

**Body Space:** thumb touches chin (female area of face)

**Movement:** move hand forward, making two small bounces

**Memory Aid:** indicating another generation

**Date Introduced:** _____

**Date Produced:** _____

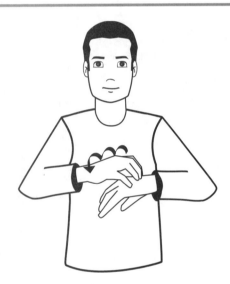

# grapes

**Hand Shape:** "5" claw shape with right hand, "B" shape with left hand, palms downward

**Body Space:** at chest level

**Movement:** bounce right hand down back of left hand

**Memory Aid:** indicating a bunch of grapes

**Date Introduced:** _____

**Date Produced:** _____

# grass

**Hand Shape:** "5" claw shape with right hand, palm up

**Body Space:** at chin

**Movement:** brush heel of right hand forward from chin a few times

**Memory Aid:** indicating an animal eating grass close to the ground

**Date Introduced:** _____

**Date Produced:** _____

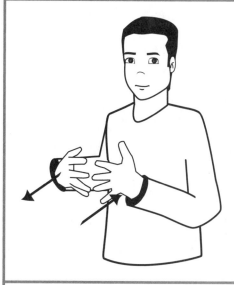

# gray

**Hand Shape:** "5" shape with both hands, palms facing you

**Body Space:** at chest level

**Movement:** move fingers through each other a few times

**Memory Aid:** indicating fingers moving between each other, just as gray is a color between black and white

Date Introduced: _____

Date Produced: _____

# green

**Hand Shape:** "G" shape with right hand

**Body Space:** at shoulder level

**Movement:** twist wrist forward a few times

**Memory Aid:** "G" is for green!

Date Introduced: _____

Date Produced: _____

# ground

**Hand Shape:** "B" shape with both hands, palms down

**Body Space:** at chest level

**Movement:** right hand circles left forearm

**Memory Aid:** indicating an area of ground

Date Introduced: _____

Date Produced: _____

# grow

**Hand Shape:** flat "O" shape, right hand; "C" shape left hand

**Body Space:** just below chest level

**Movement:** move your right hand up through your other hand and open it into a "5" shape

**Memory Aid:** this shows a plant growing

**Date Introduced:** _____

**Date Produced:** _____

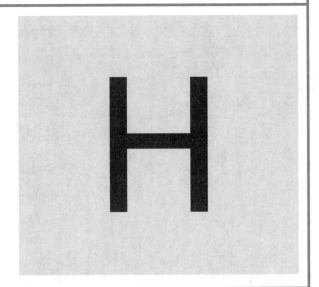

# hair

**Hand Shape:** "F" shape with right hand

**Body Space:** at the side of your head

**Movement:** grasp a small amount of your hair and gently tug a few times

**Memory Aid:** indicating where your hair is on the body

**Date Introduced:** _____

**Date Produced:** _____

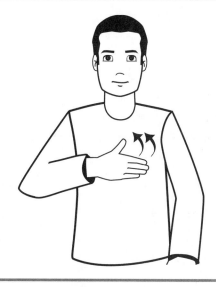

# happy

**Hand Shape:** "B" shape with right hand, palm facing your body

**Body Space:** at chest level

**Movement:** brush hand up and out two times, quickly

**Memory Aid:** as if the happiness is coming out of you; accompany with appropriate facial expression

**Date Introduced:** _____

**Date Produced:** _____

# hat

**Hand Shape:** "B" shape with right hand

**Body Space:** on top of head

**Movement:** pat head twice

**Memory Aid:** indicating where you place your hat

**Date Introduced:** _____

**Date Produced:** _____

# head

**Hand Shape:** bent "B" shape with right hand

**Body Space:** fingertips on head

**Movement:** move downward and tap against top of head

**Memory Aid:** indicating where your head is located

**Date Introduced:** _____

**Date Produced:** _____

# hear

**Hand Shape:** "1" shape with right hand, palm facing left

**Body Space:** at right ear

**Movement:** tap finger against ear

**Memory Aid:** as if pointing to sound going into your ear

**Date Introduced:** _____

**Date Produced:** _____

# helicopter

**Hand Shape:** "5" shape with right hand, palm touching left hand in "1" shape

**Body Space:** at shoulder level

**Movement:** shake right wrist in small rapid movements

**Memory Aid:** right fingers imitating the blades of a helicopter

**Date Introduced:** _____

**Date Produced:** _____

# hello

**Hand Shape:** "B" shape with right hand

**Body Space:** at right temple

**Movement:** move right forearm forward and to the right

**Memory Aid:** as if saluting someone

**Date Introduced:** _____

**Date Produced:** _____

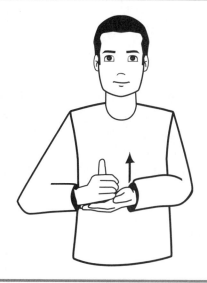

# help

**Hand Shape:** "A" shape with right hand, sitting on upturned palm of left hand

**Body Space:** at chest level

**Movement:** move hands up and forward

**Memory Aid:** as if the left hand is helping the right hand

Date Introduced: _____

Date Produced: _____

# here

**Hand Shape:** "B" shape with both hands, palms up

**Body Space:** at chest level

**Movement:** move both hands in small circles at the same time

**Memory Aid:** indicating you are here

Date Introduced: _____

Date Produced: _____

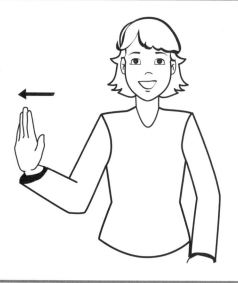

# hers

**Hand Shape:** "B" shape, right hand, palm facing away from body

**Body Space:** at chest level

**Movement:** move hand outward

**Memory Aid:** you are moving your hand toward the female you are referring to

Date Introduced: _____

Date Produced: _____

# hide

**Hand Shape:** "A" shape with right hand; cup "B" shape with left hand, palm down

**Body Space:** right hand at mouth, left hand at chest level

**Movement:** move right hand under cupped left hand

**Memory Aid:** as if hiding something under your left hand; accompanying facial expression should match idea of hiding

Date Introduced: _____

Date Produced: _____

# high

**Hand Shape:** "B" shape with both hands, palms down

**Body Space:** at chest level

**Movement:** raise hands upward at the same time

**Memory Aid:** as if you are showing something rising or getting higher

Date Introduced: _____

Date Produced: _____

# hill

**Hand Shape:** "B" shape with right hand, palm down

**Body Space:** at chest level

**Movement:** move right hand to the right in an up and then down motion

**Memory Aid:** as if outlining the shape of a hill

Date Introduced: _____

Date Produced: _____

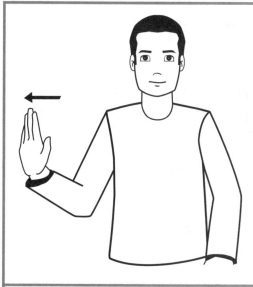

## his

**Hand Shape:** "B" shape, right hand, palm facing away from body

**Body Space:** at chest level

**Movement:** move hand outward

**Memory Aid:** you are moving your hand toward the male you are referring to

Date Introduced: _____

Date Produced: _____

## hippo

**Hand Shape:** "Y" shape with both hands, palms facing each other

**Body Space:** at chest level

**Movement:** move hands together and apart

**Memory Aid:** imitating the opening and closing of a hippo's mouth

Date Introduced: _____

Date Produced: _____

## home

**Hand Shape:** "O" shape with right hand, palm facing you

**Body Space:** at mouth

**Movement:** move right hand from mouth to cheek area, near ear

**Memory Aid:** combining of the signs for EAT and SLEEP

Date Introduced: _____

Date Produced: _____

# hooray! (yeah!)

**Hand Shape:** "5" shape both hands, palms facing each other

**Body Space:** raised over head

**Movement:** from wrists, twist hands back and forth quickly

**Memory Aid:** indicating the Deaf sign for APPLAUSE; accompany with appropriate facial expression

**Date Introduced:** _____

**Date Produced:** _____

# horse

**Hand Shape:** "H" shape with right hand, thumb extended, palm facing forward

**Body Space:** thumb at right temple

**Movement:** flick two fingers of "H" shape up and down

**Memory Aid:** imitating a horse flicking its ears; sounds are optional but encouraged!

**Date Introduced:** _____

**Date Produced:** _____

# hot

**Hand Shape:** clawed "5" shape with right hand, palm facing you

**Body Space:** at mouth

**Movement:** move hand away from mouth and downward quickly

**Memory Aid:** as if removing something hot from your mouth; accompany with appropriate facial expression

**Date Introduced:** _____

**Date Produced:** _____

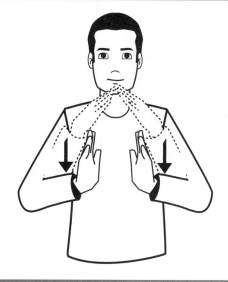

# house

**Hand Shape:** "B" shape with both hands, fingertips touching and hands at an angle

**Body Space:** at chest level

**Movement:** move hands apart and downward

**Memory Aid:** as if outlining the shape of roof and walls

**Date Introduced:** _____

**Date Produced:** _____

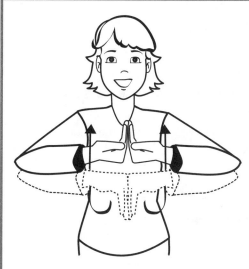

# how

**Hand Shape:** curved hands, palms down, knuckles touching

**Body Space:** at chest level

**Movement:** roll your hands forward until palms are facing up

**Memory Aid:** as if you are revealing how something is done

**Date Introduced:** _____

**Date Produced:** _____

# hug

**Hand Shape:** "5" shape with both hands, relaxed, crossed at wrist, palms facing body

**Body Space:** against chest

**Movement:** press hands firmly against chest and shrug shoulders

**Memory Aid:** as if giving someone a hug

**Date Introduced:** _____

**Date Produced:** _____

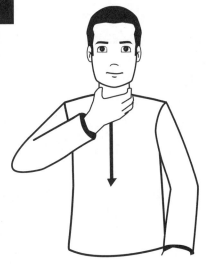

# hungry

**Hand Shape:** "C" shape with right hand, palm facing body

**Body Space:** just below your neck

**Movement:** move hand downward firmly one time

**Memory Aid:** indicating your esophagus; where you would like food to go

**Date Introduced:** _____

**Date Produced:** _____

# hurry

**Hand Shape:** "H" shapes both hands

**Body Space:** at chest level

**Movement:** move both hands up and down quickly

**Memory Aid:** the movement suggests a rushing action

**Date Introduced:** _____

**Date Produced:** _____

# hurt

**Hand Shape:** "1" shape with both hands, both hands facing body

**Body Space:** at chest level or near the hurt area of your body, at your knee, at your head, etc.

**Movement:** tap fingertips together

**Memory Aid:** indicating the site of the hurt; also used as the sign for PAIN

**Date Introduced:** _____

**Date Produced:** _____

## I

**Hand Shape:** "1" shape, right hand

**Body Space:** at chest level

**Movement:** point your finger to yourself

**Memory Aid:** just as you would show a gesture toward yourself. Also, the sign for ME

**Date Introduced:** _____

**Date Produced:** _____

## I love you

**Hand Shape:** "Y" shape with right hand, index finger extended, palm outward

**Body Space:** at shoulder level

**Movement:** move hand slightly in direction of person being signed to

**Memory Aid:** combining the letters "I," "L," and "Y" makes this phrase; also used for friendly greetings and goodbyes

**Date Introduced:** _____

**Date Produced:** _____

# ice cream

**Hand Shape:** "S" shape with right hand, palm facing left

**Body Space:** at mouth

**Movement:** twist wrist downward at least two times

**Memory Aid:** as if you are licking an ice cream cone

**Date Introduced:** _____

**Date Produced:** _____

# in

**Hand Shape:** "C" shape with left hand, palming facing body; flat "O" shape with right hand, palm down

**Body Space:** at chest level

**Movement:** move fingers of right hand into fingers of left hand

**Memory Aid:** as if putting something into a container, such as blocks into an empty cup

**Date Introduced:** _____

**Date Produced:** _____

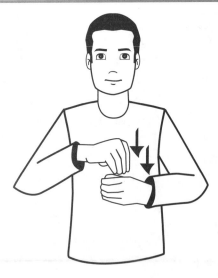

# inside

**Hand Shape:** "C" shape with left hand, palm facing body; flat "O" shape with right hand, palm down

**Body Space:** at chest level

**Movement:** move fingers of right hand into fingers of left hand twice, but use a smaller motion the second time

**Memory Aid:** as is you are stuffing something "inside" a container

**Date Introduced:** _____

**Date Produced:** _____

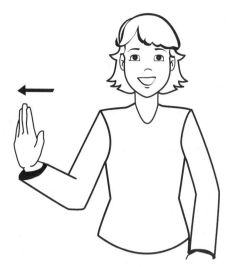

# its

**Hand Shape:** "B" shape, right hand, palm facing away from body

**Body Space:** at chest level

**Movement:** move hand outward

**Memory Aid:** you are moving your hand toward the object you are referring to

**Date Introduced:** _____

**Date Produced:** _____

# juice

**Hand Shape:** "J" shape with right hand

**Body Space:** at cheek

**Movement:** twist the hand back and forth a few times

**Memory Aid:** as if you are drawing a "J" at your cheek

**Date Introduced:** _____

**Date Produced:** _____

# jump

**Hand Shape:** "V" shape with right hand, fingertips down; open "B" shape with left hand, palm up

**Body Space:** at chest level

**Movement:** bend right "V" finger on left palm and bring upward quickly

**Memory Aid:** as if your fingers are jumping on a platform

**Date Introduced:** _____

**Date Produced:** _____

# kangaroo

**Hand Shape:** bent "B" shape with both hands, palms facing down

**Body Space:** at chest level

**Movement:** at the same time, move hands up and down with a lot of energy

**Memory Aid:** imitating the jumping movement of a kangaroo

**Date Introduced:** _____

**Date Produced:** _____

# key

**Hand Shape:** "X" shape with right hand, palm facing you; open "B" shape with left hand, palm to the right

**Body Space:** at chest level

**Movement:** twist "X" shape of right hand into palm up left hand

**Memory Aid:** as if inserting a key into a door

**Date Introduced:** _____

**Date Produced:** _____

# kiss

**Hand Shape:** flat "O" shape with both hands

**Body Space:** right hand at mouth, left hand at chest level

**Movement:** move fingertips of right hand to fingertips of left hand while moving toward the person being kissed

**Memory Aid:** as if taking a kiss from your mouth and putting it onto your hand

**Date Introduced:** _____

**Date Produced:** _____

# knife

**Hand Shape:** "H" shape right hand, palm toward your body. "1" shape, left hand

**Body Space:** at chest level

**Movement:** move fingers of right hand downward, striking the tip of the left hand pointer finger

**Memory Aid:** as if slicing the tip of your other finger

**Date Introduced:** _____

**Date Produced:** _____

# know

**Hand Shape:** bent "B" with right hand, palm facing you

**Body Space:** at right side of forehead

**Movement:** tap temple with fingertips of right hand

**Memory Aid:** as if putting knowledge into your head; same sign for KNOWLEDGE

**Date Introduced:** _____

**Date Produced:** _____

# laugh

**Hand Shape:** "L" shape with both hands, palms facing you

**Body Space:** at sides of mouth

**Movement:** move hands backward several times

**Memory Aid:** imitating the corner of the mouth moving up and down when laughing; accompany with appropriate facial expression

**Date Introduced:** _____

**Date Produced:** _____

# leaf

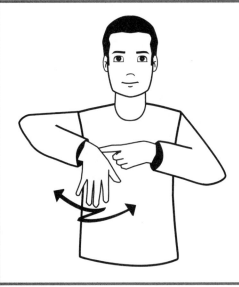

**Hand Shape:** "5" shape with right hand, palm facing you, fingertips downward; "1" shape with left hand

**Body Space:** at chest level

**Movement:** place tip of left hand at wrist of right hand while right hand moves from side to side

**Memory Aid:** indicating a leaf moving in the breeze

**Date Introduced:** _____

**Date Produced:** _____

# lie down

**Hand Shape:** "V" shape with right hand, palm up; open "B" shape with left hand, palm up

**Body Space:** at chest level

**Movement:** rest back of right hand in palm of left hand

**Memory Aid:** imitating a person lying down

**Date Introduced:** _____

**Date Produced:** _____

# life

**Hand Shape:** "L" shape with both hands, palms facing you

**Body Space:** at chest level

**Movement:** move both hands up chest at the same time

**Memory Aid:** as if growing up; "L" is for life

**Date Introduced:** _____

**Date Produced:** _____

# light off

**Hand Shape:** "5" shape with right hand

**Body Space:** at head

**Movement:** close right hand into a flat "O" shape

**Memory Aid:** as if closing or stopping the rays of light coming from a light bulb

**Date Introduced:** _____

**Date Produced:** _____

# light on

**Hand Shape:** flat "O" shape with right hand

**Body Space:** at shoulder level

**Movement:** open right hand into a "5" shape

**Memory Aid:** as if opening the rays of light coming from a light bulb

**Date Introduced:** _____

**Date Produced:** _____

# like

**Hand Shape:** starts with a "5" shape, with your right hand and ends in an "8" shape

**Body Space:** at your chest

**Movement:** hold your "5" shape, palm to chest. Move your hand forward and into an "8" shape

**Memory Aid:** as if you are taking just a little bit of your heart, to "like" something

**Date Introduced:** _____

**Date Produced:** _____

# line up

**Hand Shape:** "4" shapes both hands, right hand facing toward you, left hand facing outward. Pinkie finger of right hand touching thumb of left hand

**Body Space:** at chest level

**Movement:** slide your right hand backward

**Memory Aid:** your fingers represent a line up of people

**Date Introduced:** _____

**Date Produced:** _____

# lion

**Hand Shape:** clawed "5" shape with right hand, palm facing downward

**Body Space:** starts at forehead

**Movement:** draw hand toward back of head

**Memory Aid:** as if outlining a lion's mane; accompanying facial expressions and sounds are optional but encouraged!

**Date Introduced:** _____

**Date Produced:** _____

# look

**Hand Shape:** "V" shape with right hand, palm facing forward

**Body Space:** at shoulder level

**Movement:** move hand forward toward object being looked at

**Memory Aid:** fingertips representing your eyes looking at an object

**Date Introduced:** _____

**Date Produced:** _____

# loud

**Hand Shape:** "1" shape with right hand, "S" shape with left hand

**Body Space:** right hand at ear, left hand at chest

**Movement:** move right hand away from ear into "S" shape and shake both hands repeatedly

**Memory Aid:** combining signs for HEAR and NOISE; accompany with appropriate facial expression

**Date Introduced:** _____

**Date Produced:** _____

# love

**Hand Shape:** "S" shapes with both hands, wrists crossed, palm facing you

**Body Space:** at chest

**Movement:** press hands to chest

**Memory Aid:** as if holding something you love to your heart; accompany with appropriate facial expression; also used as the sign for DEAR

**Date Introduced:** _____

**Date Produced:** _____

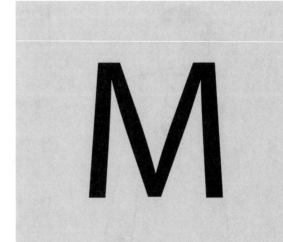

# mad

**Hand Shape:** clawed "5" shape with right hand, palm facing you

**Body Space:** at face

**Movement:** bring hand toward face abruptly

**Memory Aid:** as if showing anger coming from your face; accompany with appropriate facial expression. May be used for GRUMPY

**Date Introduced:** _____

**Date Produced:** _____

# man

**Hand Shape:** "5" shape with right hand, palm facing left

**Body Space:** at forehead (male area of face)

**Movement:** touch thumb of right hand to forehead and move hand down so thumb touches chest

**Memory Aid:** ends in the sign for FIVE ("5" shape at your chest)

**Date Introduced:** _____

**Date Produced:** _____

# me

**Hand Shape:** "1" shape, right hand

**Body Space:** at chest level

**Movement:** point your finger to yourself

**Memory Aid:** just as you would show a gesture toward yourself. Also, the sign for "1"

**Date Introduced:** _____

**Date Produced:** _____

# meat

**Hand Shape:** open "B" with left hand, palm facing you; "F" shape with right hand

**Body Space:** at chest level

**Movement:** use right hand to grasp skin on left hand between thumb and forefinger, shaking hands slightly

**Memory Aid:** indicating meat hanging on a hook in a butcher shop

**Date Introduced:** _____

**Date Produced:** _____

# medicine

**Hand Shape:** tip of right middle finger touches upturned palm of left hand

**Body Space:** at chest level

**Movement:** with right finger, make a small circle in palm of left hand

**Memory Aid:** as if outlining a small pill in the palm of your hand

**Date Introduced:** _____

**Date Produced:** _____

# meet

**Hand Shape:** "1" or "D" shape both hands

**Body Space:** at chest level, hold hands roughly shoulder width apart

**Movement:** move hands together until finger tips of thumbs touch

**Memory Aid:** as if two people are meeting each other

**Date Introduced:** _____

**Date Produced:** _____

# melon

**Hand Shape:** "8" shape with right hand, palm down; "S" shape with left hand, palm down

**Body Space:** at chest level

**Movement:** tap back of left hand with a flicking motion

**Memory Aid:** as if testing a melon for ripeness

**Date Introduced:** _____

**Date Produced:** _____

# milk

**Hand Shape:** "S" shape with right hand, palm facing left

**Body Space:** at chest level

**Movement:** open and close "S" shape several times (can be signed with two hands)

**Memory Aid:** as if milking a cow

**Date Introduced:** _____

**Date Produced:** _____

# mine/my

**Hand Shape:** open "B" shape with right hand, palm toward you

**Body Space:** at chest level

**Movement:** tap chest firmly

**Memory Aid:** indicating possession

**Date Introduced:** _____

**Date Produced:** _____

# mitten (version 1)

**Hand Shape:** open "B" shape with both hands, left palm facing right

**Body Space:** at chest level

**Movement:** move right hand fingertips to outline left hand

**Memory Aid:** as if outlining the shape of a mitten on your hand

**Date Introduced:** _____

**Date Produced:** _____

# mitten (version 2)

**Hand Shape:** "B" shape, left hand, with your thumb extended, palm toward body. "B" shape, right hand

**Body Space:** at chest level

**Movement:** the fingertips of your right hand move along the outside of your left hand

**Memory Aid:** as if tracing the shape of a mitten around your hand

**Date Introduced:** _____

**Date Produced:** _____

# mommy

**Hand Shape:** "5" shape with right hand, palm facing left

**Body Space:** at chin (female area of face)

**Movement:** tap chin twice

**Memory Aid:** indicating the female area of your face

**Date Introduced:** _____

**Date Produced:** _____

# Monday

**Hand Shape:** "M" shape right hand, palm facing up

**Body Space:** at shoulder or chest level

**Movement:** move your hand in a small circle

**Memory Aid:** "M" is for Monday and the circle represents a full day

**Date Introduced:** _____

**Date Produced:** _____

# monkey

**Hand Shape:** clawed "5" shape with both hands, palms facing body

**Body Space:** at waist

**Movement:** move both hands up and down at the same time

**Memory Aid:** imitating a monkey scratching; accompanying sounds and funny faces are optional but encouraged!

**Date Introduced:** _____

**Date Produced:** _____

# moon

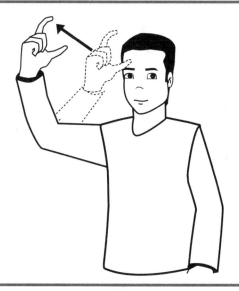

**Hand Shape:** bent "L" shape with right hand

**Body Space:** at right side of forehead

**Movement:** move hand upward

**Memory Aid:** imitating the shape of a crescent moon in the sky

**Date Introduced:** _____

**Date Produced:** _____

## more

**Hand Shape:** flat "O" shape with both hands, fingertips touching

**Body Space:** at chest level

**Movement:** tap fingertips together

**Memory Aid:** as if adding more to a pile; great sign to start with

Date Introduced: _____

Date Produced: _____

## morning

**Hand Shape:** open "B" shape with right hand, palm upward; place left hand in crook of right elbow

**Body Space:** at chest level

**Movement:** raise right hand upward

**Memory Aid:** indicating the sun coming up at the horizon

Date Introduced: _____

Date Produced: _____

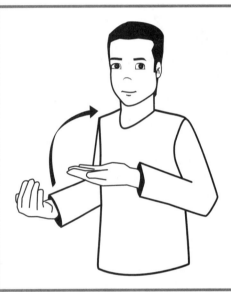

## mountain

**Hand Shape:** "A" shape with both hands, palms down and wrists crossed

**Body Space:** at chest level

**Movement:** tap wrists of hand twice and then move into open "B" shapes and raise hands upward

**Memory Aid:** uses sign for ROCK and then hands move upward, indicating the slope of the side of a mountain

Date Introduced: _____

Date Produced: _____

# mouse

**Hand Shape:** "1" shape with right hand, palm facing left

**Body Space:** at your nose

**Movement:** brush tip of index finger against nose twice

**Memory Aid:** indicating a mouse's nose twitching; accompanying sounds are optional but encouraged!

**Date Introduced:** _____

**Date Produced:** _____

# mower

**Hand Shape:** "S" shape with both hands, palms down and held parallel to ground

**Body Space:** at chest level

**Movement:** move hands forward at the same time

**Memory Aid:** imitating pushing a lawn mower; accompanying sounds are optional. Without sound can also be sign for STROLLER

**Date Introduced:** _____

**Date Produced:** _____

# muffin

**Hand Shape:** small claw shape, right hand, palm downward. "B" shape left hand, palm facing upward

**Body Space:** at chest level

**Movement:** move small claw shape into palm of left hand

**Memory Aid:** as if outline the shape of a cupcake. This is also the sign for CUPCAKE

**Date Introduced:** _____

**Date Produced:** _____

# music

**Hand Shape:** open "B" shape with right hand, palm down, above left forearm; left hand palm up

**Body Space:** at chest level

**Movement:** move right hand at wrist back and forth over left forearm

**Memory Aid:** as if you are strumming some sort of instrument; also used as the sign for SING and SONG

**Date Introduced:** _____

**Date Produced:** _____

# name

**Hand Shape:** "U" shape with both hands, right palm angled leftward from body, left palm angled rightward

**Body Space:** at chest level

**Movement:** tap right fingers on top of left fingers two times

**Memory Aid:** indicating the noun, as in "My NAME is Sabrina"

**Date Introduced:** _____

**Date Produced:** _____

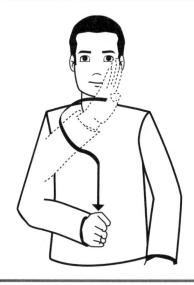

## never

**Hand Shape:** "B" shape with right hand, palm left

**Body Space:** near face

**Movement:** curve hand downward with emphasis

**Memory Aid:** indicating a sharp message; depending on context, accompanying facial expression is important

**Date Introduced:** _____

**Date Produced:** _____

## night

**Hand Shape:** bent "B" shape with right hand, palm downward; left hand, palm down, under right wrist

**Body Space:** at chest level

**Movement:** move right hand downward over left wrist

**Memory Aid:** indicating the sun setting below the horizon

**Date Introduced:** _____

**Date Produced:** _____

## no

**Hand Shape:** "3" shape with right hand, palm out

**Body Space:** at shoulder level

**Movement:** open and close right fingers (may be repeated), shaking head at the same time

**Memory Aid:** comes from fingerspelling "N" and "O" quickly; accompany with appropriate facial expression

**Date Introduced:** _____

**Date Produced:** _____

# none

**Hand Shape:** "O" shapes both hands, palms facing toward each other and forward slightly

**Body Space:** at chest level

**Movement:** move both hands towards each other and then quickly move them forward and down slightly

**Memory Aid:** as if there is nothing there. Can also be used, with one hand or two, to mean "nothing"

**Date Introduced:** _____

**Date Produced:** _____

# now

**Hand Shape:** bent "B" shape with both hands, hands apart and palms upward

**Body Space:** at chest level

**Movement:** lower hands at the same time

**Memory Aid:** depending on context, movement may be sharper; also made with "Y" shapes

**Date Introduced:** _____

**Date Produced:** _____

# ocean

**Hand Shape:** "5" shape with both hands, palms down

**Body Space:** at chest level

**Movement:** move hands up and down at the same time and move them forward slightly

**Memory Aid:** indicating the waves of an ocean

Date Introduced: _____

Date Produced: _____

# off

**Hand Shape:** open "B" with right hand, on back of open "B" with left hand, palm down

**Body Space:** at chest level

**Movement:** move right hand up and off left hand

**Memory Aid:** indicating your hand moving off your other hand

Date Introduced: _____

Date Produced: _____

# old

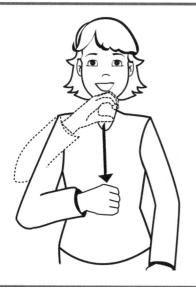

**Hand Shape:** "C" shape with right hand, palm left

**Body Space:** at your chin

**Movement:** move right hand down firmly from chin and close to an "S" shape

**Memory Aid:** as if outlining the shape of an old man's beard

Date Introduced: _____

Date Produced: _____

# Old MacDonald

**Hand Shape:** "M" shape with right hand

**Body Space:** at the side of your forehead

**Movement:** move right hand out away from temple sharply

**Memory Aid:** as if you are saluting with an "M" shape

Date Introduced: _____

Date Produced: _____

# on

**Hand Shape:** open "B" shape with right hand, palm facing left

**Body Space:** at chest level

**Movement:** move right hand onto left hand

**Memory Aid:** indicating one of your hands moving toward and resting on the other

Date Introduced: _____

Date Produced: _____

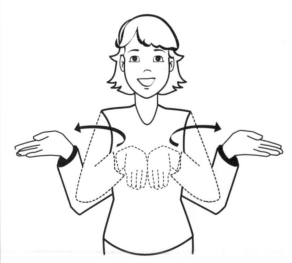

# open

**Hand Shape:** "B" shape with both hands, side by side and palms down

**Body Space:** at chest level (position of hands may move depending on what is being opened)

**Movement:** move hands outward at the same time, ending with palms up

**Memory Aid:** indicating the lid of a box being opened

Date Introduced: _____

Date Produced: _____

# orange

**Hand Shape:** "S" shape with right hand, palm left

**Body Space:** at your chin

**Movement:** open and close hand in small motions

**Memory Aid:** indicating squeezing an orange at your mouth to get the juice; can be used for the color or the fruit

Date Introduced: _____

Date Produced: _____

# O-shaped cereal

**Hand Shape:** "F" shape with right hand; "B" shape with left hand, palm up

**Body Space:** at chest level

**Movement:** bounce right hand on left palm several times

**Memory Aid:** indicating small circular shapes in the palm of your hand

Date Introduced: _____

Date Produced: _____

# out

**Hand Shape:** "C" shape with left hand, palm facing body; flat "O" shape with right hand, palm down

**Body Space:** at chest level

**Movement:** move right hand up and out of left hand

**Memory Aid:** indicating one hand coming out of the other

Date Introduced: _____

Date Produced: _____

# outside

**Hand Shape:** "O" shape with right hand, palm down; "C" shape with left hand, palm toward body

**Body Space:** at chest level

**Movement:** move right hand out of left hand twice

**Memory Aid:** indicating the motion of pulling out

Date Introduced: _____

Date Produced: _____

# over

**Hand Shape:** "4" shape with left hand, palm facing body; bent "V" shape with right hand, palm down

**Body Space:** at chest level

**Movement:** move right hand over the left hand

**Memory Aid:** indicating one hand moving over the other, as in the baby crawled over the pillow

Date Introduced: _____

Date Produced: _____

# paint

**Hand Shape:** open "B" shape with left hand, palm facing right; open "B" shape with right hand, palm down

**Body Space:** at chest level

**Movement:** move right hand at the wrist so right fingertips brush up and down of left palm

**Memory Aid:** as if painting the palm of one hand with the other

Date Introduced: _____

Date Produced: _____

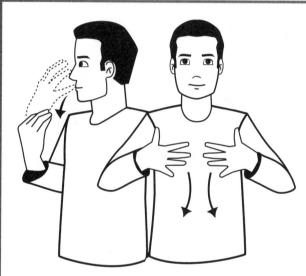

# pajamas

**Hand Shape:** relaxed "5" shape with right hand, palm toward face

**Body Space:** on your face and then at chest level

**Movement:** close right hand to an "O" shape, then move both hands to "5" shapes, and brush down sides of chest

**Memory Aid:** combining the signs for SLEEP and CLOTHES

Date Introduced: _____

Date Produced: _____

# pancake

**Hand Shape:** open "B" shape with both hands, left palm up, right palm up on left palm

**Body Space:** at chest level

**Movement:** flip right hand over so that right palm is facing down

**Memory Aid:** as if flipping a pancake

Date Introduced: _____

Date Produced: _____

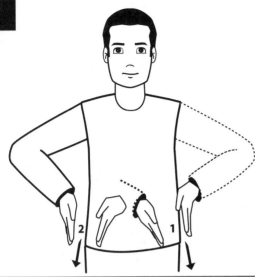

# pants

**Hand Shape:** open "B" shape with both hands, fingers downward

**Body Space:** on either side of left thigh

**Movement:** move hands down outside of left thigh, then down outside of right thigh

**Memory Aid:** indicating where your pants are worn

**Date Introduced:** _____

**Date Produced:** _____

# paper

**Hand Shape:** relaxed "5" shape with right hand, palm down; open "B" shape with left hand, palm up

**Body Space:** at chest level

**Movement:** brush hands against each other twice

**Memory Aid:** as if clapping two pieces of paper together to separate them

**Date Introduced:** _____

**Date Produced:** _____

# parrot

**Hand Shape:** bent "L" shape with right hand, palm facing out

**Body Space:** at your mouth

**Movement:** bend open and close repeatedly the pointer finger and thumb

**Memory Aid:** indicating the curved beak of a parrot; based on the sign for BIRD; accompanying sounds are optional but encouraged!

**Date Introduced:** _____

**Date Produced:** _____

# party

**Hand Shape:** "P" shape with both hands, palms facing each other

**Body Space:** at chest level

**Movement:** swing hands in and out at the wrists

**Memory Aid:** "P" is for party!

**Date Introduced:** _____

**Date Produced:** _____

# pasta

**Hand Shape:** "I" shape with both hands, fingertips touching, palms facing body

**Body Space:** at chest level

**Movement:** move hands apart while rotating up and down

**Memory Aid:** indicating twirly or curvy pasta; can be used for SPAGHETTI or NOODLES as well

**Date Introduced:** _____

**Date Produced:** _____

# peach

**Hand Shape:** relaxed "5" shape with right hand, palm toward face

**Body Space:** at your right cheek

**Movement:** move hand away from cheek and close into a flat "O" shape

**Memory Aid:** as if touching a soft, fuzzy cheek, just like the skin of a soft, fuzzy peach

**Date Introduced:** _____

**Date Produced:** _____

# peanut

**Hand Shape:** "A" shape, right hand, palm facing to your left

**Body Space:** place the tip of your thumb behind your two front teeth

**Movement:** move your hand forward, brushing your thumb against your teeth

**Memory Aid:** as if cracking a nut between your teeth. Pair this sign with the sign for BUTTER to sign PEANUT BUTTER

Date Introduced: _____

Date Produced: _____

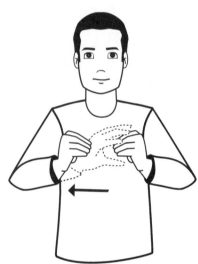

# pear

**Hand Shape:** flat "O" shape with left hand, palm facing right; relaxed "5" shape with right hand

**Body Space:** at chest level

**Movement:** close fingers of right hand over left hand and move to the right into a flat "O" shape

**Memory Aid:** indicating the curved shape of a pear

Date Introduced: _____

Date Produced: _____

# peas

**Hand Shape:** "1" shape with both hands, palms facing body

**Body Space:** at chest level

**Movement:** while left hand points to right and stays still, right index finger bounces across left index finger

**Memory Aid:** as if pointing to little peas in a pod

Date Introduced: _____

Date Produced: _____

# picnic

**Hand Shape:** open "B" shape with both hands, palms facing you

**Body Space:** at your mouth

**Movement:** place right fingers on top of left fingers and move hands toward mouth a few times

**Memory Aid:** as if putting a sandwich or other food into your mouth

**Date Introduced:** _____

**Date Produced:** _____

# pig (version 1)

**Hand Shape:** open "B" shape with right hand, palm down

**Body Space:** under your chin

**Movement:** flap right-hand fingers up and down

**Memory Aid:** similar to sign for DIRTY; accompanying sounds are optional but encouraged! Sign may vary by region

**Date Introduced:** _____

**Date Produced:** _____

# pig (version 2)

**Hand Shape:** "S" shape with right hand, palm facing left

**Body Space:** at your nose

**Movement:** open and close "S" shape a few times

**Memory Aid:** indicating a pig's nose or snout; accompanying sounds are optional but encouraged!

**Date Introduced:** _____

**Date Produced:** _____

# pillow

**Hand Shape:** relaxed "5" shape with both hands, palms facing and apart

**Body Space:** at the side of your head

**Movement:** tilt head and move hands toward each other and then apart

**Memory Aid:** indicating the shape of a pillow under your head

**Date Introduced:** _____

**Date Produced:** _____

# pink

**Hand Shape:** "P" shape with right hand, palm toward body

**Body Space:** just below your mouth

**Movement:** brush middle finger down against lip twice

**Memory Aid:** as if putting on pink lipstick

**Date Introduced:** _____

**Date Produced:** _____

# play

**Hand Shape:** "Y" shape with both hands, held apart, palms facing body

**Body Space:** at chest level

**Movement:** swing hands up and down at the wrists

**Memory Aid:** similar to the sign for PARTY; use to invite a friend to play

**Date Introduced:** _____

**Date Produced:** _____

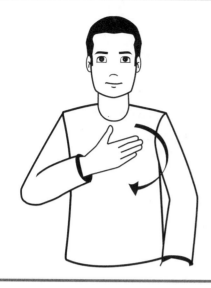

# please

**Hand Shape:** open "B" shape with right hand, palm facing body

**Body Space:** at chest level

**Movement:** move hand in circle over heart

**Memory Aid:** as if asking politely; accompany with appropriate facial expression

Date Introduced: _____

Date Produced: _____

# popcorn

**Hand Shape:** "S" shapes with both hands, palms up

**Body Space:** at chest level

**Movement:** alternate hands bouncing upward into "1" shapes and down again several times

**Memory Aid:** indicating popcorn kernels popping up and down

Date Introduced: _____

Date Produced: _____

# potato

**Hand Shape:** bent "V" shape with right hand, palm down; "5" shape with left hand, palm down

**Body Space:** at chest level

**Movement:** tap back of left hand with fingertips of right bent "V"

**Memory Aid:** as if you are testing a potato with a fork to see if it's cooked

Date Introduced: _____

Date Produced: _____

# potty

**Hand Shape:** "T" shape with right hand, palm facing outward

**Body Space:** at shoulder level

**Movement:** shake hand from side to side

**Memory Aid:** "T" is for toilet; the more you shake the sign, the more urgent it is!

**Date Introduced:** _____

**Date Produced:** _____

# proud

**Hand Shape:** "A" shape with right hand, thumb pointing downward

**Body Space:** at your stomach

**Movement:** move hand upward to upper chest

**Memory Aid:** as if swelling with pride; accompany with appropriate facial expression

**Date Introduced:** _____

**Date Produced:** _____

# purple

**Hand Shape:** "P" shape with right hand

**Body Space:** at chest level

**Movement:** shake hand back and forth at wrist (hand may also be moved in a circle)

**Memory Aid:** "P" is for purple

**Date Introduced:** _____

**Date Produced:** _____

## quiet

**Hand Shape:** "B" shape with both hands, one hand in front of the other

**Body Space:** starts in front of your mouth

**Movement:** move hands down and apart

**Memory Aid:** similar to the gesture for "shhh"; accompany with appropriate facial expression

**Date Introduced:** _____

**Date Produced:** _____

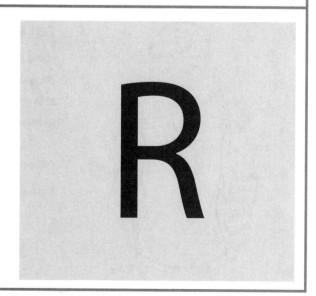

# rain

**Hand Shape:** claw shape with both hands, palms down

**Body Space:** at upper chest level

**Movement:** move hands downward in a bouncing motion twice

**Memory Aid:** indicating that rain is coming down in sheets

**Date Introduced:** _____

**Date Produced:** _____

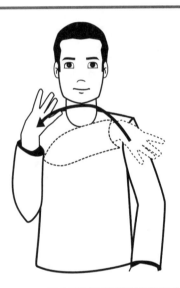

# rainbow

**Hand Shape:** "4" shape with right hand, palm toward body

**Body Space:** at chest level, on left side

**Movement:** move right hand upward and to the right in an arc

**Memory Aid:** as if tracing the varied colors and the arc of a rainbow

**Date Introduced:** _____

**Date Produced:** _____

# rattle

**Hand Shape:** "R" shape with right hand

**Body Space:** at shoulder level

**Movement:** shake hand from side to side

**Memory Aid:** as if you are shaking a rattle in your hand

**Date Introduced:** _____

**Date Produced:** _____

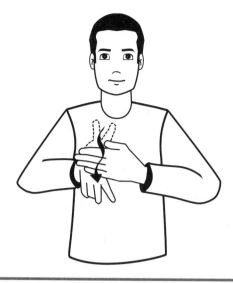

# read

**Hand Shape:** "V" shape with right hand behind left hand

**Body Space:** at chest level

**Movement:** move right wrist up and down

**Memory Aid:** as if your fingertips are your eyes reading what's on a piece of paper

**Date Introduced:** _____

**Date Produced:** _____

# ready

**Hand Shape:** "R" shape with both hands, held apart, palms down

**Body Space:** to the left side of the chest

**Movement:** at the same time, move hands to the right

**Memory Aid:** "R" is for ready to go!

**Date Introduced:** _____

**Date Produced:** _____

# red

**Hand Shape:** "1" shape with right hand, palm facing you

**Body Space:** at your lips

**Movement:** brush index finger down lower lip into an "X" shape

**Memory Aid:** as if putting on red lipstick

**Date Introduced:** _____

**Date Produced:** _____

# rocket

**Hand Shape:** "R" shape with right hand, fingertips upward, on "B" shape with left hand, palm down

**Body Space:** starts at chest level

**Movement:** move right hand upward a few times

**Memory Aid:** indicating a rocket ship blasting upward; accompanying sounds are optional but encouraged!

**Date Introduced:** _____

**Date Produced:** _____

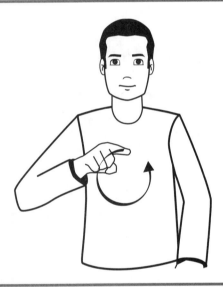

# round

**Hand Shape:** "1" shape with right hand

**Body Space:** at chest level

**Movement:** move hand in a circle from the wrist

**Memory Aid:** as if drawing a round shape with your finger; may vary depending on the circle being described

**Date Introduced:** _____

**Date Produced:** _____

# row

**Hand Shape:** "S" shape with both hands, held apart, palms down

**Body Space:** at chest level

**Movement:** at the same time, move both hands up, forward, and down in a circular motion a few times

**Memory Aid:** as if rowing a boat

**Date Introduced:** _____

**Date Produced:** _____

# run

**Hand Shape:** bent "L" shape with both hands, forefinger of right hand hooked on thumb of left hand

**Body Space:** at chest level

**Movement:** move hands forward quickly while wiggling right thumb and left index finger

**Memory Aid:** as if the fingers of one hand are running after the fingers of the other

Date Introduced: _____

Date Produced: _____

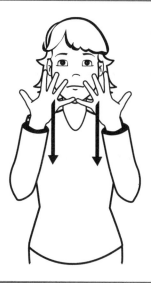

# sad

**Hand Shape:** bent "5" shape with both hands, palms toward face

**Body Space:** start just under your eyes

**Movement:** move hands downward at the same time

**Memory Aid:** as if you are feeling "down"; accompany with appropriate facial expression

Date Introduced: _____

Date Produced: _____

# same

**Hand Shape:** "Y" shape with right hand, palm forward

**Body Space:** at chest level

**Movement:** move hand back and forth in small motion between items being compared

**Memory Aid:** as if saying, "This is the same as that one," with your thumb pointing to something that is the same as what your little finger is pointing to

**Date Introduced:** _____

**Date Produced:** _____

# sand

**Hand Shape:** flat "O" shape with both hands, palms up

**Body Space:** at chest level

**Movement:** rub thumbs and fingertips together

**Memory Aid:** as if you are feeling grains of sand between your fingers

**Date Introduced:** _____

**Date Produced:** _____

# sandwich

**Hand Shape:** open "B" shape with both hands, left palm downward, palms together, fingertips facing mouth

**Body Space:** at your mouth

**Movement:** move hands toward mouth twice

**Memory Aid:** as if holding two slices of bread and moving them to your mouth

**Date Introduced:** _____

**Date Produced:** _____

# Saturday

**Hand Shape:** "S" shape, right hand, palm facing upward

**Body Space:** at chest or shoulder level

**Movement:** move your hand in a small circular motion

**Memory Aid:** "S" is for Saturday and the circle represents a full day

Date Introduced: _____

Date Produced: _____

# say/tell

**Hand Shape:** "1" shape with right hand, palm facing you

**Body Space:** starts from your mouth

**Movement:** move hand outward from mouth

**Memory Aid:** as if you are pointing to the words coming out of your mouth

Date Introduced: _____

Date Produced: _____

# scared

**Hand Shape:** "S" shape with both hands, palms facing body

**Body Space:** hands start at side of body

**Movement:** open hands into "5" shapes and move toward center of body with force

**Memory Aid:** accompany with a fearful facial expression

Date Introduced: _____

Date Produced: _____

# seek

**Hand Shape:** "C" shape with right hand, palm facing left

**Body Space:** in front of face

**Movement:** move hand in circular motion to the left or toward item being sought

**Memory Aid:** as if you are looking for something; accompanying facial expression should appear inquisitive

**Date Introduced:** _____

**Date Produced:** _____

# share

**Hand Shape:** open "B" shape with left hand, palm facing body; open "B" shape with right hand, palm facing left

**Body Space:** at chest level

**Movement:** sweep right hand back and forth between thumb and index finger of left hand

**Memory Aid:** as if your right hand is dividing something equally

**Date Introduced:** _____

**Date Produced:** _____

# sheep

**Hand Shape:** "K" shape with right hand, palm toward body; left arm, palm up in front of body

**Body Space:** at chest level

**Movement:** move right hand in circular motion near elbow

**Memory Aid:** indicating a sheep being sheared; "Baa" sounds are optional but encouraged!

**Date Introduced:** _____

**Date Produced:** _____

# shine

**Hand Shape:** Left hand, palm down. "5" shape, right hand, with middle finger curved forward

**Body Space:** at chest level

**Movement:** the middle (or touch) finger of the right hand touches the ring finger of your left hand and wiggles upward

**Memory Aid:** as if rays of light are shining off your ring finger

**Date Introduced:** _____

**Date Produced:** _____

# shirt

**Hand Shape:** "F" shape with right hand, palm facing body

**Body Space:** at chest level

**Movement:** with right hand, pull up shirt twice

**Memory Aid:** indicating on the body where a shirt is worn

**Date Introduced:** _____

**Date Produced:** _____

# shoe

**Hand Shape:** "S" shape with both hands, palms down and held parallel to ground

**Body Space:** at chest level

**Movement:** tap both hands together twice

**Memory Aid:** as if two shoes are tapping together; think of Dorothy in *The Wizard of Oz* chanting, "There's no place like home."

**Date Introduced:** _____

**Date Produced:** _____

# shovel

**Hand Shape:** "S" shape with both hands, left palm down, right palm up

**Body Space:** at chest level

**Movement:** move both hands downward, sharply, and then up

**Memory Aid:** as if using a shovel to dig sand or shovel snow

**Date Introduced:** _____

**Date Produced:** _____

# show

**Hand Shape:** open "B" shape with left hand, palm facing right; "1" shape with right hand, fingertip on left palm

**Body Space:** at chest level

**Movement:** move both hands forward or toward the person being shown the item

**Memory Aid:** as if pointing to a picture in your hand that you want to show

**Date Introduced:** _____

**Date Produced:** _____

# sick

**Hand Shape:** middle fingers of both hands are bent (sometimes made with the right hand only)

**Body Space:** left hand at stomach, right hand at forehead

**Movement:** tap stomach with left middle finger while tapping forehead with right middle finger

**Memory Aid:** indicating site of sickness; accompany with appropriate facial expression

**Date Introduced:** _____

**Date Produced:** _____

# sign (verb)

**Hand Shape:** "1" shape with both hands

**Body Space:** at chest level

**Movement:** move hands alternately toward your body in a circular motion

**Memory Aid:** as if sending a message with your hands

**Date Introduced:** _____

**Date Produced:** _____

# silly

**Hand Shape:** "Y" shape with right hand

**Body Space:** at your nose

**Movement:** twist right hand a few times at wrist

**Memory Aid:** as if making a silly face; accompany with an appropriate facial expression

**Date Introduced:** _____

**Date Produced:** _____

# sister

**Hand Shape:** "L" shape with both hands

**Body Space:** left hand at chest level, right hand at chin to start

**Movement:** move right hand from chin to top of left hand

**Memory Aid:** uses a modified version of the sign CARE in the female area of the face; your sister is a female you care about

**Date Introduced:** _____

**Date Produced:** _____

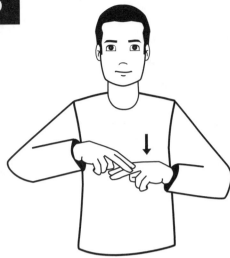

# sit

**Hand Shape:** "U" shape with left hand, palm down; "U" shape with right hand, palm down

**Body Space:** at chest level

**Movement:** with right-hand fingers, tap left-hand fingers once

**Memory Aid:** as in "sit on the bench;" use with CHAIR as verb/noun pair (CHAIR uses a double movement)

Date Introduced: _____

Date Produced: _____

# sky

**Hand Shape:** open "B" shape with right hand

**Body Space:** starts at chest level

**Movement:** sweep right hand upward and over body in an arc

**Memory Aid:** indicating where the sky is

Date Introduced: _____

Date Produced: _____

# sleep

**Hand Shape:** relaxed "5" shape with right hand, palm toward face

**Body Space:** at head level

**Movement:** close fingers of right hand into a flat "O" shape

**Memory Aid:** as if closing your eyes; accompany with appropriate facial expression; close your eyes as your hand closes

Date Introduced: _____

Date Produced: _____

## slide

**Hand Shape:** bent "V" shape with right hand, palm down

**Body Space:** at chest level

**Movement:** move right hand forward and down, outlining the shape of a child's slide

**Memory Aid:** as if the fingers are the legs of someone going down a slide

Date Introduced: _____

Date Produced: _____

## slow

**Hand Shape:** "B" shape with both hands, palms down

**Body Space:** at chest level

**Movement:** move right hand up left forearm

**Memory Aid:** indicating one hand moving slowly up the other

Date Introduced: _____

Date Produced: _____

## small

**Hand Shape:** open "B" shape with both hands, held apart, palms facing each other

**Body Space:** at chest level

**Movement:** move both hands together (hands may also be held horizontally)

**Memory Aid:** indicating the size of the object as your hands move together

Date Introduced: _____

Date Produced: _____

# smile

**Hand Shape:** "L" shape with both hands (also done with "1" shape)

**Body Space:** at sides of mouth

**Movement:** move both hands upward at the same time

**Memory Aid:** as if you are pulling the corners of your mouth up to smile; accompany with appropriate facial expression

**Date Introduced:** _____

**Date Produced:** _____

# snake

**Hand Shape:** bent "V" shape with right hand, palm down

**Body Space:** at your mouth

**Movement:** move right hand out and away from mouth in circular motion

**Memory Aid:** indicating a snake's fangs moving forward; accompanying sounds are optional but encouraged!

**Date Introduced:** _____

**Date Produced:** _____

# sneeze

**Hand Shape:** "1" shape with right hand, palm down

**Body Space:** under your nose

**Movement:** move right index finger under nose and move head back and then forward sharply

**Memory Aid:** accompany with appropriate facial expression; sound is optional. Bless you!

**Date Introduced:** _____

**Date Produced:** _____

# snore

**Hand Shape:** Bent "V" shape with right hand

**Body Space:** near mouth

**Movement:** move hand in "Z" shape, moving up

**Memory Aid:** as if a snoring sound is coming out of your mouth; accompany with a snoring sound

**Date Introduced:** _____

**Date Produced:** _____

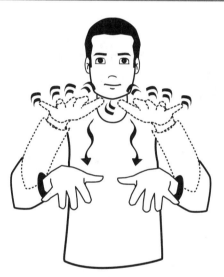

# snow

**Hand Shape:** relaxed "5" shape with both hands, palms facing downward

**Body Space:** at upper chest level

**Movement:** move both hands downward while making finger-fluttering motion

**Memory Aid:** indicating snowflakes floating down

**Date Introduced:** _____

**Date Produced:** _____

# soap

**Hand Shape:** open "B" shape with left hand, palm up; "B" shape with right hand, palm toward left hand

**Body Space:** at chest level

**Movement:** with right-hand fingertips, brush palm of left hand twice

**Memory Aid:** as if you are rubbing a bar of soap

**Date Introduced:** _____

**Date Produced:** _____

# socks

**Hand Shape:** "1" shape with both hands, palms down, fingertips angling downward

**Body Space:** at chest level

**Movement:** with index fingers of both hands, brush against each other in a back and forth motion

**Memory Aid:** indicating two knitting needles knitting a pair of socks

**Date Introduced:** _____

**Date Produced:** _____

# son

**Hand Shape:** "B" shape, right hand, palm slightly facing forward

**Body Space:** at side of forehead

**Movement:** move "B" shape to the crook of the other arm's elbow

**Memory Aid:** the first part of this sign looks as if you are saluting. This sign evolved from the signs for BOY and BABY

**Date Introduced:** _____

**Date Produced:** _____

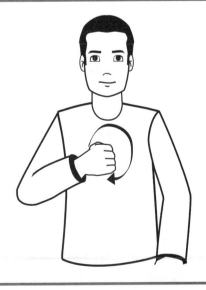

# sorry

**Hand Shape:** "S" shape with right hand, palm facing body

**Body Space:** at chest level

**Movement:** move hand in a circle

**Memory Aid:** accompany with appropriate facial expression

**Date Introduced:** _____

**Date Produced:** _____

# special

**Hand Shape:** 1 shape, left hand, palm toward your body

**Body Space:** at chest level

**Movement:** the index finger of the left hand is pulled up by the opposite hand

**Memory Aid:** as if one finger is special

Date Introduced: _____

Date Produced: _____

# spider

**Hand Shape:** relaxed "5" shape with both hands, palms down, little fingers crossed

**Body Space:** at chest level

**Movement:** wiggle fingers of both hands forward

**Memory Aid:** as if your fingers are a spider's legs

Date Introduced: _____

Date Produced: _____

# spoon

**Hand Shape:** relaxed "B" shape with left hand, palm up; "U" shape with right hand, palm up, resting in left palm

**Body Space:** starts at chest level

**Movement:** move "U" shape of right hand from left hand up toward mouth

**Memory Aid:** as if lifting food to your mouth with a spoon

Date Introduced: _____

Date Produced: _____

# squirrel

**Hand Shape:** bent "V" shape with both hands, palms facing each other

**Body Space:** just below chin

**Movement:** move fingers toward each other in small motions

**Memory Aid:** indicating the motion a squirrel makes with its mouth while holding and chewing a nut

Date Introduced: _____

Date Produced: _____

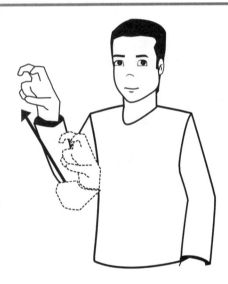

# stairs

**Hand Shape:** bent "V" shape with right hand, palm down

**Body Space:** at chest level

**Movement:** move hand upward at an angle, while "V" fingers move up and down

**Memory Aid:** as if climbing a set of stairs

Date Introduced: _____

Date Produced: _____

# stand

**Hand Shape:** "V" shape with right hand, fingertips down; open "B" shape with left hand, palm up

**Body Space:** at chest level

**Movement:** with right "V" fingers, tap palm of left hand once

**Memory Aid:** fingers imitating legs standing up

Date Introduced: _____

Date Produced: _____

# star

**Hand Shape:** palms forward, fingertips pointing upward

**Body Space:** at shoulder level

**Movement:** brush index fingers of both hands against each other in a back and forth motion

**Memory Aid:** fingers imitating a shooting star in the sky

Date Introduced: _____

Date Produced: _____

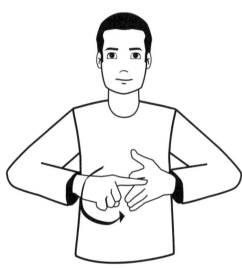

# start

**Hand Shape:** "1" shape right hand, fits between the pointer and middle (or touch) fingers of the left hand

**Body Space:** at chest level

**Movement:** twist your right hand toward your body

**Memory aid:** as if you are turning a key to start a car

Date Introduced: _____

Date Produced: _____

# stop

**Hand Shape:** open "B" shape with right hand, palm facing left; open "B" shape with left hand, palm up

**Body Space:** at chest level

**Movement:** move side of right hand sharply down onto left palm

**Memory Aid:** accompany with appropriate facial expression

Date Introduced: _____

Date Produced: _____

# store

**Hand Shape:** flat "O" shape with both hands, palms down

**Body Space:** at chest level

**Movement:** swing fingertips of both hands forward a few times

**Memory Aid:** as if money is going away from you when you buy something at a store

**Date Introduced:** _____

**Date Produced:** _____

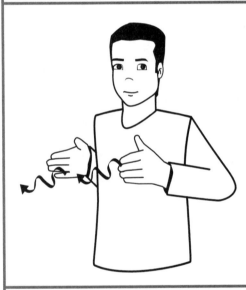

# stream

**Hand Shape:** open "B" shape with both hands, palms facing each other, fingertips forward

**Body Space:** at chest level

**Movement:** move both hands forward in a wavy side-to-side motion

**Memory Aid:** hands imitating water moving down a stream

**Date Introduced:** _____

**Date Produced:** _____

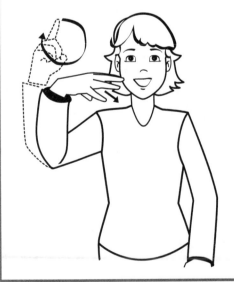

# sun

**Hand Shape:** "1" shape with right hand, palm forward

**Body Space:** above your head to the right

**Movement:** with index finger, outline a circle and then move into an "O" shape that opens into a relaxed "5" shape

**Memory Aid:** hand and fingers indicating the round sun and rays of sunshine coming from it

**Date Introduced:** _____

**Date Produced:** _____

# Sunday (version 1)

**Hand Shape:** "5" shapes both hands, palms facing forward

**Body Space:** over your head

**Movement:** move your hands in small circular motions

**Memory Aid:** as if you are washing windows

**Date Introduced:** _____

**Date Produced:** _____

# Sunday (version 2)

**Hand Shape:** "5" shapes both hands, palms facing forward

**Body Space:** hold your hands in front and at the sides of your face

**Movement:** move your hands down at the same time to the front of your chest

**Memory Aid:** as if you are lifting up your hands at church

**Date Introduced:** _____

**Date Produced:** _____

# sweet

**Hand Shape:** "U" shape

**Body Space:** at your chin

**Movement:** brush your fingertips down your chin once or twice

**Memory Aid:** this is also the sign for CUTE. Pair this sign with the sign for POTATO to sign SWEET POTATO

**Date Introduced:** _____

**Date Produced:** _____

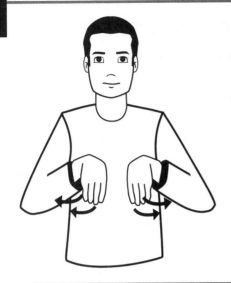

# swim

**Hand Shape:** open "B" shape with both hands, palms facing down, fingertips forward

**Body Space:** at chest level

**Movement:** move both hands from the wrists, forward and to the side a few times

**Memory Aid:** indicating a simple swimming motion

Date Introduced: _____

Date Produced: _____

# swing

**Hand Shape:** "U" shape with left hand, palm down; bent "V" shape with right hand, palm down on "U" fingers

**Body Space:** at chest level

**Movement:** rest right hand "V" fingers on left hand "U" fingers and swing both hands back and forth

**Memory Aid:** as if sitting on a swing and moving forward and back

Date Introduced: _____

Date Produced: _____

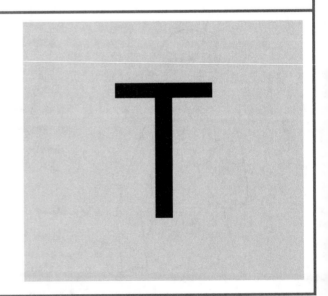

# table

**Hand Shape:** open "B" shape with both hands, right forearm on top of left forearm

**Body Space:** at chest level

**Movement:** with right forearm, tap top of left forearm a few times

**Memory Aid:** as if resting both forearms on a table

**Date Introduced:** _____

**Date Produced:** _____

# talk

**Hand Shape:** "4" shape

**Body Space:** at the chin

**Movement:** tap your chin twice

**Memory Aid:** as if words are coming out of your mouth

**Date Introduced:** _____

**Date Produced:** _____

# telephone

**Hand Shape:** "Y" shape with right hand

**Body Space:** at your ear

**Movement:** move right hand up to right ear

**Memory Aid:** as if holding a telephone to your ear

**Date Introduced:** _____

**Date Produced:** _____

# thank you

**Hand Shape:** open "B" shape with right hand, palm toward you

**Body Space:** starts with fingertips at mouth

**Movement:** move hand away and down from mouth

**Memory Aid:** indicating hand moving toward the person you are thanking

Date Introduced: _____

Date Produced: _____

# then

**Hand Shape:** "L" shape with left hand, palm facing right; "1" shape with right hand

**Body Space:** at chest level

**Movement:** move forefinger of right hand from left thumb to left forefinger

**Memory Aid:** a natural follow-up to the sign for FIRST

Date Introduced: _____

Date Produced: _____

# think

**Hand Shape:** "1" shape with right hand

**Body Space:** to the right of your forehead

**Movement:** touch forefinger of right hand to right temple

**Memory Aid:** as if something is going on in your mind

Date Introduced: _____

Date Produced: _____

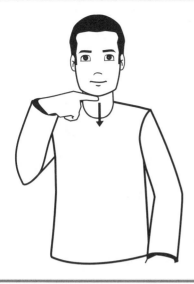

# thirsty

**Hand Shape:** "1" shape with right hand

**Body Space:** starts at the top of your throat

**Movement:** slowly move hand down throat

**Memory Aid:** as if liquid is running down your throat; accompanying facial expression shows that you are thirsty

**Date Introduced:** _____

**Date Produced:** _____

# Thursday

**Hand Shape:** "H" shape, right hand, fingertips pointing upward slightly

**Body Space:** at shoulder level

**Movement:** moves in a small circular motion

**Memory Aid:** "H" is for the H in Thursday (because T is used for Tuesday) and the circle represents a full day

**Date Introduced:** _____

**Date Produced:** _____

# tiger

**Hand Shape:** claw shape with both hands, palms toward face

**Body Space:** hands in front of face

**Movement:** draw hands apart at the same time and repeat a few times

**Memory Aid:** accompany with a ferocious facial expression; sounds are optional but encouraged!

**Date Introduced:** _____

**Date Produced:** _____

# time

**Hand Shape:** "1" shape, right hand

**Body Space:** just below chest level

**Movement:** pointer finger of your right hands taps the other wrist twice

**Memory Aid:** as if tapping your watch

**Date Introduced:** _____

**Date Produced:** _____

# tired

**Hand Shape:** bent open "B" shape with both hands, fingertips touching chest

**Body Space:** on either side of chest

**Movement:** rotate wrists downward while fingertips still touch chest and your head droops

**Memory Aid:** accompany with appropriate facial expression and body language; the more emphasis on body language, the more tired you are

**Date Introduced:** _____

**Date Produced:** _____

# toilet

**Hand Shape:** "T" shape with right hand, palm facing outward

**Body Space:** at shoulder or chest level

**Movement:** shake hand from side to side

**Memory Aid:** "T" is for toilet; the more you shake the sign, the more urgent it is

**Date Introduced:** _____

**Date Produced:** _____

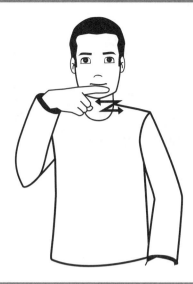

# toothbrush

**Hand Shape:** "1" shape with right hand

**Body Space:** at your mouth

**Movement:** move hand back and forth in a rapid motion in front of your teeth

**Memory Aid:** as if brushing your teeth

**Date Introduced:** _____

**Date Produced:** _____

# touch

**Hand Shape:** middle finger of right hand is bent downward, palm down; left hand palm down

**Body Space:** at chest level, at the back of your hand

**Movement:** with fingertip of right hand, tap back of left hand

**Memory Aid:** use in combination with the sign for NO for curious babies and toddlers

**Date Introduced:** _____

**Date Produced:** _____

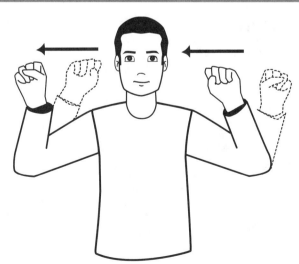

# towel

**Hand Shape:** "S" shape with both hands, palms facing forward

**Body Space:** at shoulder level

**Movement:** move hands from side to side a few times

**Memory Aid:** as if drying your back with a towel

**Date Introduced:** _____

**Date Produced:** _____

# town

**Hand Shape:** open "B" shape with both hands, palms facing

**Body Space:** at chest level

**Movement:** tap fingertips of both hands twice

**Memory Aid:** indicating the many rooftops in a town

**Date Introduced:** _____

**Date Produced:** _____

# toy

**Hand Shape:** "T" shape with both hands

**Body Space:** at chest level

**Movement:** swing hands in and out at the wrists

**Memory Aid:** similar to the sign for PLAY

**Date Introduced:** _____

**Date Produced:** _____

# train

**Hand Shape:** "U" shape with both hands, palms down, extended fingers of right hand on top of extended fingers of left

**Body Space:** at chest level

**Movement:** move fingers of right hand back and forth across fingers of left hand several times

**Memory Aid:** indicating a train running on tracks; "Choo choo" sounds are optional but encouraged!

**Date Introduced:** _____

**Date Produced:** _____

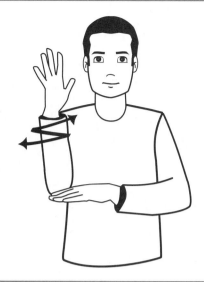

# tree

**Hand Shape:** "5" shape with right hand, fingertips upward; left hand palm down with elbow of right arm on left hand

**Body Space:** at chest level

**Movement:** twist right hand at wrist several times

**Memory Aid:** indicating the ground with tree branches moving in the breeze

**Date Introduced:** _____

**Date Produced:** _____

# trip

**Hand Shape:** bent "V" shape with right hand, palm down

**Body Space:** just below chest level

**Movement:** move forward and upward in a winding movement

**Memory Aid:** indicating a person riding and moving around as if on a journey

**Date Introduced:** _____

**Date Produced:** _____

# truck

**Hand Shape:** "S" shape with both hands, palms facing you (held farther apart than sign for CAR)

**Body Space:** at chest level

**Movement:** move hands up and down alternately

**Memory Aid:** as if driving a vehicle with a big steering wheel

**Date Introduced:** _____

**Date Produced:** _____

# Tuesday

**Hand Shape:** "T" shape, right hand

**Body Space:** at shoulder or chest level

**Movement:** move hand in a circular motion

**Memory Aid:** "T" is for Tuesday and the circular motion represents a full day

Date Introduced: _____

Date Produced: _____

# turkey

**Hand Shape:** "G" shape, right hand

**Body Space:** at or just under your chin

**Movement:** move your hand downward in a wiggling motion

**Memory Aid:** as if you are moving your hand like the skin under a turkey's beak

When you are eating turkey or looking at pictures of turkeys. "Gobbling" is optional!

Date Introduced: _____

Date Produced: _____

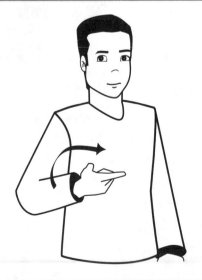

# turn

**Hand Shape:** "L" shape with right hand, palm up

**Body Space:** at chest level

**Movement:** turn hand over so palm is facing down

**Memory Aid:** as if you are turning something over; versions of this are used for MY TURN and YOUR TURN

Date Introduced: _____

Date Produced: _____

# turn (my)

**Hand Shape:** "L" shape with right hand, palm toward you

**Body Space:** at chest level

**Movement:** move hand forward toward you

**Memory Aid:** to show your possession of the turn in a game or with a toy, move sign toward you

Date Introduced: _____

Date Produced: _____

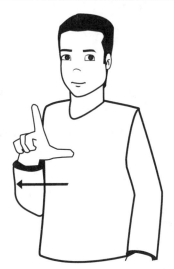

# turn (your)

**Hand Shape:** "L" shape with right hand, palm outward

**Body Space:** at chest level

**Movement:** move hand forward

**Memory Aid:** for YOUR TURN, move toward your baby's chest

Date Introduced: _____

Date Produced: _____

# turtle

**Hand Shape:** "A" shape with right hand, palm left, held under "C" shape with left hand

**Body Space:** at chest level

**Movement:** wiggle thumb of right hand

**Memory Aid:** indicating the turtle under its shell wiggling its head

Date Introduced: _____

Date Produced: _____

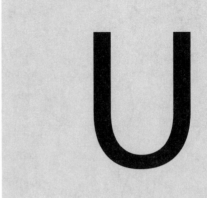

## uncle

**Hand Shape:** "U" shape with right hand, palm facing forward

**Body Space:** at the side of your forehead (male area of face)

**Movement:** move right hand up and down in short movements twice

**Memory Aid:** "U" is for uncle!

**Date Introduced:** _____

**Date Produced:** _____

## under

**Hand Shape:** "A" shape with right hand, palm facing left; "B" shape with left hand, palm down

**Body Space:** at chest level, left hand in front of right hand

**Movement:** move right hand forward and under left hand

**Memory Aid:** as if moving one hand under the other

**Date Introduced:** _____

**Date Produced:** _____

# up

**Hand Shape:** "1" shape with right hand, palm facing forward

**Body Space:** starts at chest level

**Movement:** move hand upward once

**Memory Aid:** indicating your hand moving up

**Date Introduced:** _____

**Date Produced:** _____

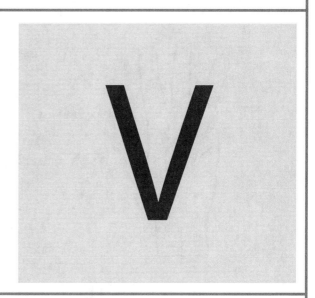

# vegetable

**Hand Shape:** "V" shape with right hand, palm facing forward

**Body Space:** index finger touches right cheek

**Movement:** twist right hand forward from wrist, with index finger staying in contact with cheek

**Memory Aid:** Similar to sign for FRUIT, but "V" is for vegetable!

**Date Introduced:** _____

**Date Produced:** _____

# violin

**Hand Shape:** "F" shape, right hand; "8" shape, left hand

**Body Space:** at shoulder level

**Movement:** move your right hand back and forth toward your non-dominant arm

**Memory Aid:** as if moving the bow of a violin you are holding. Use it when talking about and listening to violin music

**Date Introduced:** _____

**Date Produced:** _____

# wait

**Hand Shape:** relaxed "5" shape with both hands, hands apart and palms facing up

**Body Space:** at chest level

**Movement:** wiggle fingers of both hands a few times

**Memory Aid:** as if drumming your fingers while waiting for someone, but palms are turned upward or else you'd be signing PIANO

**Date Introduced:** _____

**Date Produced:** _____

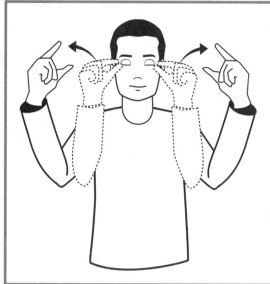

# wake up

**Hand Shape:** closed "G" shape with both hands, palms facing each other

**Body Space:** at outer corners of eyes

**Movement:** open both hands to "L" shapes and move outward a short distance

**Memory Aid:** also the sign for SURPRISE when fingers open quickly

**Date Introduced:** _____

**Date Produced:** _____

# walk

**Hand Shape:** open "B" shape with both hands, palms down

**Body Space:** at chest level

**Movement:** alternate moving hands forward a few times

**Memory Aid:** indicating your feet walking

**Date Introduced:** _____

**Date Produced:** _____

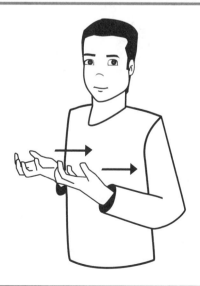

# want

**Hand Shape:** bent "5" shape with both hands, held apart, with palms facing up

**Body Space:** at chest level

**Movement:** pull hands toward you at the same time, while hand shapes change to a claw shape

**Memory Aid:** as if bringing something that you want toward you

**Date Introduced:** _____

**Date Produced:** _____

# warm

**Hand Shape:** "S" shape with right hand, palm facing you

**Body Space:** starts from your mouth

**Movement:** move hand up and forward gently, opening into relaxed "5" shape

**Memory Aid:** indicating warm breath coming out of your mouth on a cold day

Date Introduced: _____

Date Produced: _____

# wash (hair)

**Hand Shape:** claw shape with both hands, palms facing hair

**Body Space:** at sides of head

**Movement:** alternately move hands forward and back a few times

**Memory Aid:** indicating the motion of washing or shampooing your hair; also the sign for SHAMPOO

Date Introduced: _____

Date Produced: _____

# wash (general)

**Hand Shape:** "S" shape with both hands, palms touching

**Body Space:** at chest level

**Movement:** rub hands together

**Memory Aid:** as if washing your hands

Date Introduced: _____

Date Produced: _____

# water

**Hand Shape:** "W" shape with right hand, palm facing left

**Body Space:** at your mouth

**Movement:** tap twice at chin

**Memory Aid:** "W" is for water, something you can drink

**Date Introduced:** _____

**Date Produced:** _____

# Wednesday

**Hand Shape:** "W" shape, right hand

**Body Space:** at shoulder or chest level

**Movement:** move hand in a circular motion

**Memory Aid:** "W" is for Wednesday and the circular motion represents a full day

**Date Introduced:** _____

**Date Produced:** _____

# wet

**Hand Shape:** relaxed "5" shape with both hands, apart and palms upward

**Body Space:** at chest level

**Movement:** move both hands gently downward into flat "O" shapes

**Memory Aid:** as if something is dripping wet

**Date Introduced:** _____

**Date Produced:** _____

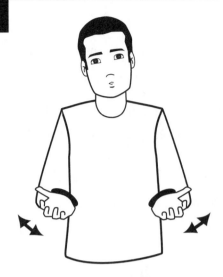

# what

**Hand Shape:** relaxed "S" shape with both hands, palms up

**Body Space:** at lower chest level

**Movement:** move hands side to side slightly

**Memory Aid:** accompany with a questioning face; use when offering choices, such as "MILK or JUICE. WHAT do you want?" Signs may vary by region

Date Introduced: _____

Date Produced: _____

# where

**Hand Shape:** "1" shape with right hand, palm facing out

**Body Space:** at shoulder level

**Movement:** shake right hand from side to side a few times

**Memory Aid:** accompany with a questioning face; great for playing silly hiding games with a baby

Date Introduced: _____

Date Produced: _____

# white

**Hand Shape:** relaxed "5" shape with right hand, palm toward chest

**Body Space:** at your chest

**Movement:** move hand outward and close into a flat "O" shape

**Memory Aid:** indicating a white T-shirt

Date Introduced: _____

Date Produced: _____

## who

**Hand Shape:** "L" shape with right hand, palm facing left; lips are rounded

**Body Space:** thumbtip touching below lower lip

**Movement:** move index finger up and down quickly

**Memory Aid:** indicating the movement of your mouth when you say "who"; accompany with a questioning face

**Date Introduced:** _____

**Date Produced:** _____

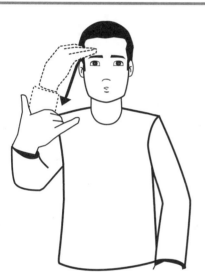

## why

**Hand Shape:** open "B" shape with right hand, fingertips touching forehead

**Body Space:** at right side of forehead

**Movement:** move hand out and downward, changing into "Y" shape, palm up

**Memory Aid:** as if your mind is trying to figure out why; accompany with a questioning face

**Date Introduced:** _____

**Date Produced:** _____

## wind

**Hand Shape:** "5" shape with both hands, palms facing each other

**Body Space:** at shoulder level

**Movement:** swing your hands back and forth at the same time; a gentle movement is a soft breeze, while a stronger movement is a strong wind

**Memory Aid:** indicating the wind blowing

**Date Introduced:** _____

**Date Produced:** _____

# window

**Hand Shape:** "B" shapes both hands, palms facing your body. The right hand on top of the other

**Body Space:** at chest level

**Movement:** your right hand slides up and down

**Memory Aid:** as if the sash of a window is being lifted up

Date Introduced: _____

Date Produced: _____

# with

**Hand Shape:** "A" shape with both hands, palms facing each other

**Body Space:** at chest level

**Movement:** move hands together until touching

**Memory Aid:** showing that one hand is with the other; move this sign in a circle to sign TOGETHER

Date Introduced: _____

Date Produced: _____

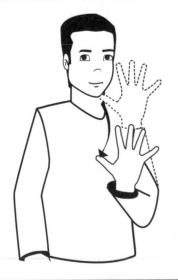

# woman

**Hand Shape:** "5" shape with right hand, palm facing left

**Body Space:** at chin (female area of face)

**Movement:** touch thumb of right hand to chin and move hand down so thumb touches chest

**Memory Aid:** ends in the sign for FIVE ("5" shape at your chest

Date Introduced: _____

Date Produced: _____

# wonder

**Hand Shape:** "1" shape with right hand, palm toward face

**Body Space:** at right side of your forehead

**Movement:** with right hand, make small circles

**Memory Aid:** as if something has come from your mind; accompany with a questioning look

**Date Introduced:** _____

**Date Produced:** _____

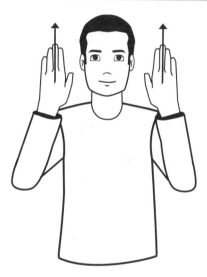

# wonderful

**Hand Shape:** open "B" shape with both hands, palms facing forward

**Body Space:** hands apart and above your shoulders

**Movement:** with force, move both forearms upward a small distance twice

**Memory Aid:** accompany with appropriate facial expression

**Date Introduced:** _____

**Date Produced:** _____

# work

**Hand Shape:** "S" shape with both hands, palms down, right wrist on left wrist

**Body Space:** at chest level

**Movement:** with right wrist, strike left wrist twice

**Memory Aid:** indicating something that is hard; may also be used as the sign for JOB

**Date Introduced:** _____

**Date Produced:** _____

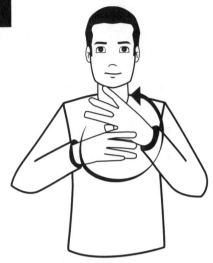

# world

**Hand Shape:** "W" shapes both hands, right hand on top of your left hand

**Body Space:** at chest level

**Movement:** move hands in circular motions around each other, at first your right hand moves downward and your left hand moves upward

**Memory Aid:** "W" for world and the circular motion outlines the shape of the world

Date Introduced: _____

Date Produced: _____

# worm

**Hand Shape:** open "B" shape with left hand, palm facing right; "1" shape with right hand, palm down, fingertip to left

**Body Space:** at chest level

**Movement:** "squirm" extended right finger across left palm

**Memory Aid:** indicating a worm moving across your palm

Date Introduced: _____

Date Produced: _____

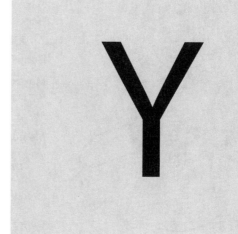

## yellow

**Hand Shape:** "Y" shape with right hand, palm facing forward

**Body Space:** at chest level

**Movement:** twist at the wrist several times

**Memory Aid:** "Y" is for yellow!

**Date Introduced:** _____

**Date Produced:** _____

## yes

**Hand Shape:** "S" shape with right hand, palm facing forward

**Body Space:** at shoulder level

**Movement:** move right hand up and down from wrist several times

**Memory Aid:** as if you are nodding yes

**Date Introduced:** _____

**Date Produced:** _____

# yogurt

**Hand Shape:** "Y" shape with right hand, palm down; "C" shape with left hand, palm facing right

**Body Space:** starts at chest level

**Movement:** move tip of little finger on right hand into "C" shape of left hand and then move right hand up to mouth

**Memory Aid:** as if bringing yogurt from a small cup to your mouth; based on the signs for CUP and SOON

**Date Introduced:** _____

**Date Produced:** _____

# you

**Hand Shape:** "1" shape, right hand, palm facing down

**Body Space:** at chest level

**Movement:** move your hand toward the person you are referring to

**Memory Aid:** just like you are pointing to someone

**Date Introduced:** _____

**Date Produced:** _____

# your

**Hand Shape:** "B" shape, right hand, palm facing forward

**Body Space:** at chest level

**Movement:** move your hand toward the person you are referring to

**Memory Aid:** the open palm represents ownership

**Date Introduced:** _____

**Date Produced:** _____

## ZOO

**Hand Shape:** index finger writes a "Z"

**Body Space:** at shoulder level

**Movement:** move right hand into "O" shape that slides slightly to right

**Memory Aid:** combining of the letters for "Z" and "O"; also fingerspelled Z-O-O

**Date Introduced:** _____

**Date Produced:** _____

# PART 3

# Songs for Signing

# How to Sign and Sing

I N THE SONGS THAT FOLLOW, WORDS AND LETTERS in SMALL CAPS highlight the key words you will sign while singing. If you don't have a great singing voice, don't worry. If you make mistakes while signing the songs, that's all right too. Your baby or toddler will not mind. If you cannot remember the tunes to some of the songs, visit www.kididdles.com for sound bites of most of the traditional songs we sing with our children. Most importantly, have fun while signing, singing, and interacting with your child.

## Songs to Sign and Sing

### The ABC Song
A B C D E F G H I J K L M N O P Q R S T U and
    V W X Y and Z.
NOW I KNOW my ABCs.
Next time, will you SIGN with ME!

ant

### The Ants Go Marching
The ANTs go marching ONE by ONE, hurrah, hurrah
    [sign WONDERFUL]
The ANTs go marching ONE by ONE, hurrah, hurrah
    [sign WONDERFUL]
The ANTs go marching ONE by ONE,
And the little [sign SMALL] ONE stops to suck his THUMB,
And they all go MARCHing down to the ground
To get out of the RAIN, boom! boom! boom! [sign LOUD]

TWO by TWO . . . to tie his SHOE.
THREE by THREE . . . to climb a TREE.
FOUR by FOUR . . . to shut the DOOR.
FIVE by FIVE . . . to take a dive [sign SWIM].

### Are You Hungry?
*(Sung to the tune of "Frère Jacques")*

Are you HUNGRY? Are you HUNGRY?
BABY mine. BABY mine.
Now it's time for MILK. Now it's time for MILK.
Time to EAT. Time to EAT.

hungry

## Are You Sleeping?

Are you SLEEPing,
Are you SLEEPing?
BABY John [substitute your baby's name]?
BABY John [substitute your baby's name]?
MORNING BELLS are ringing,
MORNING BELLS are ringing.
Ding ding dong,
Ding ding dong.

## Are You Sleepy?

*(Sung to the tune of "Frère Jacques")*

Are you SLEEPy? Are you SLEEPy?
BABY mine. BABY mine.
Now it's time for SLEEP. Now it's time for SLEEP.
Time to SLEEP. Time to SLEEP.

**sleep**

## Baby's Fingers

BABY's fingers UP
And BABY's fingers DOWN.
BABY's fingers DANCE-ing
All around the TOWN.
DANCE-ing on your shoulders,
DANCE-ing on your head,
DANCE-ing on your knees,
then tuck them into BED.

*[repeat with MOMMY's or DADDY's fingers]*

**dance**

## The Bear Went over the Mountain

The BEAR went over the MOUNTAIN,
The BEAR went over the MOUNTAIN,
The BEAR went over the MOUNTAIN,
To see [sign LOOK] what he could see [sign LOOK].

To see [sign LOOK] what he could see [sign LOOK],
To see [sign LOOK] what he could see [sign LOOK].
The BEAR went over the MOUNTAIN,
To see [sign LOOK] what he could see [sign LOOK].

The other side of the MOUNTAIN,
The other side of the MOUNTAIN,
The other side of the MOUNTAIN,
Was all that he could see [sign LOOK].

Was all that he could see [sign LOOK],
Was all that he could see [sign LOOK],
The other side of the MOUNTAIN,
Was all that he could see [sign LOOK]!

**bear**

**diaper**

### Change Your Diaper Song
*(Sung to the tune of "She'll Be Coming 'Round the Mountain")*

It is time to CHANGE your DIAPER 'cause it's WET.
Oh, it's time to CHANGE your DIAPER 'cause it's WET.
Yes, it's time to CHANGE your DIAPER,
It is time to CHANGE your DIAPER,
Oh, it's time to CHANGE your DIAPER 'cause it's WET.

It is time to CHANGE your DIAPER 'cause it's FULL.
Oh, it's time to CHANGE your DIAPER 'cause it's FULL.
Yes, it's time to CHANGE your DIAPER,
It is time to CHANGE your DIAPER,
Oh, it's time to CHANGE your DIAPER 'cause it's FULL.

**duck**

### Five Little Ducks
FIVE little DUCKs went out [sign GO] one day,
Over the HILL and far away.
MOTHER DUCK said, "Quack, quack, quack."
But only FOUR little DUCKs came back [sign COME].

*Repeat the verse, substituting FOUR, THREE, TWO, and ONE.*
*Then, sign and sing:*

SAD MOTHER DUCK went out [sign GO] one day,
Over the HILL and far away.
SAD MOTHER DUCK said, "Quack, quack, quack."
And all of the FIVE little DUCKs came back [sign COME].

**frog**

### Five Little Frogs
FIVE little FROGs sat on a shore.
ONE went for a SWIM, and then there were FOUR.

FOUR little FROGs LOOKed out to sea [sign OCEAN].
Another went SWIMming, and then there were THREE.

THREE little FROGs said, "WHAT can we do?"
ONE JUMPed in the WATER, and then there were TWO.

TWO little FROGs sat in the SUN.
Another SWAM off, and then there was ONE.

ONE little FROG said, "This is NO FUN!"
He dove in the WATER, and then there were none
　　　[sign FINISH].

## Five Little Monkeys

FIVE little MONKEYs JUMPing on the BED,
One fell off [sign FALL] and bumped his HEAD.
So MOMMY called the DOCTOR and the DOCTOR said,
NO more MONKEYs JUMPing on the BED!

*Repeat the verse, substituting FOUR, THREE, and TWO.*
*Then sign and sing:*

ONE little MONKEY JUMPing on the BED,
He fell off [sign FALL] and bumped his HEAD.
So MOMMY called the DOCTOR and the DOCTOR said,
Put those MONKEYs right to BED!

**monkey**

## Happy Birthday

HAPPY BIRTHDAY to you [point to your child].
HAPPY BIRTHDAY to you [point to your child].
HAPPY BIRTHDAY, DEAR [use the sign for
      LOVE and fill in your child's name]
HAPPY BIRTHDAY to you [point to your child].

## Head and Shoulders

*This is a classic song/chant, and children love it. Point to*
*each of the body parts. You can sign during this song by*
*stopping in the middle and asking your toddler, "WANT*
*MORE?" At the end of the song, sign and say, "FINISHED!*
*NO? You WANT MORE? MORE MUSIC!" You can even use*
*ASL numbers to count up to the song, signing and*
*saying, "MORE MUSIC? READY, 1, 2, 3 . . ." Then start*
*the song again.*

**happy**

Head, shoulders, knees and toes,
Knees and toes.
Head, shoulders, knees and toes,
Knees and toes.

And eyes and ears and mouth and nose,
Head, shoulders, knees and toes.

**more**

**smile**

### If You're Happy and You Know It

If you're HAPPY and you KNOW it, show a SMILE.
If you're HAPPY and you KNOW it, show a SMILE.
If you're HAPPY and you KNOW it,
Then your FACE will surely SHOW it.
If you're HAPPY and you KNOW it, show a SMILE.

If you're SAD and you KNOW it, CRY a tear.
If you're SAD and you KNOW it, CRY a tear.
If you're SAD and you KNOW it,
Then your FACE will surely SHOW it.
If you're SAD and you KNOW it, CRY a tear.

### The I Love You Song

I LOVE you, you LOVE me,
We're a HAPPY FAMILY.
With a great big HUG
And a KISS from me to you,
Won't you say you LOVE me too?

**I love you**

### It's Raining, It's Pouring

It's RAINing, it's pouring,
The old MAN is SNORE-ing.
He went to BED
And he bumped [sign HURT] his HEAD
And he couldn't get UP in the MORNING.

### Itsy Bitsy Spider

The itsy bitsy [sign SMALL] SPIDER
Crawled up the water spout [mime the sign SPIDER
    crawling up].
Down came the RAIN
And washed the SPIDER out [mime the sign SPIDER
    being washed down].
Out came the SUN
And dried up all the RAIN.
And the itsy bitsy [sign SMALL] SPIDER
Crawled up the spout again [mime the sign SPIDER
    crawling up].

**spider**

## Miss Polly Had a Dolly

Miss Polly had a DOLLy
Who was SICK, SICK, SICK,
So she called for the DOCTOR
To be quick, quick, quick [sign FAST, FAST, FAST].
The DOCTOR came
With his bag and his HAT,
And he knocked at the DOOR
With a rat-a-tat-tat [mime knocking].

He looked at the DOLLy and he shook his head,
And he said, "Miss Polly, put her straight to BED."
He wrote out a PAPER
For a pill, pill, pill [sign MEDICINE].
"That'll make her better, YES it will, will, will!"

**doll**

## My Baby Lies over the Ocean

*(Sung to the tune of "My Bonnie Lies over the Ocean")*

My BABY lies over the OCEAN.
My BABY lies over the sea [sign OCEAN].
My BABY lies over the OCEAN
O BRING back my BABY to me.

BRING back, BRING back,
O BRING back my BABY to me.
BRING back, BRING back,
O BRING back my BABY to me.

**ocean**

## Old MacDonald

OLD MACDONALD had a FARM,
E-I-E-I-O! [fingerspell these]
And on his FARM he had some CHICKENs,
E-I-E-I-O! [fingerspell these]
With a cluck-cluck here,
And a cluck-cluck there,
Here a cluck, there a cluck,
Everywhere a cluck-cluck,
OLD MACDONALD had a FARM
E-I-E-I-O! [fingerspell these]

*Repeat the verse, substituting the following animals and sounds:*

COW: moo-moo
HORSE: neigh-neigh
PIG: oink-oink
DOG: woof-woof

**Old MacDonald**

## On Top of Spaghetti
*(Sung to the tune of "On Top of Old Smokey")*

On top of spaghetti [sign PASTA]
All covered with CHEESE,
I lost my poor meatball
When somebody SNEEZEd.

It rolled off the TABLE
And onto the FLOOR,
And then my poor meatball
Rolled out of the DOOR.

It rolled in the GARDEN
And under a bush [sign TREE],
And then my poor meatball
Was nothing but mush [sign WET/SOFT].

## Pat-a-Cake
Pat-a-cake, pat-a-cake, baker's man
    [clap your hands together]
Bake me a CAKE as fast as you can.
Roll it and knead it [mime rolling and kneading]
And mark it with a "B" [show the sign for the letter "B"]
And put it in the oven for BABY and ME.

## Rain, Rain, Go Away
RAIN, RAIN, go away [sign FINISH].
Come again some other DAY.
We want to go OUTSIDE and PLAY.
So RAIN, RAIN, go away [sign FINISH].

**cheese**

**cake**

**rain**

## The Rainbow Song
*(Sung to the tune of "Hush Little Baby")*

RAINBOW PURPLE
RAINBOW BLUE
RAINBOW GREEN
And YELLOW too
RAINBOW ORANGE
and RAINBOW RED
RAINBOW shining overhead.

COME and count
The COLORS with me
How many COLORS
Do you SEE?
1-2-3 on down to GREEN
4-5-6 COLORS can be seen.

RAINBOW PURPLE
RAINBOW BLUE
RAINBOW GREEN
And YELLOW too
RAINBOW ORANGE
and RAINBOW RED
RAINBOW shining overhead.

**rainbow**

## Ring Around the Rosie
Ring around the rosie [sign FLOWER],
A pocketful of posies [sign FLOWER],
Husha, husha [sign SNEEZE],
We all FALL DOWN.

*Join hands and recite the chant again while skipping in one direction (it's okay — you can't sign while holding hands). When you fall down, sign and say "MORE?" If your child indicates in some way that she wants more, play the game again.*

**color**

**flower**

**baby**

**row**

**cry**

### Rock-a-Bye Baby
Rock-a-bye BABY, in the TREEtop,
When the WIND blows, the cradle [sign BABY] will rock.
When the bough breaks, the cradle [sign BABY] will FALL,
And down will come BABY, cradle and all.

From the HIGH rooftops, DOWN to the sea [sign OCEAN],
No one's as LOVED, as BABY to me.
Wee little fingers, EYEs wide and bright,
Now sound ASLEEP, until MORNING light.

### Round and Round the Garden
Round and round the GARDEN
Like a teddy BEAR;
ONE step, TWO step,
TICKLE under there! [tickle your baby]

### Row, Row Your Boat
ROW, ROW, ROW your BOAT
Gently down the STREAM.
Merrily, merrily, merrily, merrily [sign HAPPY],
Life is but a DREAM.

### Ten in the Bed
There were TEN in a BED
And the little ONE said [sign SAY],
"ROLL over, ROLL over."
So they all ROLLed over
And one fell out [sign FALL].

*Continue to sign and sing for each number down to 1.*

There was ONE in the BED
And the little ONE said [sign SAY]
"GOOD NIGHT"!

### This Little Piggy Went to Market
This little PIGgy went to market [sign STORE].
This little PIGgy stayed HOME.
This little PIGgy had roast beef [sign MEAT].
This little PIGgy had NONE [sign NO].
And this little PIGgy cried [sign CRY], "Wee! Wee! Wee!"
    all the way HOME.

## Twinkle, Twinkle, Little Star

Twinkle, twinkle, little [sign SMALL] STAR,
How I WONDER what you are!
UP above the world so HIGH,
Like a DIAMOND in the SKY.
Twinkle, twinkle, little STAR,
How I WONDER what you are!

**star**

## Two Little Blackbirds

TWO little blackBIRDS sat on a HILL,
ONE named Jack and ONE named Jill.
FLY away, Jack; FLY away, Jill.
COME back, Jack; COME back, Jill.
TWO little blackBIRDS sat on a HILL,
ONE named Jack and ONE named Jill.

## Wash, Wash
*(Sung to the tune of "Row, Row Your Boat")*

WASH, WASH, WASH your _____ [fill in the blank].
WASH your little _____.
Pour the WATER on your _____.
And WASH your little _____.

**bath**

## The Wheels on the Bus
*(I've included just a few lyrics here, but you can add as many as you like. To sign WHEEL or ROUND, draw a circle in the air.)*

The WHEELs on the BUS go ROUND and ROUND,
ROUND and ROUND, ROUND and ROUND.
The WHEELs on the BUS go ROUND and ROUND,
All through the TOWN.

The DOOR on the BUS goes OPEN and CLOSE,
OPEN and CLOSE, OPEN and CLOSE.
The DOOR on the BUS goes OPEN and CLOSE,
All through the TOWN.

The BABY on the BUS goes wah, wah, wah [sign CRY],
Wah, wah, wah [sign CRY], wah, wah, wah [sign CRY].
The BABY on the BUS goes wah, wah, wah [sign CRY],
All through the TOWN.

The MOMMY on the BUS goes sh, sh, sh [sign QUIET],
Sh, sh, sh [sign QUIET], sh, sh, sh [sign QUIET].
The MOMMY on the BUS goes sh, sh, sh [sign QUIET],
All through the TOWN.

**bus**

**sun**

**fast**

### You Are My Sunshine

You are my SUNshine, my only SUNshine,
You make me HAPPY when SKIES are GRAY.
You'll never [shake your head to indicate negation]
    KNOW, DEAR,
How much I LOVE YOU.
Please don't [shake your head to indicate negation]
    take my SUNshine away.

### Zoom, Zoom, Zoom

Zoom, zoom, zoom [sign FAST],
We're going to the MOON.
Zoom, zoom, zoom [sign FAST],
We're going to the MOON.
If you want to take a TRIP,
Climb aboard my ROCKET ship.
Zoom, zoom, zoom [sign FAST],
We're going to the MOON.
5, 4, 3, 2, 1, blast off! [sign ROCKET]

# Resources

## Sign Language Dictionaries

*The Gallaudet Dictionary of American Sign Language* (with DVD).
Gallaudet University Press, 2005.

*My First Book of Sign Language.*
Scholastic, 2004.

*Random House Webster's American Sign Language Dictionary.*
Random House Reference, 1994.

*Signs for Me: Basic Sign Vocabulary for Children, Parents & Teachers.*
Dawnsign Press, 2003.

*Teach Your Tot to Sign: The Parents' Guide to American Sign Language.*
Gallaudet University Press, 2005.

## Resources for All Ages

*WeeHands At Home* (DVD)
www.weehands.com
The *WeeHands At Home* DVD, Volume I, features more than
33 American Sign Language (ASL) signs to use at home with your
child (age 0 to 6 years), language development tips and strategies,
as well as 10 children's songs signed from start to finish in American
Sign Language!

*WeeHands At Home* (Music CD)
www.weehands.com
The WeeHands At Home music CD introduces fun and functional
vocabulary related to activities that you do every day at home with
your baby!

*Dancing with Words: Signing for Hearing Children's Literacy*
by Dr. Marilyn Daniels. Bergin & Garvey, 2000.

## Resources for Toddlers

### Sign Language Board Books

Includes the associated American Sign Language sign and may include
more than one concept per page.

*A Book of Colors: A Baby's First Sign Book*
by Kim Votry. Gallaudet University Press, 2003.

*I Want . . . : Teaching Your Baby to Sign* (Baby Fingers series)
by Lora Heller. Sterling, 2006.

*Let's Sign: Every Baby's Guide to Communicating with Grownups*
by Kelly Ault and Leo Landry. Houghton Mifflin, 2005.

*Out for a Walk: A Baby's First Sign Book*
by Kim Votry. Kendall Green Publications, 2003.

*Teaching Your Baby to Sign* (Baby Fingers series)
by Lora Heller. Sterling, 2004.

*Twinkle, Twinkle, Little Star* (Sign & Singalong series)
by Annie Kubler. Board edition. Child's Play, 2005.

### Other Books for Toddlers

Many of these are classics, and all contain text that is appropriate for toddlers age 1 to 3 years. These are not sign language books, but they are great when signed!

*Counting Kisses: A Kiss & Read Book*
by Karen Katz. Little Simon, 2003.

*Goodnight Moon*
by Margaret Wise Brown. HarperCollins, 2005.

*The Very Hungry Caterpillar*
by Eric Carle. Puffin Books, 1994.

*The Going to Bed Book*
by Sandra Boynton. Little Simon, 2004.

*Open the Barn Door, Find a Cow* (A Chunky Book)
by Christopher Santoro. Random House Books for Young Readers, 1993.

# Resources for Preschoolers

### Sign Language Books for Preschoolers

*The Handmade Alphabet*
by Laura Rankin. Puffin Books, 1996.

*Help Me Learn: Counting 1–10 in American Sign Language*
by Joan Silvey and Allen Silvey. Silvey Book Publishers, 2005.

*Moses Goes to a Concert*
by Isaac Millman. Farrar, Straus and Giroux, 2002.

*Moses Goes to School*
by Isaac Millman. Farrar, Straus and Giroux, 2000.

*Moses Sees a Play*
by Isaac Millman. Farrar, Straus and Giroux, 2004.

### DVDs and CDs for Preschoolers

*Sign-a-Lot, The Big Surprise! A "Hands On" Adventure!* (DVD)
See Me Sign, LLC, 2005.
Go on an adventure with a group of children learning to sign.

*Sign-a-Lot, ABC Games* (DVD)
See Me Sign, LLC, 2006.
Continues the signing adventures of a group of children learning to sign. Includes the alphabet and a number of fun games to reinforce learning.

# Online Sign Language Resources

ALPHAbuddies
Color and black-and-white coloring pages you can print off.
www.dltk-teach.com/alphabuddies/asl/index.htm

American Sign Language Slider
A simple site with photographs of ASL hand shapes.
http://asl.gs

Fingerspelling Quiz
www.asl.ms

Fingerspelling Resources
From the PBS Kids show *Arthur Teaches Sign*. Several fun activities to help practice fingerspelling.
http://pbskids.org/arthur/print/signdesign

Lifeprint
Information about fingerspelling, quizzes, and games.
www.lifeprint.com/asl101/fingerspelling

WeeHands
Links to WeeHands classes, signing resources, and support.
www.weehands.com

# Online Sign Language Support Groups

WeeHands on Twitter
https://twitter.com/WeeHands
Need to ask a quick baby sign language question? Follow and ask Sara Bingham on Twitter!

WeeHands on Facebook
http://www.facebook.com/weehandsbabysignlanguage
Want to ask questions and share your family's signing stories, 'like' WeeHands on Facebook.

Signing with Baby Meetup Groups
Meet other local parents and caregivers, online and off, who are teaching their babies sign language.
http://babysigning.meetup.com

# Online ASL Resources

ASL Browser
www.commtechlab.msu.edu/sites/aslweb/browser.htm

ASL Dictionary
www.lifeprint.com/asl101/pages-layout/signs.htm

Handspeak
www.handspeak.com

Lifeprint ASL University
A series of free, self-paced ASL classes. Fee-based if you need a certificate upon completion.
www.lifeprint.com

Signing Online
Web-based courses, for a fee, designed to teach ASL at your own pace.
www.signingonline.com

Sign Genius
Sells ASL software for US$55, but you can use the demo download version to learn and practice the alphabet and hand shapes.
www.signgenius.com

WeeHands on YouTube
www.youtube.com/MyWeeHands

# Speech and Language Development Resources

American Speech-Language-Hearing Association (ASHA)
www.asha.org

Canadian Association of Speech-Language Pathologists and Audiologists (CASLPA)
www.caslpa.ca

# Resources for Special Needs Children

American Society for Deaf Children (ASDC)
A non-profit organization that advocates rights and education for deaf children.
www.deafchildren.org

Autism Society of America (ASA)
Raises and allocates funds to address the many unanswered questions about autism.
www.autism-society.org

Autism Society Canada (ASC)
A national non-profit organization committed to advocacy, public education, information and referral, and support for its regional societies.
www.autismsocietycanada.ca

Canadian Hearing Society (CHS)
Provides services that enhance the independence of deaf, deafened, and hard-of-hearing people and encourage prevention of hearing loss.
www.chs.ca

Canadian Down Syndrome Society (CDSS)
A support group for the families of children with Down syndrome.
www.cdss.ca

Childhood Apraxia of Speech Association of North America
(CASANA)
A non-profit organization whose mission is to strengthen the support
systems for children with apraxia so that each child is afforded the
best opportunity to develop speech.
www.apraxia-kids.org

Expressive Communication Help Organization (ECHO)
A volunteer-run non-profit organization established by parents for
parents and caregivers of late-talking children diagnosed with or
suspected of having apraxia of speech, dyspraxia, dysarthria, or oral
motor speech disorders.
www.apraxia.ca

Hands & Voices
A parent-driven non-profit organization dedicated to providing
unbiased support to families with children who are deaf or hard of
hearing.
www.handsandvoices.org

International Society for Augmentative and Alternative
Communication (ISAAC)
Supports and encourages the best possible communication methods
for people who find communication difficult.
www.isaac-online.org

National Down Syndrome Society (NDSS)
A non-profit organization supporting research in the United States.
Includes details of education and advocacy programs.
www.ndss.org

Ontario Association for Families of Children with Communication
Disorders (OAFCCD)
A parent support group that has useful information for families
anywhere.
www.oafccd.com

# References

"communication." Dictionary.com Unabridged (v 1.1). Based on the *Random House Unabridged Dictionary*, Random House, Inc., 2006. Retrieved January 14, 2007, from http://dictionary.reference.com/browse/communication.

"language." Dictionary.com Unabridged (v 1.1). Based on the *Random House Unabridged Dictionary*, Random House, Inc., 2006. Retrieved January 14, 2007, from http://dictionary.reference.com/browse/language.

"speech." Dictionary.com Unabridged (v 1.1). *The American Heritage Dictionary of the English Language*, 4th ed., Houghton Mifflin Company, 2006. Retrieved January 14, 2007, from http://dictionary.reference.com/browse/speech.


Barinaga M. New insights into how babies learn language. *Science*, 1997; 227(5326):641.

Brereton A. Alana: How one hearing child used sign language to move from 'disruptive' student to a classroom expert. *Early Childhood Education Journal*. Feb 2009;461-65. doi:10.1007/s10643-008-0297-5.

Bonvillian JD, Orlansky MD, Novack LL. Developmental milestones: Sign language acquisition and motor development. *Child Development*, December 1983; 54(6):1435–45.

Boyatzis CJ. An introduction to the special issue. *Journal of Nonverbal Behavior, Gesture, and Development*, Summer 2000; 24(2):59–62.

Capone NC, McGregor KK. Gesture development: A review for clinical and research practices. *Journal of Speech, Language & Hearing Research*, February 2004; 47(1):173–86.

Church RB, Kelly SD, Lynch K. Immediate memory for mismatched speech and representational gesture across development. *Journal of Nonverbal Behavior*, Summer 2000; 24(2):151–74.

Church RB, Ayman-Nolley S, Mahootian S. The role of gesture in bilingual education: Does gesture enhance learning? *International Journal of Bilingual Education & Bilingualism*, 2004; 7(40):303–19.

Daniels M. *Dancing with Words: Signing for Hearing Children's Literacy*. Westport, CT: Bergin & Garvey, 2000.

Daniels M. Seeing language: The effect over time of sign language on vocabulary development in early childhood. *Child Study Journal*, 1996; 26(3):193.

Davis T. *Hearing Children and Signing*. 2007. Available by email: signwithyourbaby@yahoogroups.com from signingstore@shaw.ca.

Dougherty D. *How to Talk to Your Baby*. New York: Perigee Trade, 1999.

Downing JE. *Teaching Communication Skills to Students with Severe Disabilities*. 2nd ed. Baltimore: Brookes Publishing Company, 2005.

Drake M. *Take Home: Preschool Language Development*. East Moline, IL: LinguiSystems, 1998.

Durand VM. *Severe Behavior Problems: A Functional Communication Training Approach*. New York: The Guilford Press, 2002.

Eliot, L. *What's Going On in There? How the Brain and Mind Develop in the First Five Years of Life*. New York: Bantam, 2000.

Garcia J, White B. *Sign with Your Baby Complete Learning Kit: How to Communicate with Infants Before They Can Speak* (with DVD). Mukilteo, WA: Northlight Communications, 2004.

Goodwyn SW, Acredolo LP, Brown CA. Impact of symbolic gesturing on early language development. *Journal of Nonverbal Behavior*, Summer 2000; 24(2):81–103.

Greene A, Hanley K. *The Parent Soup A-to-Z Guide to Your Toddler*. Chicago: McGraw-Hill/Contemporary Books, 1999.

Jitendra A, DaCosta J. Teaching sign language to children with behavior disorders: A direct instruction approach. *Preventing School Failure*, Spring 1997; 41(3):137.

Hopmann MR. The use of signs by children with Down syndrome. *Down Syndrome Today*, Spring 1993; 2(2):22–23.

Ingersoll B, Lewis E, Kroman E. Teaching the imitation and spontaneous use of descriptive gestures in young children with autism using a naturalistic behavioral intervention. *Journal Of Autism & Developmental Disorders*, 2007;37(8):1446-56. doi:10.1007/s10803-006-0221-z

Iverson JM, Tencer HL, Lany J, Goldin-Meadow S. The relation between gesture and speech in congenitally blind and sighted language-learners. *Journal of Nonverbal Behavior*, Summer 2000; 24(2):105–30.

Krentz U C, Corina D P. Preference for language in early infancy: the human language bias is not speech specific. *Developmental Science*, 2008;11(1):1-9. doi:10.1111/j.1467-7687.2007.00652.x

Larson B C, Chang I. Enhancing hearing children's memory with American sign language. *Intervention in School and Clinic*, 2007;42(4):239-42.

Lee FR. A child's adventure in a deaf world. *The New York Times*. Monday, January 22, 2007.

Leech E, Cress C J. Indirect facilitation of speech in a late talking child by prompted production of picture symbols or signs. *AAC: Augmentative & Alternative Communication,* 2011;27(1):40-52. doi:10.3109/07434618.2010.55006

Liszkowski U, Carpenter M, Henning A, Striano T, Tomasello M. Twelve-month-olds point to share attention and interest. *Developmental Science,* June 2004; 7(3):297–307.

Manolson A. *It Takes Two to Talk: A Parent's Guide to Helping Children Communicate.* Toronto: The Hanen Centre, 1992.

*Meet the Fokkers.* Universal Studios, 2004.

McNeil NM, Alibali MW, Evans JL. The role of gesture in children's comprehension of spoken language: Now they need it, now they don't. *Journal of Nonverbal Behavior,* Summer 2000; 24(2):131–50.

Michnick Golinkoff R, Hirsh-Pasek K. *How Babies Talk: The Magic and Mystery of Language in the First Three Years of Life.* New York: Penguin Books, 1999.

Namy LL, Acredolo L, Goodwyn S. Verbal labels and gestural routines in parental communication with young children. *Journal of Nonverbal Behavior,* Summer 2000; 24(2):63–79.

Nelson LH, White K R, Grewe J. Evidence for website claims about the benefits of teaching sign language to infants and toddlers with normal hearing. *Infant & Child Development,* 2012;21(5):474-502. doi:10.1002/icd.1748

O'Neill M, Bard KA, Linnell M, Fluck M. Maternal gestures with 20-month-old infants in two contexts. *Developmental Communications,* July 2005; 8(4):352–59.

Pizer G, Walters K, Meier R P. Bringing up baby with baby signs: Language ideologies and socialization in hearing families. *Sign Language Studies,* 2007;7(4):387-430.

Radford A. *Transformational Grammar: A First Course.* New York: Cambridge University Press, 1997.

Robb MB, Richert RA, Wartella EA. Just a talking book? Word learning from watching baby videos. *British Journal of Developmental Psychology,* 2009;27(1):27-45. doi:10.1348/026151008X320156

Rowland C. *Observing and Enhancing Communication Skills for Individuals with Multisensory Impairments.* Tucson: Communication Skill Builders, 1992.

Spencer TD, Petersen DB, Gillam SL. Picture exchange communication system (PECS) or sign language. *Teaching Exceptional Children,* 2008;41(2):40-47.

Thompson RH, McKerchar PM, Dancho KA. The effects of delayed physical prompts and reinforcement on baby sign language acquisition. *Journal of Applied Behavior Analysis,* Fall 2004; 37(3):379–83.

Thompson SA, Nelson-Metlay V. *Teach Your Tot to Sign: The Parents' Guide to American Sign Language*. Washington, DC: Gallaudet University Press, 2005.

Topping K, Dekhinet R, Zeedyk S. Hindrances for parents in enhancing child language. *Educational Psychology Review,* 2011;23(3):413-55. doi:10.1007/s10648-011-9169-4

Toth A. Bridge of signs: Can sign language empower non-deaf children to triumph over their communication disabilities? *American Annals Of The Deaf,* 2009;154(2):85-95.

Vallotton CD, Ayoub CC. Symbols build communication and thought: The role of gestures and words in the development of engagement skills and social-emotional concepts during toddlerhood. *Social Development,* 2010;19(3):601-26. doi:10.1111/j.1467-9507.2009.00549.x

Vallotton CD. Signs of emotion: What can preverbal children "say" about internal states?. Infant Mental Health Journal, 2008;29(3):234-558. doi:10.1002/imhj.20175

Vallotton C. Babies open our minds to their minds: How 'listening' to infant signs complements and extends our knowledge of infants and their development. Infant Mental Health Journal, 2011;32(1):115-133. doi:10.1002/imhj.20286

Wetherby AM, Prizant BM. *Autism Spectrum Disorders: A Transactional Developmental Perspective* (Communication and Language Intervention Series). Baltimore: Brookes Publishing, 2000.

Wong VN, Kwan Q. Randomized controlled trial for early intervention for autism: A pilot study of the Autism 1-2-3 Project. *Journal of Autism & Developmental Disorders,* 2010(6):677-88. doi:10.1007/s10803-009-0916-z

**Library and Archives Canada Cataloguing in Publication**

Bingham, Sara
    The baby signing book : includes 450 ASL signs for babies & toddlers / Sara Bingham ; illustrated by Jamie Villanueva. — 2nd ed.

Includes bibliographical references and index.
ISBN 978-0-7788-0451-2

1. Nonverbal communication in infants.  2. Interpersonal communication in infants.  3. American Sign Language.  4. Sign language.  I. Villanueva, Jamie  II. Title.

BF720.C65B55 2013        419'.70832        C2012-907482-9

# Index